THE 3% SIGNAL

JASON KELLY is the author of *The Neatest Little Guide to Stock Market Investing*, a perennial bestseller. Every Sunday morning, he delivers *The Kelly Letter* by e-mail, providing what many subscribers call the best read of the week. Having realized his dream of being able to live and work anywhere in the world, Jason moved to Japan in 2002, where he works from his office in the countryside about two hours from Tokyo.

After the March 2011 earthquake and tsunami, he started Socks for Japan, a volunteer organization that hand-delivered 160,000 care packages from around the world to survivors. More than 70 percent of donations came from the United States. In that moment of crisis, seeing return labels from churches, Brownie troops, neighborhood coffee shops, small-town light and power departments, Mrs. Wilson's fourth-grade class, and other mainstays of American culture filled him with pride for his country.

He keeps busy writing new books and *The Kelly Letter*. With his sister and business partner, Emily, he co-owns Red Frog Coffee in Longmont, Colorado. Visit his website at jasonkelly.com.

THE 3% SIGNAL

THE INVESTING TECHNIQUE THAT WILL CHANGE YOUR LIFE

JASON KELLY

A PLUME BOOK

PLUME
Published by the Penguin Group
Penguin Group (USA) LLC
375 Hudson Street
New York, New York 10014

USA | Canada | UK | Ireland | Australia | New Zealand |
India | South Africa | China
penguin.com
A Penguin Random House Company

First published by Plume, a member of Penguin Group (USA) LLC, 2015

LIBRARY OF CONGRESS CATALOGING-IN-PUBLICATION DATA
Kelly, Jason.
The 3% signal : the investing technique that will change your life / Jason Kelly.
pages   cm
Includes index.
ISBN 978-0-14-218095-2 (paperback)
1. Investments—Handbooks, manuals, etc.   2. Portfolio management—
Handbook, manuals, etc.   I. Title.   II. Title: Three percent signal.
HG4527.K437   2015
332.67'8—dc23   2014039340

Printed in the United States of America
10 9 8 7 6 5 4 3 2 1

Set in Minion Pro Reg

For my mother,
on whose behalf I first studied stocks

CONTENTS

Acknowledgments   xi

A Note on Performance Calculations   xiii

Introduction: Financial Floundering   xv

Chapter One: Why Markets Baffle Us   **1**

    The Zero-Validity Environment   4

    Coin Toss Forecasting   15

    Evidence of Inability   24

    Paging Peter Perfect   27

    What We Think versus What Is Real   33

    Executive Summary of This Chapter   34

Chapter Two: Harnessing Fluctuation   **36**

    The 3 Percent Signal   37

    Volatility Is Opportunity   40

    Retreat to the Index   42

    Nudging the Coin Toss Line   44

    Reactive Rebalancing   47

    Executive Summary of This Chapter   51

Chapter Three: Setting a Performance Goal　　　**53**

What's a Good Performance?　53

Gauging Fluctuations Against Our Goal　59

Executive Summary of This Chapter　78

Chapter Four: What Investments to Use　　　**80**

Small Companies for Growth　80

Bonds for Safety　84

The Performance Advantage　87

Beating the Heroic Holding　94

Beating Dollar-Cost Averaging　103

30 Down, Stick Around　111

Variations on the Plan　117

Executive Summary of This Chapter　130

Chapter Five: Managing Money in the Plan　　　**133**

Starting with a Large Cash Balance　134

Your Living, Breathing Bond Balance　135

Keep a Bottom-Buying Account　147

Adjusting Your Bond Balance as You Grow Older　152

Pulling It All Together　155

Executive Summary of This Chapter　156

Chapter Six: The Plan in Action　　　**159**

The Quarterly Procedure　160

Little Expenses Are a Big Deal　164

Tax Considerations　168

Individual Retirement Accounts　170

Typical Brokerage Accounts　172

Employer Retirement Accounts　185

The Plan Works Where You Work   211
Executive Summary of This Chapter   212

Chapter Seven: The Life of the Plan   **214**

The Setup   215
Year 1   227
Year 2   235
Years 3–7   241
Years 8–9   256
Years 10–13   269
Analysis   286
Executive Summary of This Chapter   295

Chapter Eight: Happy Signaling   **297**

Appendix 1: Mark's Plan   299

Appendix 2: Tools   304

Appendix 3: Rights and Permissions   305

Appendix 4: The Kelly Letter   306

Index   307

ACKNOWLEDGMENTS

I'm surrounded by fabulous people.

I can't imagine life without Doris Michaels, the only agent I've ever had. I was one of her first clients, and I'll be one of her last. It's a joy to still work together after all these years, and to see her and her incomparable husband, Charlie, on every trip to New York.

My editor at Plume, Kate Napolitano, worked with me on *The Neatest Little Guide to Stock Market Investing.* At lunch one December day just before the fifth edition debuted, she listened to my impassioned speech about a game-changing new way for people to invest using just two index funds and what I called "the 3 percent signal"—and here we are. She was there when it began and walked every step of the way with me.

Many researchers contributed to the body of work that helped me create the plan, but in this limited space I'll mention just three. Behavioral psychologist Daniel Kahneman showed me why stock market success eludes people, and the value of following a formula. In the formula department, I'm indebted to Michael Edleson's value-averaging concept of rebalancing to a fixed performance goal. John Bogle at Vanguard has been a tireless champion of index fund investing for the past four decades, and such low-cost funds are all that the 3 percent signal needs. Thank you, gentlemen. I wish there were more like you on Wall Street.

A special thank-you to Roger Crandell, whom I first met when he subscribed to *The Kelly Letter* but who later became a friend and research collaborator. His expert coding provided many of the historical plan results presented in this book, and his software double-checked output from my spreadsheets. You would be amazed at the volume of data crunching necessary to present what appear to be simple conclusions. Roger made this task easier for me.

Finally, thanks to Fidelity, the Investment Company Institute, Morningstar, Standard & Poor's, Vanguard, and Yahoo! Finance for supplying me with information.

A NOTE ON PERFORMANCE CALCULATIONS

Historical stock and fund prices change over time due to splits and dividends. This book shows values adjusted through autumn 2013. If you check historical prices of the investments you see in this book, many will have changed. Rest assured that this does not affect historical performance. Something that grew 20 percent back in 2005 still did so whether calculated using prices in 2005, 2013, or a future year. In the performance calculations not shown in the text, I used unadjusted prices with dividend payments to better reflect the change in balances that investors experienced at the time. For this reason, some of the prices discussed in Chapter 7, "The Life of the Plan," are different from those shown in adjusted price tables elsewhere in the book.

This book's primary time period is the fifty calendar quarters from the beginning of 2001 to the middle of 2013. To begin the period, the closing prices from December 2000 are used for the initial buys, and I usually refer to the period as the fifty quarters from December 2000 to June 2013. This sometimes confuses people, as they wonder if the time period includes 2000. No, it just uses December 2000 closing prices as the starting point for a clean look at the period from the first quarter of 2001 through the end of the second quarter of 2013, a fifty-quarter, or 12.5-year, time frame.

Except for the Medifast tables in Chapter 4 (where the December 2000 closing price plays a critical role in the example), price tables begin with the first quarter of 2001 to display exactly fifty prices for the time period.

Finally, the 3 percent signal plan produces trading guidance for buying and selling two funds at the same time. In real life, the trades won't happen at exactly the same time, but they can get pretty close these days due to fast order execution. I calculated past performance with all trades using the closing prices of the period in question. While real-world performance will vary based on slightly different order execution prices, it shouldn't vary by much. Follow the plan, and it will basically do for you what it's shown doing here.

INTRODUCTION
Financial Floundering

One day long ago, I found my mother sitting befuddled behind a stack of stock market ideas. She pushed one of the reports my way and said, "I can't make heads or tails of this. What do you think?" Heads or tails. That was an appropriate way to put it, I later discovered, because stock market advice is wrong half the time. My mother couldn't make heads or tails of the ideas in front of her—and neither could the people who'd written about them. They were all just guessing.

So I embarked on a two-decade quest in search of a better way for ordinary people to tap the profit potential of the stock market. I wanted to free them from the unreliable advice of market pundits, steer them away from investment mistakes that cause stress in their personal lives, and show them how to avoid overpaying for underperformance. I spoke with widely praised professional money managers, read every book on the subject, subscribed to newsletters, wrote my own books and newsletter, and appeared in media.

My research revealed that parts of the investment industry are connected in a clever system designed to tease money from investor accounts and into the accounts of firms and advisers. It goes like this: Entice people onto the treacherous trail of stock picking and market timing, knowing they'll fail; present alternatives that look more sophisticated than going it alone; then overcharge for those alternatives that actually perform worse than the unmanaged market itself.

What the experts don't want you to know—but what you'll never forget after reading this book—is that prices are all that matter. Ideas count for nothing; opinions are distractions. The only thing that matters is the price of an investment and whether it's below a level indicating a good time to buy or above a level indicating a good time to sell. We can know that level and monitor prices on our own, no experts required, and react appropriately to what prices and the level tell us. Even better, we can automate the reaction because it's purely mathematical.

This is the essence of the 3 percent signal. We set it as a constant performance line to return to each quarter, and then we either buy our way up to it or sell our way down to it. Used with common market indexes, this simple plan beats the stock market. Because most supposed pros lose to the market, the plan greatly outperforms them as well. This may seem too good to be true, and the pros want you to think so, but it's not, and this book will prove it to you. The performance advantage of the 3 percent signal can be yours after just four fifteen-minute calculations per year, without a single moment of your life wasted on meritless market chatter.

Unlike most automated plans, this one acknowledges your emotional side, which sees news and wants to take action. To appease this impulse, the plan will show you the right action to take at a pace that's perfect. You won't jump in too often and create disorder; nor will you stay away too long and feel you've abandoned your investments. You'll show up just frequently enough to keep your finances on track and yourself assured that everything is fine. This plan is all about getting the most out of the market for you in a way that satisfies your emotional needs as well as your portfolio needs.

We'll begin with a look at how our instincts lead us astray in the stock market, and how so-called experts prey on these vulnerabilities. You'll learn that the stock market is a zero-validity environment, and begin referring to pundits offering opinions on its future direction as "z-vals."

Next, we'll outline this book's superior approach, the 3 percent signal. It requires only a stock fund, a bond fund, and a signal line. You'll discover how to check in quarterly to see whether the stock fund's growth is below target, on target, or above target, and then move money in the appropriate direction between the stock fund and the bond fund. This action, using the unperturbed clarity of prices alone, automates the investment masterstroke of buying low and selling high—with no z-val interference of any kind.

From there, we'll explore the parts of the plan in more detail so you know what types of funds are ideal, why a quarterly schedule works best, how to manage cash contributions to the plan and occasional imbalances between its two funds, and when to implement a special "stick around" rule that keeps the plan fully invested for recovery after a market crash. You'll see that the plan works in any account, even a 401(k). Finally, you'll watch it alongside other investment approaches in a real-life scenario that brings together everything you've learned.

Are you ready? Come with me on a journey to a better way to invest.

THE 3% SIGNAL

CHAPTER ONE
Why Markets Baffle Us

There you are managing your career with a few financial goals in mind, following the basics of spending less than you earn and saving the rest, when one day you're told that putting your savings into the stock market will make it grow over time. "Grow?" you think. "That sounds good." You bet, the experts assure, by about 10 percent a year on average over time. That means your savings will double every seven years! If you pay attention and are a little smarter than other people—and we know you are, wink—you could do even better.

So it begins. Things go well for a few years after you move your savings into the stock market (probably in mutual funds and probably in a retirement account at work), and then the market goes down. Headlines announce a recession. Unemployment is rising. You read about the Federal Reserve, which you never thought about before, and aren't sure what to make of the minutes from its latest open-market committee meeting. The experts now say it was obvious a recession was on the way. "Just look at history," one opines wisely on TV. "The smart money is on the sidelines."

You're supposed to be the smart money, but you are most assuredly not on the sidelines. You're in the game and losing by the day. You follow your gut, which tells you to follow the experts, and get to the sidelines ASAP. Everything is moved to cash, and you feel good at lunch that day, just to not be losing anymore. "Whew! Let all those other suckers not smart enough to read about the Federal Reserve"—or just "the Fed," as you like to call it now—"stay in and get hammered day after day. I'm out. I'll buy back in when prices are lower later." You figure 20 percent wasn't too terrible a loss in the grand scheme of things. You'll make it back.

The news stays bad. Every article you read profiles a company laying people off. The Fed is taking all kinds of steps you've never heard of, and economists are worried. The bad news makes you happy to be on the sidelines, but the prices of the mutual funds and stocks you were hoping to buy again keep going up. By the time the economy seemingly stabilizes, they've recovered to prices higher than they were before the trouble began. Not only did you miss out on recovering your lost 20 percent, but you now have to decide whether to buy back in at higher prices. You refuse to do so at first, just because it kills you. Who wants to pay a high price to buy back something he sold at a lower price before? Three months go by, then six, then nine, and prices are much higher than when you decided not to buy back in. "Stocks are rising because there's nothing worrisome on the horizon," observe the experts on TV. "The smart money is all in."

What? *You are* the smart money, but you are decisively out of the market and missing gains. The experts say it's not too late. The lows are behind, but this is a long trend and it's still early. One talking head says it's like a baseball game, and the market's only in the third inning. Makes sense, you think, and so you buy back into the investments you sold at a 20 percent loss.

You know what happens next, I'll bet. The news stays good and prices rise for a while longer, but then they start falling, even as the news remains good. When the news turns bad again, they fall even faster. Before you know it, you're down another 20 percent in the middle of another recession filled with bad news and hearing from the same experts that getting out was obvious to the smart money, whoever they are. (I'll spare you the research: They don't exist. They're a fiction of the financial media, irrelevant for planning purposes.)

You might conclude from this brief junket to buy when news is bad and sell when it's good. The idea is great on paper and sensible in spirit, but try it. Begin by asking yourself what constitutes enough bad news. Is it the first frightening headline, or the tenth? One week of coverage? A month? A year? Sure, buying cheap prices that accompany bad news makes sense, but nobody knows what depth of bad news will deliver optimum buy prices. "Buy the lows," people chirp offhandedly as if it's that simple, to which a battered veteran of wiggling price lines should reply, "Which lows?" This is to say nothing of the same difficulty in knowing what constitutes enough good news for selling. The market is equally tricky at bottoms and tops, and each new tricky moment provides investors with a fresh chance to blow it.

Reading the predicament spelled out in these pages in compact form without real emotions makes it plain to see, and tempting to mock. You know what, though? This path is trod by countless investors, but the financial industry lures them back time and again. The destructive cycle looks obvious in retrospect, but is not at all obvious when it's happening. There's no end to the slipperiness of the stock market.

We are very vulnerable when it comes to money, experiencing depression when we lose it and euphoria when we gain it, and we're awful at timing. This combination makes financial markets a poisonous prescription for most people, yet millions are forced to participate as the only way they'll ever be able to buy a bigger home, send a child to college, or retire one day.

In this book, we're going to construct a plan that puts your savings on a reliable growth path without the need to time the market. Before we get there, however, it's important for you to understand why you shouldn't bother trying to time the market. The majority of investors learn this lesson the expensive way. You won't.

You'll learn in this chapter the myth of the perfect timer, a fictional character who buys bottoms and sells tops without fail. We're going to call him Peter Perfect. His influence over the investment industry has cost innocent people their fortunes. Why? Because they've been told that anything less than Peter Perfect can achieve is a failure and that they should strive to emulate him, even though he doesn't exist. They chase unrealistically high gains and end up losing, just as a person trying to copy Tinker Bell might leap off a cliff, expecting to fly. The Tinker Bell copycat loses her life. The Peter Perfect copycat loses his fortune.

Our journey to a plan that boosts your savings through thick and thin begins by looking at what doesn't work. Doing so will force us to examine unpleasant truths about our nature, which is hard for successful people to do. Generally, investors are smart and used to succeeding in life. They assume that what works elsewhere (hard work, studying, standing apart from the crowd) will work in the market, too. Yet it doesn't because the market lacks the regularities needed to improve intuition with experience. Succeeding in stocks comes down to accepting that nobody can know the future, and then adopting an investment system that wins by reacting rather than predicting. We'll get to the winning system soon enough, but first we're going to take a sober look in the mirror to see why we need it.

The Zero-Validity Environment

Have you ever wondered why experts get financial markets wrong, and why you make mistakes, too? The experts are not stupid; neither are you. Why is it that human beings can invent electricity, design airplanes, cure diseases, write literature, and craft cabinetry, but don't have the foggiest clue where stock prices are heading?

There's a simple answer, actually. Notice that all of these examples of human accomplishment follow set patterns and laws. The lessons we learn when researching electricity and other parts of the physical universe are applicable for all time. The reason an airplane flies is the same now as it was a hundred years ago. Medical research builds on past discoveries within a framework of unchanging rules. The kinds of stories people like are surprisingly fixed, which is why we still appreciate the works of Shakespeare four hundred years after he died. A master carpenter learns how to work with a certain grain of wood, and every time he sees that grain of wood again he knows what to do, because the wood behaves the same way each time.

In these areas of human endeavor, pattern recognition pays off. What we learn from past experience can help us in future experiences. This is not so in the stock market, where fluctuations follow no patterns precisely, despite what you might have heard. The lessons you learned in the last crash won't necessarily help you in this one. Same with the last rally. Experience in the stock market doesn't accumulate to create disciplinary wisdom the way it does in other walks of life. In fact, the very lessons we learn from past markets can lead us astray in future markets.

The Way We're Wired

The study of how our minds and emotions work in the realm of money is called "behavioral economics" or "behavioral finance." Among other things, it's taught us that we hate losing money more than we love gaining it, and that we're so averse to losing it that we'll inadvertently lose more by taking too much risk to try recouping what we lost.

Three leading contributors to behavioral economics are Daniel Kahneman, Richard Thaler, and Amos Tversky. Kahneman, a psychologist who won the 2002 Nobel Prize in Economics, summarizes the findings of his life's work in collaboration with Thaler, Tversky, and others in his 2011 book, *Thinking, Fast and Slow.*

The book offers insight into several areas of decision making given our emotional vulnerabilities and our tendency to draw hasty conclusions from limited sets of evidence, which Kahneman refers to as What You See Is All There Is (WYSIATI). He presents two ways that our minds process the world. System 1 thinking is fast, instinctive, automated, and emotional. System 2 thinking is slow, logical, deliberate, and rational. System 1 is easy and requires little effort; hence we use it most of the time in daily life. System 2 is hard and requires much more effort; hence we're reluctant to switch over to it unless we absolutely must.

We Believe What We've Experienced

Kahneman's work proved that our minds are not good at considering base rates and sample sizes when making decisions.

A base rate is the frequency with which something occurs. If 3 percent of people have an eye twitch while 97 percent do not, then the base rate of eye twitching is 3 percent. You will forget this, however, when asked if you think the guy sitting by the window has an eye twitch. He's a stranger to you. You'll size him up from a distance and ask yourself if he seems like an eye twitcher. You'll run through your mental inventory of all the eye twitchers you've ever known. The way he sits reminds you of an eye twitcher you used to sit next to on the school bus. He sure looks like an eye twitcher, you conclude, and answer in the affirmative: he's definitely an eye twitcher. Yet you actually know nothing about the man by the window. With such a low base rate of eye twitchers, the only reasonable guess for you to make is that he's not an eye twitcher, but you made an unreasonable guess that he is one based on your limited personal experience. All of us are vulnerable to this kind of hasty, sloppy decision making.

A sample size is the number of units studied. The larger a sample size, the more units we study and the more accurate our results become. We know this instinctively but forget it in practice. You would not take a medicine that boasted a 100 percent cure rate with no side effects if you knew it had been tried on just five people. If all five were cured with no side effects, then the statistics are right, but the problem is the sample size. We get it. What we don't get as easily is that when we tap into our personal experience, the most vivid collection of life data at our disposal, we're relying on a similarly small sample size to draw conclusions. In the stock market, we remember that last year we lost money after the Fed's June meeting, so we're cautious going into future June meetings. We overlook the Junes that did not portend trouble because they didn't personally affect us.

We're quick to form an opinion based on the limited part of life we've experienced firsthand, and we lose perspective on the thimble of ocean water these personal lessons represent. Kahneman reminds us that large samples are more precise than small samples, and that small samples yield extreme results more often than large samples do. Thus our thimble of experience is going to expose us to extreme results, and we're going to draw conclusions based on them in full confidence because they're all we know firsthand. We'll frequently proceed with certainty in the wrong direction based on what's been right in our limited past. In the stock market, this becomes even worse because there's an extra layer of uncertainty. Not only is our experience just a tiny slice of market history, even what has been true in market history is not necessarily going to be true again. This inconvenient fact spawned a favorite saying among traders: "It works until it doesn't."

Our minds create plausible stories from limited data sets. In the market, this happens daily. At the end of each day, pundits report confidently why the market rose or fell. Even they know, however, that the reason proffered is usually arbitrary. I once appeared on a financial television program that invited two people to be on call for that day's market wrap. One guest was the guy prepared to explain why the market had gone up; the other was the guy prepared to explain why the market had gone down. They were, respectively, the bull and the bear. Since nobody knows where the market will go on a given day, the station covered its bases by inviting a person who could say something convincing no matter what happened. Telling, isn't it?

Kahneman writes that it's natural for our System 1 thinking (the fast, instinctive, automated, emotional type) to "generate over-confident judgments, because confidence, as we have seen, is determined by the coherence of the best story you can tell from the evidence at hand. Be warned: your intuitions will deliver predictions that are too extreme and you will be inclined to put far too much faith in them."

We Think We Knew It All Along

Even more discouraging, when we're proven wrong and change our minds, we can't recall very well what led us to the wrong conclusions to begin with. We rationalize them away, sometimes convincing ourselves in cases related to stocks that *we* weren't wrong, *the market* was wrong. It should have gone down, or it should have gone up; if only it were more rational and understood the evidence as well as we understood it. Eventually, we decide that not only were we not wrong in our incorrect belief, but it wasn't even our belief. No, we actually believed—knew, rather—that the market would go down. It's so obvious, looking back. So, the next time we're convinced by the evidence, we proceed as confidently as we did the last time we got it wrong, believing that our track record is better than it actually is and that what we know this time is bankable.

This mistaken belief that we knew it all along is called "hindsight bias." We use it to improve ourselves in retrospect, believing we knew in the past things we didn't actually know at the time but that we know now only with the help of hindsight. We compound the problems of this tendency by thinking that if we got it right last time, we'll probably get it right this time, even though we didn't get it right last time and have no business thinking we'll get it right this time. Can you imagine a creature less suited for rational market analysis? We're just smart enough to get ourselves into a heap of trouble, all too often with money that matters.

About our hindsight bias, Kahneman writes that the human mind suffers an imperfect ability to recall past levels of knowledge and previous beliefs that have changed. When we arrive at new conclusions, we lose our grasp of previous conclusions and settle into thinking we've always believed what we believe now. This minimizes in our memory the extent to which past developments caught us off guard, and creates the illusion that we understood the past as it unfolded. Then, we think that if we navigated the past pretty well we'll probably be able to predict the outcome of current events, too. We take comfort in this illusion that we understood the past and can forecast the future. It's more reassuring than admitting that we actually have no idea why things went the way they did, or what's going to happen next.

We Mistake Luck for Skill

To really have some fun, toss a person a few random successes in the market. Witness their confidence rise, their pride swell. More important, tabulate the increasing amount of money they allocate to their next ideas. "It worked last time," they think. "Too bad my idea that gained thirty percent did so with only ten thousand dollars. What if I used fifty thousand next time?" What if, indeed.

On top of not understanding that winning streaks in the market happen randomly, on top of not seeing that two-thirds of professional money managers lose to the market, on top of not realizing that a few recent successes do not override a mountain of forecasting folly, we don't recognize the ability of a single mistake with too much money to erase all the gains we accumulated in the past. You can get it right four times in a row, but if you get it wrong badly enough the fifth time, you'll return to square one with nothing but a tax write-off to show for all your painstaking work and stress.

Even though randomness says successes are bound to happen

now and again among even the least skillful participants, we apply our successes toward a personal skill assessment upgrade. We're not lucky; we're good. This could be fine if we downgraded our skill assessment with each failure, but we don't. When we're right, we're smart. When we're wrong, it's not our fault—we explain our failures away. Our assessment of ourselves rises toward "master" designation, ratcheting up with each success but only pausing its ascent with each failure.

Here's how Kahneman summarizes what is probably the most willfully ignored conclusion of behavioral finance studies: "There is general agreement among researchers that nearly all stock pickers, whether they know it or not—and few of them do—are playing a game of chance. The subjective experience of traders is that they are making sensible educated guesses in a situation of great uncertainty. In highly efficient markets, however, educated guesses are no more accurate than blind guesses." Why? Because everybody competing is in possession of the same information, so there's no edge to be found.

Newcomers to the market think they're breaking new ground by reading balance sheets, dissecting management discussions, meeting with competitors, and so on. What they miss is that everybody else is doing the same things. Understanding a company's prospects or the market's prospects is not enough to make a wise decision on the future direction of prices. Whatever is known by us is known by others, too, reducing the stock picker's job to speculating on what fickle humans will do with the information they possess. Nobody knows, so our decisions are reduced along with everybody else's to meaninglessly educated guesses. We'll win some, we'll lose some, just like others in the crowd, but we'll somehow conclude we're more skillful than most—even as we achieve average results.

Illusions of skill can be convincing, though. Say you made the top 3.1 percent of investment managers, joining a group of just 313 out of 10,000 who earned money five years in a row. You'd be proud of yourself—rightfully so, most people would grant. Nassim Nicholas Taleb would disagree. He shows in his 2001 book, *Fooled by Randomness*, that the outcome could be ascribed to chance. "No," you object, but work through a simple experiment offered by Taleb.

Imagine a fair contest in which managers have a 50 percent chance of turning a profit each year and a 50 percent chance of posting a loss. After a manager loses, we remove him from the contest. Toss a coin for each manager the first year—heads means profit, tails means loss—and 5,000 of them will lose and drop out. Do this again in each subsequent year. The group of 5,000 remaining at the end of the first year will be reduced by half at the end of the second year, to leave us with 2,500. At the end of year three we'll have 1,250; year four, 625; and year five, 313. Taleb concluded the experiment: "We have now, simply in a fair game, 313 managers who made money for five years in a row. Out of pure luck."

They won't be called lucky, though. They'll be called brilliant and will probably appear on magazine covers. They'll become the subjects of articles purporting to reveal the secrets of stock market success, which will contain contradictory advice such as "buy more of what's working" but "average down into winners on sale." The articles will exhibit survivorship bias, the mistake of focusing on traits of people and companies who made the cut without comparing them to the ones that didn't. It's how we hear that a runner won a race because he practiced for hours before sunrise every day, ignoring that the loser did the same thing. It's how a reporter tells us with great fanfare that winning investment managers talked with presidents of companies in their portfolios, ignoring that the losers did the same thing.

These investing winners will be celebrated and sought out. Not one of them will discuss the many moments of uncertainty they faced along the way, the countless items over which they had no control but that went their way by mere chance. Kahneman writes that "the admission that one is merely guessing is especially unacceptable when the stakes are high. Acting on pretended knowledge is often the preferred solution."

Pretended knowledge and luck are better known in the stock market as skill.

Limits of Pattern Recognition

We have evolved to recognize patterns. Once we recognize them, we learn the best way to react to them so we're ready the next time they appear. Wet roads are slippery, so we learn to drive more carefully on them. Stoves can be hot, so we approach them cautiously. Even if a wet road is not especially slippery, it doesn't hurt to drive carefully. Caution around stoves is never a bad idea.

Why, then, does pattern recognition fail us in the stock market? Because we think we see patterns in randomness where none actually exist, and even the market patterns that do exist fail to repeat reliably. Just as wildly different days share a basic structure of morning, daytime, and night, so do wildly different market trajectories share similar features. These catch the attention of our pattern recognition instincts, which tell us we're in familiar territory and know what to do, but then the course of current events branches to a different path.

Confirmation Bias

Science writer Michael Shermer explains this pattern recognition tendency in the November 25, 2008, issue of *Scientific American*. He calls our brains "belief engines" and "pattern-recognition machines" that assign meaning to the patterns we think we see in nature. Sometimes different events are connected, sometimes not. Where relationships exist, such as stoves being hot and therefore deserving caution, we've gained something valuable in noticing them and can adjust our behavior in ways that aid our survival and ability to perpetuate the species. We are descendants of the most successful pattern detectors. This association learning is a trait we share with other animal survivors. It's a core part of who we are.

Because our pattern recognition capability has helped us survive, no wonder we turn to it in just about every situation. We're not good at seeing its limits, though, and use it even when the environment is not conducive to creating reliable patterns. The stock market is one such environment.

Our pattern detector is so sensitive that it can even find meaningful patterns in meaningless noise. Shermer calls this tendency "patternicity." In his 2011 book, *The Believing Brain*, he argues that people often concoct beliefs first and *then* find evidence to support them. Our belief engines sift through sensory inputs in search of patterns, pick them out, and create a narrative around them to support our interpretation. If a belief is strong enough, it sprouts from our head as invisible antennae tuned to a frequency for corroborating evidence. It misses contrary evidence, which is on a different frequency, and gradually builds an ever stronger case for the initial belief. This stronger case makes the belief more believable, which enlarges the antennae, which gather more evidence, which strengthens the case, and so on, in a feedback loop that transmogrifies the belief into a permanent fixture of a person's psyche, in some cases.

What we're discussing is called "confirmation bias," the selective interpretation of information to match a preconceived belief. If you were burned by stocks last summer, you're apt to be cautious in the market this summer. You believe stocks are going to fall again, and will tune your antennae to hear bearish commentary and focus on bad economic data to reinforce your belief. You're biased toward confirming what you've already decided, rather than taking the more useful approach of assigning equal weight to all available information.

Z-Val

Consider the high potential for damage this tendency poses in the stock market. We see patterns in random data, construct beliefs based on these meaningless patterns, and then set about gathering information to confirm our beliefs. When our pattern detector collides with stock market randomness, we tell ourselves convincing stories for why stocks will rise, equally convincing ones for why they'll fall, with the result balancing out to average performance not at all worth the effort.

Kahneman writes that there are "two basic conditions for acquiring a skill: an environment that is sufficiently regular to be predictable; an opportunity to learn these regularities through prolonged practice. When both these conditions are satisfied, intuitions are likely to be skilled." The stock market doesn't qualify, because "stock pickers and political scientists who make long-term forecasts operate in a zero-validity environment. Their failures reflect the basic unpredictability of the events that they try to forecast."

Let that term sink in: zero-validity environment. This sounds ominous, as it should. You can almost hear a Wall Street carnival barker crying, "Ladies and gentlemen, welcome to the zero-validity environment! Rev up your guessing engines! Good luck planning a future!" Financial hilarity ensues, at least for bystanders. For those in the experiment with their futures on the line, there's nothing funny about it.

The zero validity of the stock market is a key concept I'll mention repeatedly throughout the book. Let's shorthand it to z-val, a handy epithet for referring to both the market itself and the pundits offering zero-validity stock advice subject to a 50 percent failure rate, which you'll read about in the next section.

Kahneman advises that intuition is reliable only when an environment is sufficiently regular and a participant has had a chance to learn the regularities. You can trust a person's intuition if these conditions are met. They are not met in the stock market, which means you can't trust anybody's intuition regarding the market's future—including your own.

Coin Toss Forecasting

Everything you've read so far explains a most inconvenient number related to stock market investing: fifty, as in 50 percent. It's hard to get more average than that, and nearly every study of stock market participants of both the professional and part-time variety concludes that they're right only 50 percent of the time. It's the same percentage chance you get for heads or tails in a coin toss, which is why you frequently encounter the coin toss metaphor in reference to stock market participation. This is a major point that you should commit to memory because it's a foundational flaw of human behavior in the stock market. *We're wrong half the time.* It's important to incorporate this reality into your view of the stock market as a way of sensing the risk in every forecast or idea you encounter, no matter how believable it seems.

Experts are always impressive. They are professors of finance, managers of large sums of money, longtime market seers with successful calls in their selectively edited biographies, and presidents of organizations with authoritative names. They are never introduced as "somebody somewhere who said something," though their track records indicate they should be.

An investment research firm called CXO Advisory tracked nearly 6,600 forecasts of the American stock market made by 68 experts employing multiple disciplines from 2005 to 2012. I was one of the experts in the study. Some of the forecasts came from archives and some of the most recent ones in the study extended beyond 2012. The oldest one tracked in the sample was made at the end of 1998, and the final grading happened in 2013, so the study provided a good look at typical performance in different environments using various methods. What did it find? An average accuracy of just 47 percent, even worse than coin tossing. We'll give humans the benefit of the doubt, however, and grant average accuracy to be the coin toss 50 percent.

Funny things happen in a coin tossing environment, one of

which you read about earlier when it produced a convincing subset of market winners at the end of five years. This can't be random, we think, but we're wrong. Randomness doesn't look random to us. It often appears more orderly than we believe it should, with trends that are assigned stories to explain why the market keeps going up or down. In a series of coin tosses, for example, streaks of heads (H) and tails (t) are common. (I show tails in lowercase to make changes in sequence easier to spot.) Most people think a sequence such as HHHHHttttt is less random than HtHtHtHtHt, but statistically each is equally likely.

To see the illusion of predictability that this kind of randomness produces in the stock market, consider the following chart I created with a spreadsheet and coin tosses using a quarter. I began with a balance of $10,000. I tossed the coin fifty times. Heads meant a 5 percent increase in my balance, tails a 5 percent decrease. Here's a chart of the change in balance over the course of fifty tosses:

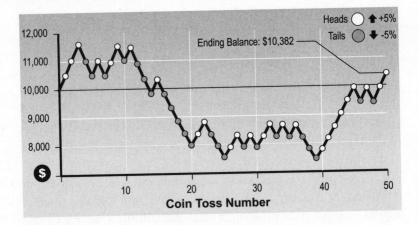

Change in $10,000 balance by coin toss.

Doesn't this look like something you might see in the stock market? It does to me, and I can just hear the experts saying when the balance falls below $9,000 that "the trend is clearly down" and suggesting that you follow what the smart money did back when the balance was above $11,000 by getting to the sidelines. When the trend "bases" along the $8,000 line, television networks will have a ball pitting bulls and bears against one another in the "battle over $8,000" as the former argue that the market is basing for a recovery while the latter say it's pausing before further downside because "the fundamentals just aren't there." When it recovers back above $9,000, the bulls will say they told us so, while the bears will say the market is on borrowed time.

We would get all this drama from a sequence of coin tosses. Here's the sequence that happened in my office:

HHH tt H t HH t H ttt H ttttt HH ttt HH t H t HH t H t H ttt HHHHHH t H t HH

Notice how many streaks happened. In just fifty tosses, I produced six streaks of three or more identical results in a row. Remember from your earlier reading that streaks of success will go to our heads, tricking us into thinking we're better at this than we actually are. Random sequences provide false evidence of skill.

A Random Walk

The most famous look at randomness in stocks is Burton G. Malkiel's *A Random Walk Down Wall Street*, first published in 1973 and updated numerous times. In what should be an uncontroversial view to you by now, Malkiel contends that the market is efficient to the point where everybody knows everything at the same time, erasing all advantages to be had, so that an investor will perform better in the long run simply by owning an index fund through ups and downs. An index fund is an unmanaged collection of stocks that enables an investor to buy the market without picking and choosing which companies will do well.

Malkiel writes in the tenth edition of his book, published in 2012, that "the market prices stocks so efficiently that a blindfolded chimpanzee throwing darts at the stock listings can select a portfolio that performs as well as those managed by the experts. Through the past forty years, that thesis has held up remarkably well. More than two-thirds of professional portfolio managers have been outperformed by the unmanaged S&P 500 Index."

His "random walk" metaphor refers to what you saw earlier when I charted the result of fifty coin tosses. Each move is independent of the last one, and the one before that, and all that came before. Every tick is random, and thus unworthy of our forecasting energies. There's no need to pay for predictive services, ponder earnings projections, or study complicated charts, because they're all useless.

Precise Imprecision

You'll never hear this in the stock business, though. No analyst sits down at a table and forewarns you that he's susceptible to several biases and fallacies when it comes to thinking about stocks, and that he has underperformed a blindfolded chimpanzee throwing darts. Instead, he'll present you with a convincing overview of industry growth rates, a company's earnings history, management's bold new plans, and projections based on what he believes are reasonable assumptions.

Asinine Assumptions

The problems lurk in the assumptions. A college professor of mine used to say, "Do not assume, gentlemen! It makes an *ass* of *u* and *me*." Yet, absent certainties, what else is an analyst to do? Investment prospectuses are required to point out that future performance cannot be guaranteed, usually with statements such as "Past performance is not indicative of future results." Fine, but pray tell how to analyze the future since it hasn't happened yet. All we have is the past. Because the past provides no guarantee, there are no guarantees in this line of work.

Analysts must assume, project, and assign values to variables. It's all they can do, and it's inherently imprecise. The result, however, offers the illusion of precision by delivering firm answers at the end of sometimes complicated formulas. The formulas, unfortunately, compute exact relationships between variables that offer no predictive power. Computer programmers call this "garbage in, garbage out." If we can't trust the predictive power of the values put into a formula, then we can't trust the predictive power of the result churned out by the formula. If this is so, what's the point of the formula?

This reminds me of an old joke about economists. A mathematician, an accountant, and an economist apply for the same job. The interviewer asks the mathematician, "What does two plus two equal?" The mathematician replies, "Four." The interviewer calls in the accountant and asks the same question, "What does two plus two equal?" The accountant says, "About four, give or take a few percent, but generally four." Finally, the interviewer calls in the economist and presents the same question, "What does two plus two equal?" The economist stands up, locks the door, draws the blinds, sits close to the interviewer, and whispers, "What do you want it to equal?" Replace the economist with a stock analyst calculating a company's fair value or future stock market earnings, and the joke still works.

There's plenty of reason to doubt somebody's guess at the future value of a stock given the many variables they can't know, but the ultimate wild card is what the market thinks and how it reacts to whatever general news and company-specific news appear in the future. Even if somebody perfectly calls the fair value of a stock by getting every variable correct in a discounted cash flow analysis, the market might never move the stock's price to the fair value. The company might deliver revenue and expenses precisely on target but still see its stock price drift away from what the on-target variables determined to be fair value. Who's to say what's fair? Only the market, that most manic-depressive of all entities.

This is a hard concept to accept because the meticulous work that goes into calculating stock valuations and market forecasts is convincing. People in suits in expensive offices really do work days and nights on this stuff, after studying the methods for years. That it could all be for naught strikes us as preposterous. That an entire industry could float in a mist of illusion and false confidence is depressing but true, and better to learn earlier than later.

Formula Follies

We're tricked by stock market formulas because we've learned to trust formula results in other areas of life, the ones where they work. Unlike the zero-validity environment of the stock market, some areas of life provide us with regularity we can measure and come to understand better after years of study and practice. These are the factors that Daniel Kahneman mentioned as being necessary for the development of sound intuition.

Medicine is a good example of a high-validity environment that routinely uses reliable formulas. I like comparing the medical field to the stock business because each operates in a sea of risk, each forces difficult decisions into the funhouse of human judgment, and each relies on formulas and calculations to improve the results of that human judgment. The difference is that medical formulas return high odds of success that instill confidence, while stock formulas return coin toss odds of success that instill little confidence. The reason is that medical formulas are based on inputs that are stable over time, while most stock formulas are based on inputs that are variable from one environment to the next and produce different outcomes at different times.

One branch of medicine that relies on convenient formulas is obstetrics, the field of pregnancy and childbirth. I'll bet you're more likely to trust the result of a common drugstore pregnancy test than the most professionally prepared stock forecast—as well you should be. Pregnancy tests are accurate 99 percent of the time; stock forecasts, 50 percent. Beyond the test, even a process as fraught with uncertainty as childbirth offers more regularity than the stock market.

In 1952 an anesthesiologist named Virginia Apgar developed a simple formula for doctors to quickly assess the health of a newborn baby. It's called "the Apgar score," in honor of its creator and also to represent the five criteria it checks: appearance, pulse, grimace, activity, and respiration. Appearance considers the baby's skin color, from dangerously pale to vigorously pink in the extremities; pulse is the heart rate, from zero to more than 100; grimace measures the baby's reaction to stimulus; activity looks at his muscle tone and strength; and respiration grades breathing power. A doctor checks the newborn baby and assigns a value of 0, 1, or 2 to each criterion, then adds them up to get an overall Apgar score. Anything 7 or higher is healthy, 4 to 6 is risky, and 3 or lower is critical. Because obstetricians observe thousands of newborns over their careers, and the biological factors affecting newborns are constant, doctors become very good at judging each Apgar criterion. Even such skilled practitioners show the most consistency in scoring the criterion that requires the least amount of personal judgment, heart rate, but become proficient at the others as well.

If a stock analyst were in charge of determining a newborn baby's health, he'd start six months ahead of time. He'd tell you what percentage of newborn babies fall into each Apgar score range, discuss the mother's health and why it suggests a certain score, and then be nowhere in sight when the baby was actually born. You know what, though? It's not his fault, because everybody is demanding to know the stock market baby's Apgar score six months in advance when *nobody*, not even Virginia Apgar herself, could know how things will turn out. The same way a doctor can tell you a baby's Apgar score only after she's born, so an analyst can tell you a stock's price only after it appears. The past and present are easy. It's the future that's tricky.

Before an Apgar is possible, doctors determine a preborn baby's health by measuring his heart rate, amniotic fluid volume, and other factors to build a biophysical profile accurate enough to greatly reduce mortality. A study in the 1990s found the false-negative rate of the modified biophysical profile to be just 0.8 per 1,000 women. Good luck finding that kind of accuracy in the stock market. Wall Street's false-negative rate would be more like 500 per 1,000.

Stock market formulas cause us great aggravation when they produce bad advice, which is frequently the case because they're unreliable. We trust the solid-looking formulas more than their fifty-fifty odds warrant, then become upset when the bad odds go against us half the time rather than the very small percentage of the time they go wrong in other parts of life, and our being upset is compounded by the financial consequences of going wrong in the stock market. The stakes are much higher in the market than in medicine, after all. Medicine just deals with life and death, but stocks deal with money.

Knowing We Can't Know the Unknowable

Is the unreliability of investment formulas the fault of stock analysts? It seems unfair to attack analysts for not knowing what nobody else could know, either. Then again, maybe they should acknowledge this limitation and stop offering bogus advice based on projections proven to be unreliable.

In *Thinking, Fast and Slow*, Daniel Kahneman writes about studying the performance data of some twenty-five wealth advisers at one investment firm over an eight-year period. The scores for each year were the main factors used to calculate annual bonuses. He ranked the advisers by their performances to find differences in skill among them. Did any consistently deliver better returns to clients? He computed correlation coefficients between the rankings in each pair of years to get a total of twenty-eight results. "I knew the theory and was prepared to find weak evidence of persistence of skill. Still, I was surprised to find that the average of the 28 correlations was .01. In other words, zero. The consistent correlations that would indicate differences in skill were not to be found. The results resembled what you would expect from a dice-rolling contest, not a game of skill."

When he and his partner on the project, Richard Thaler, presented their results to executives at the investment firm, they were surprised to find the executives unsurprised. "This should have been shocking news to them, but it was not," Kahneman remembers. Life at the firm went on as before, with everybody ignoring the information that threatened their careers and self-esteem. The careful judgment they applied to complex problems was more visceral to them than some statistical fact about their performance. One of the executives told Kahneman later, with a trace of defensiveness, that he'd done well for the firm and that nobody could take that away from him. Kahneman remained politely silent, but wondered, "If your success was due mostly to chance, how much credit are you entitled to take for it?"

The industry will never change as long as there's money to be made. There's no point wishing for a different world. We should, however, protect ourselves against the investment industry's never-ending flow of groundless advice by ignoring it. They don't know the future; their clients don't know the future. They get paid despite not knowing; their clients suffer the consequences of their not knowing.

The astute observer of the stock market concludes, "Nobody can know the future of a stock, or industry, or the market because it is inherently unknowable. However, I can be smarter than others by knowing that I can't know the unknowable, and finding a way to grow my money in the face of that uncertainty."

Life itself is uncertain, so of course the stock market is uncertain. Think of all the turning points in history when a country almost won a war, a candidate almost won an election, or a team almost won a tournament. Think of times in your own life when you might have moved east but instead went west, when you declined an invitation when you might have accepted, or when you thought a test would be positive but it came back negative. Existence is a tapestry of such arbitrariness. Its defining quality is mystery.

Life outside the stock market teaches us in vivid clarity that the future is anybody's guess. We learn to live with such uncertainty in other parts of life, but for some reason we think experts know the future of the stock market. They don't because they can't. Neither can we. Once we accept this, we can begin working toward a better approach to growing our money.

Evidence of Inability

Given everything you've read so far, it almost goes without saying that human beings have failed to beat the stock market over time. Just in case it doesn't go without saying, let's review the findings of a few representative studies proving so.

In a February 2010 paper published in *The Journal of Finance*, "False Discoveries in Mutual Fund Performance: Measuring Luck in Estimated Alphas," professors Laurent Barras, Olivier Scaillet, and Russell Wermers reported their findings after studying 2,076 fund managers over the thirty-two years from 1975 to the end of 2006. They concluded that 99.4 percent of these managers exhibited no evidence of stock-picking skill. Just 2.4 percent were skilled over the short term. Only 0.6 percent beat the stock index in the full time frame, a result the professors described as being "statistically indistinguishable from zero." Further, "the proportion of skilled fund managers has diminished rapidly over the past twenty years, while the proportion of unskilled fund managers has increased substantially." The professors found it "puzzling" that investors tolerate subpar actively managed funds "when an increasing array of passively managed funds" is readily available. In this book's plan, we'll use just such passively managed funds to achieve higher performance while paying low fees.

One reason market timers lose is that the accuracy rate they need to achieve in order to beat a passively managed index is inordinately high. William Sharpe, winner of the 1990 Nobel Prize in Economics and creator of the Sharpe ratio to measure risk-adjusted investment performance, addressed this in "Likely Gains from Market Timing," published in the March/April 1975 issue of *Financial Analysts Journal*. He found that timers need a 74 percent accuracy rate to beat a passive portfolio taking on the same amount of risk. The old saying that two out of three ain't bad doesn't work in the stock market. It takes three out of four, and almost nobody can achieve it.

In a July 2013 paper, "The Bumpy Road to Outperformance," the investment company Vanguard confirmed the "considerable research" showing that "on average, actively managed equity mutual funds underperform their respective benchmarks." Using data from Morningstar, an investment research firm based in Chicago, it found that out of 1,540 actively managed U.S. equity funds in the period 1998 to 2012, only 55 percent survived—and two-thirds of the survivors lost to their benchmark. Only 275 funds, or about 18 percent of the original group, both survived and beat their benchmark. Don't think for a moment that owning one of those 275 winners was a cakewalk. Vanguard found that "almost all of the outperforming funds—267, or 97 percent—experienced at least five individual calendar years in which they lagged their style bench-

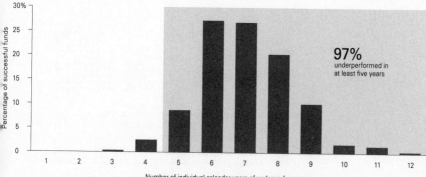

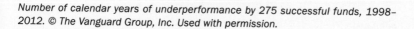

Number of calendar years of underperformance by 275 successful funds, 1998–2012. © The Vanguard Group, Inc. Used with permission.

marks. In fact, more than 60 percent had seven or more years of underperformance." It showed the distribution of winning funds across their number of single years of underperformance in the chart on page 25.

Unfortunately, this was not the most disturbing of Vanguard's findings. Noting that "For many investors, three consecutive years of underperformance represents a breakpoint after which they will divest the fund," it examined consecutive years of underperformance. It filtered for "funds that survived for fifteen years, beat their benchmarks, *and* avoided three consecutive years of underperformance." The results were "pronounced: Only 94—or 6 percent—of

1540 total funds

| | 12% | **181** funds | Survived, outperformed, and experienced at least three consecutive years of underperformance |
| | 6% | **94** funds | Survived, outperformed, and never experienced three consecutive years of underperformance |

Only 6 percent of 1,540 funds survived, outperformed, and never experienced three consecutive years of underperformance. © The Vanguard Group, Inc. Used with permission.

the initial 1,540 funds met these criteria. Stated differently, during this period, two-thirds of the outperforming funds experienced *at least* three consecutive years of underperformance." It illustrated the diminutive size of the winner's circle in the infographic on page 26.

I could fill the rest of the book with such studies, but I think you get the point. An overwhelming majority of investment managers loses to the market, and even the winners experience long losing streaks that shake a lot of investors out before they benefit from the eventual success. On top of all this, we can see only which tiny sliver of managers did better in the past. How does that help us now? It doesn't, because we have no way of knowing who the winners will be in the future.

Paging Peter Perfect

It's now time to introduce the deviant who makes it oh so hard to reach sensible conclusions about stock forecasting and timing. Meet Peter Perfect. He's the devilish voice we hear when looking at a past chart of the stock market, noting its peaks and valleys. Peter asks, "What if you'd sold at that peak, then bought at that valley, then sold at the next peak, and bought at the next valley? Wouldn't that have been amazing?" In other words, take a moment to picture perfection, achieved the way Peter consistently achieves it.

He Has Your Number

Peter preys on all our biases. He knows we'll look at those peaks and valleys in hindsight and think we knew then what we know now. He's well aware of our ability to forget the mistakes we made and remember the successes we had, and overestimate our abilities. Peter could just as well ask, "Didn't you have an inkling that trouble lay ahead back when the S&P 500 approached its high point? I'm pretty sure you did. You generally have a good feel for these things." You listen to him and find yourself nodding. "Yeah, actually, I was getting nervous as the market climbed that peak. It did seem too good to be true. I was thinking of selling." Peter smiles and claps you on the shoulder. "Of course you were!" he exclaims. "You got it right then, and you'll get it right next time, too."

The problem is, you didn't get it right then and probably won't get it right next time. You just thought about selling without actually doing it, but Peter knows your memory of the thought is enough to convince you in retrospect that you nailed it. He urges you to the timing side by constantly comparing your real results and boring index results with the results he achieved after perfectly timing his buys and sells, thereby suggesting that you pursue perfection, too.

Let's look at some real market history and how Peter plays tricks with it. Here's a chart of the S&P 500 from January 2006 to May 2008:

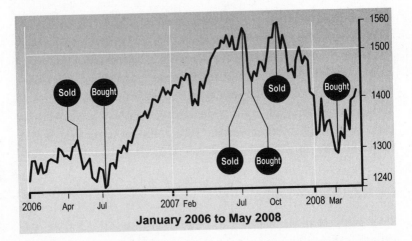

S&P 500, January 2006 to May 2008, with Peter Perfect's fictional trading history.

What Peter recalls during this time period is selling at the end of April 2006 at 1320 "because everybody knows you sell in May and go away." He started the year with $10,000 when the S&P 500 was at

1250. After the sale, he had $10,560 for a good 5.6 percent gain in four months.

He used his whole $10,560 to buy back into stocks at the beginning of the following July with the market at 1240 because the sharp drop preceding it "took the market down too far too fast." He held all the way up to the peak in February 2007 and through the short, sharp drop that followed because "the move was so fast that it was obvious the market was just relieving overbought pressure." Sure enough, less than two months later, Peter had recouped all of his paper losses incurred in February and March. Notice this little hiccup tossed into the mix. We're skeptical of truly perfect performance, but if Peter or anybody else includes a couple of minor errors in his historical report, we're more apt to let high accuracy impress us.

Onward Peter marched. He sold at 1550 at the beginning of July 2007, a year after his last buy. His $10,560 grew 25 percent, to $13,200—an amazing annual performance! Even more amazing, Peter put the entire $13,200 back to work at the end of the month, after the market fell to 1440, citing the "overly drastic drop in so tiny a time frame that I knew the rubber band had to snap back." It did, too, and just a couple of months later he thought the market "looked a little toppy" and locked in profits at 1560 in early October, growing his $13,200 by 8.3 percent, to $14,300, in only two months.

Then he stayed safely on the sidelines "with all the other smart money" as the market cascaded in fits and starts to a March 2008 low of 1290. Sure, he missed a couple of nice bounces in November and January, but "heck, you can't win 'em all," he says with a shrug, and you find yourself liking him a little more for his honesty. It was the third bottom that he decided to buy, and it turned out to be the right one. He moved his $14,300 back into the market at 1290 in March 2008, and it was up 9.3 percent, to $15,630, with the market at 1410 when you spoke with him at the beginning of May 2008.

Peter Perfect is sitting on a cool $15,630 after making just six moves in this twenty-eight-month period. They were fairly obvious moves, too, you realize when looking at the chart. Who couldn't see these major tops and bottoms? Peter got them right, and you thought about them in the right way. The rummies who bought and held, those Plain Jane indexers who started 2006 with the same $10,000 balance that Peter had, finished the time period with only $11,280 compared with his $15,630. They made only 12.8 percent, but he made 56.3 percent. He could have done even better, he interjects slyly, if only he'd caught some of those smaller moves. "Oh well," he says. "At least I caught the big ones." "That's for sure," you think.

He's Everywhere

This is how Peter Perfect operates, and what he tells you. He's rarely called Peter Perfect. In real life he'll manifest himself as your cousin Randy the know-it-all, or Greg Aguilera in accounting, or that loud-mouth in the bowling league who pretends to reach for his wallet when you pay for drinks, or a media report showcasing one lucky coin-tosser who nabbed the most recent bottom or top. (Peter rarely shows up as a woman, by the way. Women don't tell nearly as many big fish tales or stock market stories as men, and the ones they do tell are usually more accurate.)

Above all, Peter is a master publicist who charms every corner of financial media. He's the ideal go-to guy for their purposes, which are to fan flames of greed in rising markets and fear in falling markets. Between the lines of almost every stock market report is this message: "Don't you wish you had been better positioned for what's happening right now?" The answer is always yes, because nobody comes close to the perfection of Peter—except in the delusions of hindsight. So he shows up wearing a lucky coin-tosser suit in feature articles, and is described with words such as *brave* and *bold* and *prescient*. Later, after the braveness, boldness, and prescience go nowhere, follow-ups are skipped in favor of showcasing the current man at the coin boldly calling, "Heads!"

For example, here are snippets from a *Wall Street Journal* "MoneyBeat" article published on May 2, 2013, examining a forecast from a Peter appearing in the guise of a coin tossing chartist: "One brave chart watcher is calling the top. . . . Calling a top takes guts, especially in this market environment. The S&P 500 is riding a six-month winning streak—the longest such run since September 2009—and has risen in 14 of the past 17 months. . . . 'These indicators are all convincing and compelling enough to talk about and make a call at this time,' [the coin-tosser] said."

Surely, this brave coin-tosser with guts correctly called the market during its six-month winning streak, right? Wrong, but we find no mention of this when he is being praised for his bravery at calling "tails" again in a long run of the market turning up "heads." In the middle of February 2013, some two and a half months prior to his brave market-top call, he wrote to clients about his firm's "3–6 month Neutral outlook on the S&P 500," and mentioned that "The current 86 percent bullish reading is the chief reason why we believe that the best rally gains have been achieved." In the eleven weeks between this bearish note and the bearish note profiled in the *Journal*, the S&P 500 gained 5 percent. He called "tails" back in February, was wrong, then called "tails" again in May, and would undoubtedly keep calling "tails" until the market finally came up tails and he could claim to have called it right. For this, the financial media described him as brave.

I'm not picking on the *Journal* or this particular incarnation of Peter Perfect. Other publications run the same kinds of stories, and other analysts toss the same coin. Some tossers get it right along the way, of course, since the accuracy rate is 50 percent, and they are duly praised in the media. Eventually, this tosser would be right, too, and could convince himself and the rest of those not yet onto the game that he was pretty good—at calling "tails" until it happened. He had plenty of opportunities to do so. Six months after he bravely called the top on May 2, the S&P 500 was 11 percent higher and climbing. A year after, it was 18 percent higher and *still* climbing.

Beyond entertainment value, the salient point here is that this charade is no way to manage our money. The financial media create excitement by implying that forecasts work, that other people are doing better, that you should try your hand at making the right moves, and that everybody should be trying to catch Peter and his friends on their way to perfection.

Remember, Peter's perfect record doesn't really exist, and most of his professional money management friends lose to the market. When you see the word *analyst* or *chartist* or *guru* or any other title for supposed stock market pros, substitute *coin-tosser*. Whenever you read a forecast, intone the most important four syllables in the market's lexicon: 50 percent. Peter is everywhere, and he makes it hard to resist the temptation to time the market.

Peter judges all stock market results against perfection, and (no shock) they always come up short. Nobody buys the lows and sells the highs. You won't read this in many stock books or articles. Even if unstated, the implicit suggestion in stock cheerleading material is that there's so much more potential profit in the market that you can take for yourself if you just get a few more calls right. You can't, though. If you're like the majority of professional money managers, you'll get half of them right, if that, and will run up a large sum of transaction fees, a long string of tax consequences, and a high level of stress in the process of losing to the market.

This makes no difference to Peter Perfect. He'll keep reminding you about the profits of perfection and goading you onto the trapdoor of another attempt at timing. When arriving at our own sensible plan for navigating the uncertainties of stocks, the 3 percent signal, we'll need to guard against the influence of the Peters by comparing our results to less-than-perfect but more realistic outcomes. Those are the ones deemed by the media as too boring to report, but mastering them while ignoring the media brings great satisfaction and greater profits than the market.

"Where's the market heading?" you'll be asked. "Who cares?" you'll reply, and the Peters will be furious.

What We Think versus What Is Real

This chapter reaches conclusions that are hard for successful people to accept. The stock market attracts smart people who are naturally a proud bunch. Their intelligence got them to the tops of their classes; into excellent universities; recognized by their peers and the public; into high-paying positions at important companies or firms or hospitals or other organizations; hailed by their communities; and into distinctive homes and automobiles. Investors are winners in life, who are not used to middling results. Why would they accept them in the market?

"They" are really "we," of course. You and I are proud of our accomplishments, too, and have come to respect our abilities. We think we can do better than average in the stock market. Given enough exposure and practice, we think we can even beat the market itself, the same way we've risen to other challenges.

The hiccups and hang-ups of human nature fool us into thinking that predicting stocks is somehow different from predicting the future. It's not. A person predicting that the stock market will rise next month is no more believable than someone predicting that a baby will be born in your town on the third Tuesday of next month, or of another predicting the date of next year's first snowfall. The odds for each of these predictions will vary, but all are uncertain. We sense this uncertainty in the prediction of babies and weather, but are too willing to overlook it in the stock market. It's probably the speculation masquerading as research that tricks us. If people guessing when babies will be born or snow will fall in the distant future did so at the end of thick reports containing charts and tables, we'd probably believe them, too. They don't, though, because they're just guessing and don't pretend otherwise.

Some people spend years of their lives striving admirably to improve their skills and performance in a field that defies improvement, the stock market. They experience stress and frustration at each missed cycle, and many don't discover until late in life that they've given too much of their limited time to a hopeless endeavor. How many picnics, holidays, vacations, special dinners, graduations, weddings, and anniversaries must be consumed by the zero-validity vortex of the stock market to make a person realize it might not be worth it? Stock stress can become an all-consuming worry; a burrowing, hollow disappointment at what went wrong; and worse, a realization that you aren't sure how to fix it without compounding your troubles.

Imagine that weight on your shoulders during a Sunday stroll with your family, when you're supposed to be enjoying the weather and chitchatting. "Isn't this sunshine delightful?" your spouse asks. You nod absentmindedly and paste on a smile, but you're really wondering, "When will prices stop falling?" "We should do this more often," you hear, and you agree, but think, "It might be tricky when our money is draining away by the day."

But you don't have to be burdened with this stress. And that's where our plan comes in.

Executive Summary of This Chapter

We are bad at timing the stock market because we misinterpret our own limited experience as a proxy for larger complexity at work. Our memories change over time to make us think we knew in the past what we know now, and we mistake luck for skill. We see patterns where there are none, and are unable to hone our intuition in the stock market's zero-validity environment because what happened there in the past will not necessarily happen again. Key takeaways:

✔ Pattern recognition works well for us in most of life because it builds on repeating, reliable rules. Thus, we apply it to stocks, but with detrimental effect because asset price fluctuations follow no patterns precisely.

✔ Pride and poor memory make us vulnerable to hindsight bias, the mistaken belief that we knew it all along. We forget our misinterpretations or rationalize them away to conclude that we weren't wrong, the market was wrong. It should have done what we expected.

✔ We mistake luck for skill, and then become more confident in our abilities, commit more money to future ideas, and squander previous gains by losing more money in later errors.

✔ Stock market participants are correct only 50 percent of the time, the same odds involved in tossing a coin. Our pattern recognition tendency falls victim to the illusion of predictability in the randomness of this fifty-fifty environment.

✔ An overwhelming majority of investment managers loses to the market, and even the winners experience long losing streaks that shake a lot of investors out before they benefit from eventual outperformance.

✔ The stock industry is expert at tricking us into thinking we'll get better at investing than we really will. It does this by suggesting that perfect performance is within our grasp because all the information needed for us to have made a perfect decision existed at key points in the past. It leaves out that we know only in hindsight which information was correct.

CHAPTER TWO

Harnessing Fluctuation

Now that you know what doesn't work in the stock market, it's time to look at what does: the 3 percent signal, hereafter short-handed to 3Sig. You're going to tune out the z-vals in favor of running this signal's proven system just four times per year.

We'll begin this chapter with an overview of the plan. Next we'll explore price fluctuation, the market characteristic that is the powder behind 3Sig's bullet. There are only three directions the stock market can go: up, sideways, or down. It moves forward by switching among these directions at its own pace, and from this unpredictable fluctuation we're supposed to achieve profit by selling at prices higher than we paid. If we automate the process using arithmetic, even random price changes can work for us rather than against us, as you'll discover when we extend the coin toss example you saw in the last chapter. We can't know in advance what the coin will do, but we can know how we'll react to what it does.

In this sense, fluctuation is beautiful. We need prices to change in order to benefit from buying and selling. If they didn't, adding money to the stock market would be the same as depositing into and withdrawing from a bank account that paid no interest. However, fluctuation can get ugly when our powers of premonition fail us (as they're wont to do) and we end up selling things for less than we paid to buy them. These things are usually stocks, mutual funds, and exchange-traded funds. With 3Sig, we will rationally react to fluctuation in their prices by buying cheap and selling dear.

The 3 Percent Signal

There are six components to 3Sig. We'll briefly look them over here, so you can see where we're going, then spend the rest of the book becoming better acquainted with them, why they work, and most important, how amazingly they work. The six components are:

- the growth vehicle where we keep most of our capital during our working years;

- the safety vehicle where we keep a smaller portion of our capital;

- the target allocation of capital between the growth and safety vehicles;

- the safety vehicle allocation at which a rebalance back to its target is triggered;

- the timing of our growth signal; and

- the growth target.

There's flexibility in how these parts are defined. For example, the growth vehicle could be a large-company stock fund, a specialty stock fund such as one that focuses on technology companies, or a screened stock fund that invests in bargain-priced stocks. The safety vehicle could be a money market fund, a bond fund, or something else that doesn't fluctuate much. As for allocation, we could put half in growth and half in safety, or move the slider in either direction for more growth or more safety. A 20/80 division between growth and safety would be quite safe but our money wouldn't grow much, while money in an 80/20 division would grow a lot but also fluctuate widely along the way. In the timing component, we could specify how often we adjust the stock fund to its growth target: monthly, quarterly, annually, or at some other pace. Our growth target could be anything we want, such as 2 percent per month, 4 percent per quarter, or 11 percent per year.

We'll explore different permutations of these components later in the book, but there's a default, evergreen combination that I call the base case of the plan. It works for anybody during most of his working years, and it's what I mean when referring to 3Sig. In the base case of the plan, the components are:

- a small-company stock fund as the growth vehicle;

- a bond fund as the safety vehicle;

- an 80/20 target allocation between the stock and bond funds;

- a 30 percent bond allocation threshold that triggers re-balancing back to 80/20;

- a quarterly timing schedule; and

- a 3 percent growth target.

At the end of each quarter, you'll look at your stock fund balance. If it grew 3 percent, you'll do nothing. If it grew more than 3 percent, you'll sell the extra profit and put the proceeds into your bond fund. If it grew less than 3 percent or lost money, you'll use proceeds from your bond fund to buy your stock fund up to the balance it would have attained if it had grown 3 percent in the quarter. In this manner, you will mechanically extract profit from price fluctuation.

Imagine the 3 percent signal line rising up and to the right on a price chart. At the end of each quarter, your stock fund balance will be either above or below the signal line. You could shade in the distance between the two, in dark gray for a profit surplus above the signal line, in light gray for a profit shortfall below it. The quarterly procedure sells the surplus or buys the shortfall to bring your stock balance perfectly back to the signal line. It looks like this:

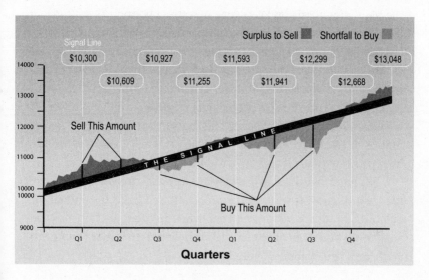

Selling surpluses and buying shortfalls along the 3 percent signal line.

This simple system beats the stock market by stripping out noise. You will not need (or want) anybody's opinion on where stocks are going, not even your own. The plan reacts to what *did* happen rather than trying to predict what *might* happen, and all it needs in order to do so are quarterly closing prices. Hard numbers, not prognostications, fuel this approach. It will help you achieve a return better than that from the supposed experts, without listening to anything they say, as you lock in the 3 percent growth rate with little work and almost no stress. This plan is going to automate an important part of your financial life to help you get back to living.

In the rest of the book, we'll look at 3Sig's components and add two addendums that boost its performance: a "stick around" rule that keeps you fully invested in stocks for recovery after a crash, and the use of a "bottom-buying" account to fund buy signals during big sell-offs.

To run 3Sig, you'll need just two cheap index funds, one for small-company stocks and one for bonds. This means you can run the plan anywhere you keep your investments, such as a 401(k), an IRA, or a regular brokerage account. A retirement account is the best place to run 3Sig because it enables you to follow sell signals without worrying about taxes on profits. We'll cover this more fully in Chapter 6. Converting your retirement and other financial goals to 3Sig will remove market nervousness from your life, lower the expenses you pay, and substantially boost your investment performance. It works so well and so painlessly, you're going to wonder how you ever made it this far without it.

Say good-bye to z-val distractions and the anxiety of indecision that haunts most investment approaches, and hello to rational calculations that take out all the guesswork on the mere four days per year you'll bother to check in. This is how the real smart money invests, and you're about to join it.

Volatility Is Opportunity

Flat lines are not conducive to profit. We need highs and lows. Our job as investors is to recognize the inevitable oscillation between highs and lows as the natural tide of the market. The media churn this movement into emotional stories of thrill and agony, but when we filter them out and simply understand that low prices are to be bought and high prices are to be sold, volatility becomes our friend.

Unfortunately, we're not naturally good at tuning out noise. We're even worse at tuning out friends and family who are tuned into noise and eager to share what they've heard. The financial media know how to make a convincing case using believable experts and compelling evidence. The latter is often couched in terms of some market measurement being at what the media claim to be some historically significant level. For instance, you might read that volume on the New York Stock Exchange topped a certain number of shares for the first time in eighteen months. You're left to believe that an important conclusion should be drawn from this information, but you'll have to draw it yourself. Combine this with an occasion where stock prices went way up or way down, and you're emotionally vulnerable to running off in a random direction. Egging you on will be experts recycling well-worn catchphrases such as "due for a rest" or "priced for perfection" on the bearish side, and "room to run" or "the bad news is baked in" on the bullish side.

All you really need to know is that stock price movement is yours for the using. It does not matter why prices are up, just that they are. It does not matter why prices are down, just that they are. Their being up or down does not influence in any way the odds of their being higher or lower in the future. You can only know what happen*ed*, not what *might* happen. Anything could happen, so why bother guessing? Leave that to the experts.

The more an investment fluctuates, the more opportunity it provides for profit, but at a higher level of stress. Low fluctuation is easy to accept emotionally, but is not very profitable. High fluctuation is hard to accept emotionally, but can be very profitable. Most planners will suggest that a balance needs to be struck by combining low-volatility assets with high-volatility, arguing that the stability of the former will provide us with confidence to stay invested for the strong performance of the latter.

I propose a different approach. Rather than relying solely on the comfort of low-volatility assets to stay the high-volatility course, why not also add an automated mechanism for putting volatility to work? Doing so makes price changes interesting and fun, not emotionally devastating, as we merrily run the automation of buying lows and selling highs. We become comfortable with the process, not fearful of losses and greedy for gains.

This comfort and the effectiveness of the automation enable us to focus the bulk of our money on a more volatile segment of the stock market for better performance in the long run. Few planners advise such a route because the higher volatility shakes most people from the plan. This is because most plans include no mechanism for signaling lows to be bought and highs to be sold. Mine does, so the automated handling of higher volatility makes it much easier to stick with the plan through ups and downs. This pays off with better performance over time for two reasons. First, because volatile parts of the market rise more than tamer parts after all is said and done; and second, because the automated buying of lows and selling of highs magnifies this already stronger performance.

We'll get to which volatile part of the market we're going to use. For now, just understand that volatility provides opportunity when it's used properly. It's not to be feared. In an investment that can't go bankrupt, falling prices are just an opportunity to deploy money for profit later. This might seem self-evident, but it's lost in the daily to-and-fro of market prognostication. By the time you're done with this book, you'll focus entirely on the prices that market volatility already delivered to you, not at all on the ones it might deliver in the future. You'll come to trust that the same automation that got you this far will take you farther still, and you'll stop worrying about where the market is heading. Wherever it goes, your automation will react appropriately.

Volatility is opportunity, and you're going to put it to work.

Retreat to the Index

Looking at the evidence in the last chapter and the shelves of research backing it up, many investors give up on timing the market and retreat to index funds. Even the great investor Warren Buffett, who amassed one of the world's largest fortunes by owning shares of companies that he believed to be undervalued, said at a press conference after his company's annual shareholder meeting in May 2007 that most investors would do better owning low-cost index funds rather than entrusting their money to managers or picking stocks on their own. "A very low-cost index is going to beat a majority of the amateur-managed money or professionally managed money," he said. He believed he could continue beating the S&P 500, but would be amazed if it were by more than "a couple of percentage points." Coming from one of the all-time best stock pickers, these observations are noteworthy. In recent years, Buffett has not outpaced the S&P 500, and he gave explicit instructions for money he's bequeathing in a trust for his wife: put 10 percent in short-term government bonds and 90 percent in a very low-cost S&P 500 index fund.

An index mutual fund or exchange-traded fund (ETF) owns the market without exercising any judgment whatsoever. It doesn't try to guess ups and downs, doesn't care what's happening in the economy, is indifferent to exciting new product launches, and so forth. In the case of the S&P 500, an index fund owns all five hundred of the large-company stocks on the list maintained by Standard & Poor's. In the case of the Russell 2000, an index fund owns all two thousand of the small-company stocks on the list. The stocks in an index are called its "components." Most index funds own all the components in the same percentage weighting as the index itself. These indexes, especially the big ones such as the Dow Jones Industrial Average and the S&P 500, are called "the market." When we own index funds, we put our money into the market itself, with no attempt to select which stocks are going to do better than the aggregate.

This works because it's cheap and it outperforms the majority of professional managers, who fall victim to all the human shortcomings you read about in the last chapter. In any given year, about two-thirds of the "pros" do worse than they would have done if they'd just bought an index fund on the first trading day in January and spent the rest of the year fishing.

Index investing, not Peter Perfect or the z-vals, is our real rival. If we can't devise a plan that beats the S&P 500 over time, then we should give up and own the index itself. The S&P 500 will be our benchmark in this book, and we'll soundly beat it. In so doing, we'll utterly trounce the legions of z-val money managers.

Nudging the Coin Toss Line

In the last chapter, we looked at a chart I created by tossing a coin fifty times and adjusting a $10,000 balance higher by 5 percent on heads and lower by 5 percent on tails. We found that it produced performance streaks that don't appear random, and that the resulting chart looked like charts from the stock market. To refresh your memory, here's the sequence of toss results and the chart it produced:

HHH tt H t HH t H ttt H ttttt HH ttt HH t H t HH t H t H ttt HHHHHH t H t HH

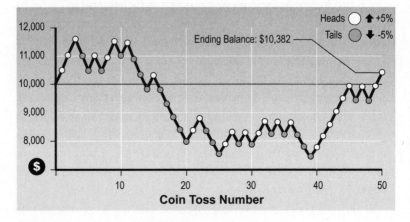

Change in $10,000 balance by coin toss.

To make the example more realistic, let's add a second layer of randomness. On top of the same sequence of heads and tails tossed previously, I tossed the coin another fifty times. Heads meant a 6 percent change in account balance, either up or down depending on the first toss, while tails meant only a 4 percent change. Here's the second sequence of toss results:

t H t HHH tt H t HH ttttt H tt HH tt H t HH t H t H t H t HH ttttt H t H tt H t

The first toss was heads in the first sequence, indicating positive change, and tails in the second sequence, indicating 4 percent. The $10,000 balance grew 4 percent, to $10,400. The second toss was heads in the first sequence, again indicating positive change, and heads in the second sequence, indicating 6 percent. The $10,400 balance grew 6 percent, to $11,024. Here's how this process played out over fifty rounds:

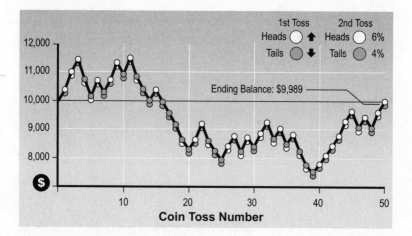

Change in $10,000 balance by double coin toss.

The pattern is very close to the one we generated before with constant 5 percent moves. The numbers are slightly different, but the pattern is almost the same. Our second layer of randomness did little to change the outcome of the first. The reason for this is that the second layer couldn't alter the direction of the chart line in each round, just the size of the move. In the first example, the chart always moved 5 percent. In the second, it moved either 4 or 6 percent, thus either a little less or a little more. That 4 and 6 average out to 5 added to the similar outcome over time, since each was equally likely.

However, larger numbers and numbers farther apart can significantly alter the outcome by forcing the same pattern over wider territory. Here's a chart of the same coin toss sequences as those just given, but with heads in the second sequence producing a 30 percent move and tails producing a 10 percent move:

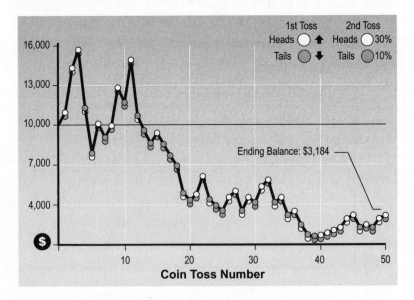

Change in $10,000 balance by double coin toss with larger moves.

This big change happened by just growing the moves. The first example, with every change at 5 percent, left us with $10,382. The second example, with heads at 6 percent and tails at 4 percent, left us with $9,989. This third example, with heads at 30 percent and tails at 10 percent, left us with $3,184.

In these examples, we achieved different outcomes on the same random pattern of ups and downs by changing the size of the moves, but it could also have happened by our changing the amount of money riding the moves. Investing more at bottoms and less at tops would nudge our performance upward even as the market followed a random path. We'll explore this in more detail next.

Reactive Rebalancing

If we believe the evidence in Chapter 1, then aren't we being hypocritical in attempting to invest more at bottoms and less at tops? If we can't know when the market has bottomed and when it has topped, how can we know when to add more money and when to sell profits?

We can't know bottoms and tops exactly, but we can know the direction the market has gone and react appropriately. This requires no prediction. Instead of guessing forward, we react backward. We determine our actions by what already happened instead of what may or may not happen. When prices rise and we find ourselves with excess profit, we sell. When prices fall and we find ourselves surrounded by bargains, we buy. I call this "reactive rebalancing," to describe reacting to where the market went by rebalancing more of our capital into and out of the stock market as appropriate—no crystal balls required. The more common attempt to profit from stocks involves predictive rebalancing, which is moving money to where a z-val's coin toss says it will grow in the future.

Consider the coin toss pattern we've looked at. In the first example, we moved 5 percent at every inflection point, up and down. In the second, we moved either 4 percent or 6 percent. In the third, 30 percent or 10 percent. We assigned the movement size randomly in the second and third examples. What would happen if, instead of reacting randomly to market moves, we reacted deliberately based on what transpired? Let's find out.

In this next example, we'll move the market randomly by the same pattern we've been using, but we'll react to it by selling after it moves higher and buying after it moves lower. We'll use the same constant 5 percent market moves from our first example, so all rises and drops will be by 5 percent. We'll begin with an 80/20 division of our $10,000 between stocks and cash, so $8,000 in stocks and $2,000 in cash. When the market rises, we'll sell 5 percent of our stock position. When the market falls, we'll use our cash balance to buy a 5 percent increase in our stock position. For example, if after a market drop of 5 percent our stock position is worth $5,000, we'll move $250 into it, which is 5 percent of $5,000. Here's the result of this plan over the same fifty coin tosses we've been following, compared with the base movement of the coin tosses themselves:

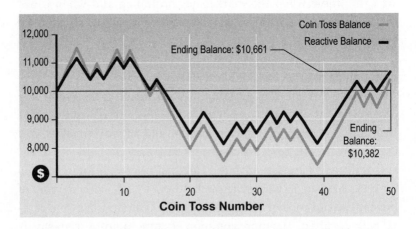

Change in $10,000 balance by coin toss vs. reactive buys and sells.

How about that? These mechanical reactions improved our performance over the performance of the coin toss market. In the first up sequence, the bold reactive line slightly underperformed because we sold the strength and therefore had less riding on stocks to benefit from the further move higher. We muted the updraft. This continued for several cycles, but even our underperformance wasn't intolerable. We were behind in that part of the journey, but not by much. The worm turned when the coin entered its tttHtttttHHttt phase, and both the market and our balance fell steadily toward the $8,000 level on all those tail tosses. Suddenly, our plan's tactic of muting the moves came in handy. It previously prevented us from getting as high as the market's peaks, but in this extended downdraft it put the brakes on our losses as the market fell freely on each tail toss. As a result, we fell less and were able to keep a performance margin over the market for the remainder of the fifty tosses.

The prognosticators of the real stock market would complicate this simple example and create the confusions that so vex us. Instead of reading about the random results of coin tosses, you would read and hear opinions from professional guessers who've spent years of their lives in the z-val environment of stocks. Thus your journey along the random market sequence would generate discussions of a "range-bound" market along the $11,000 line in the beginning. You'd hear about the bulls and the bears battling it out for control. In the tttHtttttHHttt phase, you'd hear from bears about the gathering momentum to the downside. You'd read about the unemployment rate, rising tensions in the Middle East, an overheating property market in some faraway country, the "unprecedented" decisions of the Federal Reserve or its "lack of imagination," how the president is ruining the country, the fecklessness of Congress, industrial production this month as compared with last month, dangers that are "on the radar" but not yet realized, inflation being too high or too low or on its way to one or the other, and what the price of gold says about interest rates. You would be led to believe that all this was vitally important and that wherever the market went next, it was obvious from the combination of these factors that it would do so. Come on, smart money, didn't you know that?

Then, to make forecasters look as silly as we know them to be, the market often goes sideways, as it did between coin tosses nineteen and forty-one in our example, when it fluctuated between $8,000 and $9,000. These are always the most humorous environments to watch in the media, because after the market proves everybody wrong by going neither up nor down, both sides come out in force to explain why the market is "coiling" for its next move in their pet direction. The permabulls say it's basing before going higher; the permabears say it's topping out before falling lower. It eventually breaks one way or the other, and one side or the other claims victory in that round of the coin toss contest.

We, on the other hand, beat the majority of pros and the market itself by automating our reactions to where prices actually went, and could have spent all fifty rounds of this scenario blithely disregarding the chatterboxes in favor of living our lives. At the end of the fifty rounds, we and our reactive rebalancing ended up with $10,661, the market ended up with $10,382, and the majority of pros would have ended with balances between the $9,989 of our second example (when heads produced a 6 percent move and tails a 4 percent) and the $3,184 of our third example (when heads produced a 30 percent move and tails a 10 percent).

On top of this, notice that we achieved this superior performance with a good chunk of our capital in the safety of cash. You read at the beginning of this chapter that 3Sig keeps a safe-fund target allocation of 20 percent. That's a key point that we're mimicking in this example. We began with 20 percent of our capital in cash, and the amount fluctuated later as we bought and sold, but we were never all in. Peruse the following table of key points in our journey, marked by the coin toss number in the left column and then balances after the action caused by it:

TABLE 1. Balances Through Coin Toss Market Fluctuation

Coin Toss Number	Our Cash Balance ($)	Our Stock Balance ($)	Our Overall Balance ($)	"Market" Balance ($)
1	2,420	7,980	10,400	10,500
9	3,370	7,820	11,190	11,490
25	605	7,515	8,120	7,547
36	1,890	7,348	9,238	8,649
39	886	7,257	8,143	7,415
50	3,601	7,060	10,661	10,382

See the dynamic at work? As the market fell, our automated plan steadily moved more of its cash into stocks at lower prices. When the market recovered, our plan steadily moved that money back out of stocks at higher prices. You can see the fluctuation between the cash fund and the stock fund. The cash balance fell with the market as more of it went into stocks to maintain a fairly stable balance in the $7,000 area. When the market recovered, stock profits went back into cash, so that fund's balance swelled again.

In this construct, we get ahead of the market when it falls because we fall less. If the market hits a string of heads and rises relentlessly over a long period, it could pull ahead of us because we'd be selling along the way and benefiting less from further rises. Remember, though, that the market fluctuates. Over time, the gradual tipping of the scales in our favor will nudge our performance line higher. That's all we want.

This example is simplistic because the actual stock market doesn't move in clean 5 percent increments, and setting a firm buy/sell allocation at 5 percent of our portfolio isn't the best technique. Later, we'll use real market data to develop a more elegant reaction to fluctuation. We'll also keep our safe allocation in bonds, not cash, thereby boosting performance even more while retaining much of the safety of cash. The purpose of these coin toss examples is to establish that intelligent reaction to random moves can provide a performance edge.

On this concept, we'll build a reliable system. We'll stop asking, "What *will* the market do?" and start asking, "What *did* the market do?" and then, "What should I do in response?" It's the beginning of investing wisdom, our first step away from the rabble and toward a method of making market fluctuation work for us rather than against us.

Executive Summary of This Chapter

The stock market moves at its own pace in an up, sideways, or down direction. The resulting price changes can be used to our advantage after they've happened, no prediction required. Automating the process of buying low and selling high makes market volatility a tool to be used, not a condition to be feared. Key takeaways:

✔ The 3Sig approach rebalances a stock fund back to its growth target each quarter by selling surpluses or buying shortfalls using money from a safe fund.

✔ Volatility is opportunity. We need to recognize that the oscillation between highs and lows is the natural tide of the market. It matters only that prices are where they are, not why they got there. Nobody knows why.

✔ As long as an investment won't go bankrupt, more price volatility will enable an automated system of buying low and selling high to produce more profit. This is why a volatile index, which can't go bankrupt, is our primary investment in 3Sig.

✔ Indexing beats the majority of investors, so our goal is to beat indexing. We will do so swimmingly, thereby utterly trouncing money managers.

✔ A randomly generated price line can be nudged by changing only the size of its moves; there's no need to change or predict its direction. The impact of moves on our balance can be changed by altering the amount of money riding the moves.

✔ Mechanically buying lows and selling highs adjusts the amount of money riding a price line in a helpful way, shifting performance higher than that achieved by the raw price line. This requires no forecasting, just reactive rebalancing.

CHAPTER THREE

Setting a Performance Goal

So far you've learned that we're bad at forecasting the stock market, but that an automated plan to buy low and sell high gets around this shortcoming by reacting to what already happened. In this chapter, we'll further define the automation by setting a performance goal that tells us whether the market is high or low. The market moves around all the time, so we need a signal line to put its movement in context. If the market rises above the line, we'll sell. If not, we'll buy.

This chapter explains why 3 percent per quarter is the right performance goal and how using it beats other approaches while taking less risk.

What's a Good Performance?

How much should we expect from stocks? The stories people tell are always about big successes, of course, doubling their money or owning a legendary "tenbagger," a stock that grows tenfold. These triumphs happen now and then, and they're a lot of fun, but they're not reliable and they usually don't involve enough of our capital to make a meaningful impact. The question to ask when somebody claims to have doubled their money is "How much of your money?"

We need a reliable target that we can achieve again and again as the years go by. The best way to know what's typical for the market is to look at its historical performance. There's no guarantee that it will perform similarly in the future, of course, but the past is all we have. The sea of stocks contains individual bankruptcies and ten-baggers and countless variations in between, but how much has the sea itself moved?

The Market Over Time

Various long-term studies of the stock market show its performance to have been about 10 percent per year for the past ninety years or so. This is nominal performance, which is to say before inflation is factored in. Inflation-adjusted performance is called "real performance," and it comes in at about 6.8 percent per year. The returns

Summary: January 1926–June 2012

	Nominal	Real
Geometric annualized return	10.0%	6.8%
Arithmetic annualized return	12.0	8.8
Volatility	19.3	19.4

Rolling ten-year annualized geometric returns of the broad U.S. stock market, December 1935 to June 2012. © The Vanguard Group, Inc. Used with permission.

for large companies are lower than the returns for medium-size and small companies, but the 10 percent nominal rate of return is a good approximation for what the overall market has delivered, and it's easy to remember.

The market hasn't grown as smoothly as annualized performance might make you think, though. The market's rolling ten-year returns since 1926 have fluctuated from –5 percent to 20 percent, as shown in the chart from Vanguard on page 54.

We'll use 10 percent as the basic annual growth of the stock market, and improve upon it with 3Sig.

The Outperformance Sweet Spot

"Why three percent per quarter?" you ask. It's not 1 percent per month or 12 percent per year, neither an intuitive goal nor one you see anywhere else in the investment world, thus a curiosity at first blush. It makes sense upon closer examination, though, so let's have a look.

Our goal is to beat the market, but by how much? If we assume that stocks will return about 10 percent per year, should we strive for 10.1 percent, 12 percent, 15 percent, 20 percent, or something higher?

Because we want to achieve our goal repeatedly forever, it needs to be reasonable. Steady outperformance of even a small margin produces a big advantage over time due to compounding. Look at the growth of $10,000 at various rates:

TABLE 2. Growth of $10,000 at Various Rates

Annual Rate (%)	In 5 Years, $10,000 Becomes ($)	In 15 Years, $10,000 Becomes ($)	In 25 Years, $10,000 Becomes ($)
8	14,693	31,722	64,485
10	16,105	41,772	108,347
12	17,623	54,736	170,001
14	19,254	71,379	264,619

Notice the impact of just two percentage points on your ending balance over every time frame. At 10 percent per year, your $10,000 becomes $108,347 in twenty-five years, but at 12 percent it becomes $170,001—a difference of $61,654. Even the five-year difference of $1,518 will buy two weeks' worth of dinner for two. Don't underestimate the benefit of a seemingly small 2 percent advantage. It makes a big difference.

Naturally, we'd like to earn as much as possible. With most styles of investing, the higher the desired rate of return, the higher the risk that goes with it. A safe government bond, for example, offers a low interest rate because repayment is guaranteed. Stock in a risky start-up that might become the next force in business but also might disappear offers those same twin potentials to your money: it might become a tenbagger but also might fall 90 percent. With the system we're creating, a higher desired rate of return will force us to add money to our plan more frequently because the market will be less likely to achieve our goal. This is easy to understand. If you are aiming for a 10 percent gain every month and will make up for shortfalls with new cash, you're going to be adding cash almost every month because the market rarely rises 10 percent in a month. Conversely, if you aim for 1 percent per quarter, you'll make it almost every time and will probably never need to add extra cash—but you won't grow your wealth enough over the years.

Our goal is 3 percent per quarter, thus the 3 percent signal. Growth of 3 percent per quarter produces an annual performance of 12.6 percent, which is 26 percent better than the market's annual performance of 10 percent over the past ninety years. This is a giant outperformance that produces much more profit over long periods, as you saw in the previous table. Here is the market's 10 percent annual rate compared with our 12.6 percent annual rate over the same time frames:

TABLE 3. Growth Advantage of 12.6% over 10.0%

Annual Rate (%)	In 5 Years, $10,000 Becomes ($)	In 15 Years, $10,000 Becomes ($)	In 25 Years, $10,000 Becomes ($)
10.0	16,105	41,772	108,347
12.6	18,101	59,303	194,294

The extra 2.6 percentage points of performance provide an impressive amount of profit beyond what the market has provided.

I've found this 3 percent quarterly rate to be the sweet spot of risk and reward. It's not so high that we need to take extraordinary measures to achieve it, but it's not so low that we barely notice the benefit of beating the market. It provides a reasonable boost over stock index performance that adds up to a sizable profit improvement over the years.

You need to know that I didn't just pull "3 percent per quarter" out of a hat, so let's look at how it compares with other rates of return. In the next chapter, you'll read that small-company stocks are the best category to use with our plan. Throughout later examples, we'll look at iShares Core S&P Small-Cap (IJR) as a way to invest in them, and we'll use the fifty-quarter time frame from December 2000 to June 2013. The next table shows the results of different quarterly growth targets run with our plan using IJR in this time frame, beginning with $8,000 in IJR and $2,000 in cash. "Total New Cash" refers to times the plan signaled buying with more cash than the account had, thus requiring you to deposit new cash to keep it going. As you can see, the higher the desired rate of growth, the more new cash that's occasionally needed:

TABLE 4. Results of Quarterly Growth Targets from 1% to 6%

Plan from December 2000 to June 2013	Starting Balance ($)	Total New Cash ($)	Ending Cash Balance ($)	Ending Stock Balance ($)	Ending Total Balance ($)
Rebalance to a 1% quarterly rate of growth in IJR	10,000	0	11,443	13,157	24,600
Rebalance to a 2% quarterly rate of growth in IJR	10,000	4,835	12,912	21,532	34,445
Rebalance to a 3% quarterly rate of growth in IJR	10,000	12,241	14,141	35,071	49,212
Rebalance to a 4% quarterly rate of growth in IJR	10,000	22,494	13,412	56,854	70,266
Rebalance to a 5% quarterly rate of growth in IJR	10,000	37,535	9,481	91,739	101,220
Rebalance to a 6% quarterly rate of growth in IJR	10,000	66,105	6,078	147,361	153,439

It is possible to dial in a higher ending balance by moving the growth rate target up. However, it eventually requires a lot more cash to keep the plan going. Quarterly growth rate targets higher than 3 percent ask too much of the market, and therefore frequently signal you to make up the difference with fresh cash. You could aim for a 50 percent quarterly growth rate if you wanted, but you'd end up supplying almost all of the bigger balance with new cash. The rising cash dependency is obvious when you compare the results of a 3 percent target with those of a 5 percent target. To double the ending balance from $49,212 to $101,220, you needed to invest three times the cash, from $12,241 to $37,535. This eroding efficiency persists as the growth rate is ratcheted higher.

The 3 percent quarterly target snags enough oomph from the

market to make your efforts worthwhile, but not so much that it demands excessive amounts of cash from you. It's the sweet spot, a good balance of new cash required and profit achieved.

Gauging Fluctuations Against Our Goal

Now we know how much performance we want from stocks: 3 percent per quarter. How do we go about guaranteeing we get it? By using a safe bond fund to support our stock fund when the market fails to deliver 3 percent in a quarter, and by selling the excess profit from the stock fund when the market delivers more than 3 percent in a quarter.

This strategy is a variation of value averaging, a money management technique introduced by Michael Edleson in a 1988 article and further explained in his book *Value Averaging: The Safe and Easy Strategy for Higher Investment Returns*. It's reliable because we simply provide our stock fund with whatever profit the market failed to provide in a quarter, and we replenish our bond fund with excess profits delivered by the market in other quarters. This back-and-forth keeps the stock fund growing at our 3 percent quarterly rate due to basic math, regardless of what the market does. The engine behind the long-term growth of our stock fund is provided by the market, but when that engine sputters we help it out with our safe bond fund.

You saw this concept in a chart in the last chapter on page 48, and in action when we set a system of buying price drops and selling price rises in the fictional coin toss market. Doing so produced a better performance than the market itself. In that example, the market moved in 5 percent increments, and we reacted to it by either buying or selling an amount worth 5 percent of our stock balance.

The real market moves in whatever amount it wants in whatever time frame it wants, rather than in clean 5 percent increments. Our real-life plan will respond in spirit the same way we responded in the coin toss market, by selling price rises and buying price drops at the end of each quarter. Instead of moving 5 percent of our stock balance each time, we'll buy or sell our way to the 3 percent quarterly performance goal we've set. This means the amount we buy and sell will change each quarter, which is better than the fixed reaction we used earlier because it enables our plan to reallocate in proportion to how far the market moved rather than buying and selling a set percentage of our stock fund. If the market goes up a lot, we should sell a lot. If the market goes down a lot, we should buy a lot. Our plan will do both.

How do we know how much is a lot? By comparing the rise or fall to our 3 percent quarterly goal. That's our signal, showing us both whether to buy or sell and how much to buy or sell, every quarter.

Quarterly Time Frame

"Why quarterly?" you may wonder. After all, the market is active every business day, and paychecks arrive either once or twice a month, so it might seem odd to check our portfolio only four times per year. The investment media create the impression that frequent activity increases one's control and therefore boosts performance, but as usual, the evidence runs contrary to the propaganda.

In the January/February 2013 issue of *Financial Analysts Journal*, Roger Edelen, Richard Evans, and Gregory Kadlec published a paper titled, "Shedding Light on 'Invisible' Costs: Trading Costs and Mutual Fund Performance," in which they reveal that mutual fund managers who trade frequently run up higher transaction fees and achieve worse performance.

A 1997 study by Richard H. Thaler, Amos Tversky, Daniel Kahneman, and Alan Schwartz published in *The Quarterly Journal of Economics*, "The Effect of Myopia and Loss Aversion on Risk Taking: An Experimental Test," explored the impact of information frequency on investment performance and came to similar conclusions. Participants were told to imagine they managed the endowment portfolio of a college and would invest it in a simulated financial market. At the end of the study, they would receive a sum of real money commensurate with their performance, thus encouraging everybody to do as well as possible. There were just two mutual funds in the market, A and B, and participants had to decide how many of a 100-share allotment to allocate to each. The period covered twenty-five simulated years. Participants were randomly assigned how often they would be informed of their portfolio's performance for a chance to change the allocation between the two funds: monthly, yearly, or every five years during the simulated time period.

Since nobody knew anything about the two funds, most began with a fifty-fifty division between them. As updates arrived, they adjusted their allocations. Participants receiving five-year updates could make only a handful of adjustments, while those receiving monthly updates had hundreds of chances to make moves. The end result? People receiving updates every five years more than doubled the returns of those receiving monthly updates.

One of the funds simulated the behavior of bonds, the other the behavior of stocks. The bond fund changed little month to month and almost never lost money. The stock fund was much more volatile on its path to stronger long-term performance. While the bond fund rarely slipped, the stock fund lost money in about 40 percent of the simulated months. The maximum performance would have been achieved with a complete allocation to the stock fund because its frequent losses were more than offset by higher overall gains. It delivered few losing years, for instance, and no losing five-year runs. Participants seeing monthly updates experienced the short-term losses in the stock fund, however, and reacted by moving money into the safer bond fund, thus crimping total performance. Participants receiving fewer updates saw the bigger picture of the stock fund performing better, without seeing its higher volatility between updates. By the end of the simulation, the participants updated monthly had allocated only 40 percent of their money to the stock fund, compared with 66 percent for the participants receiving updates every five years.

Add these studies to the profusion of research showing that passive investing, doing little or almost nothing with long-term investments, is the path to better performance. Why? For all the reasons you read about in Chapter 1 concluding that people are bad at picking stocks and timing the market. Humans are so prone to error in the stock market that more information leading to more activity just means more mistakes, along with higher fees incurred to make them. This fact prompts learned veterans of financial research to advise newcomers, "Don't just do something, sit there!"

Professional money managers never will, though, even as we see that the more they manage, the more fees they rack up, the more mistakes they make, and the more their performance suffers. We must learn from their mistakes, and the lesson we'll take away is that we should involve ourselves very little in the day-to-day vicissitudes of our stock account, filing those vicissitudes under the catch-all "fluctuation" label while focusing our energy on more meaningful aspects of living. We'll check in just four times per year, and in a systematic manner at that.

This quarterly schedule is just right. It gives the market three full months of moving around before we rebalance back to target. Three months is enough time for a lot of up and down to happen, for trends to get under way or wrap up. A monthly schedule tends to interrupt cycles. More important, historical testing of the plan shows that frequencies higher than quarterly ones increase activity without increasing performance. You'll buy more and sell more, but you won't make more. Our aim is to maximize profits while minimizing activity, and a quarterly pace achieves this aim.

It also provides opportunity for you to do something in reaction to what's happening in the news, but not too much. Investing doesn't take place in a vacuum, and people are proven meddlers. When we get the feeling that everybody is taking action now, we want to take some kind of action, too. Waiting until the end of the year to measure our performance against a growth target is too long for many people, and doesn't allow for the plan to react to subcurrents during the year.

Our systematic quarterly plan comes up often enough to remind us that we're not neglecting our financial duties, but infrequently enough to prevent Peter Perfect from dragging us off course and into the sand traps of whimsical judgment.

How It Works

We've established so far that we're going to aim for 3 percent growth on a quarterly basis, and that we'll buy our stock fund up to that signal line or sell it down to that signal line every quarter.

What's a SPDR?

You'll see the abbreviation SPDR here and there. It's pronounced "spider" and it stands for Standard & Poor's Depositary Receipts. The SPDR family of ETFs is managed by State Street Global Advisors in Boston. The first one in the family—and the oldest American ETF still trading—is the SPDR S&P 500, symbol SPY, introduced in January 1993. It's one of the largest ETFs in the world, and the one we'll use to monitor the broad market for our "stick around" rule.

We're going to stop tossing coins and start using real market data. Let's run through an example using the 3Sig plan with the S&P 500, the definitive index of large-company stocks, covering three-quarters of the American stock market's capitalization. The S&P 500 contains lots of companies you know, such as Apple, Chevron, Google, and Wells Fargo, in addition to many you probably haven't heard of, such as Allergan (a pharmaceutical company in California, maker of Botox), Leggett & Platt (a manufacturer in Missouri), and NiSource (a utility in Indiana).

As we did in the coin toss example in the last chapter, and consistent with the base case of 3Sig, we'll begin with an 80/20 division of our capital between a stock side and a safe side. The stock side will own the S&P 500 as represented by the SPDR S&P 500 ETF (SPY). The safe side will own the Vanguard GNMA bond fund (VFIIX). Instead of fifty coin tosses, we'll use fifty calendar quarters of adjusted SPY closing prices from the beginning of 2001 to the middle of 2013. This twelve-and-a-half-year time frame saw part of the dot-com crash, the roaring housing market recovery on Federal Reserve stimulus and lax lending standards, the subprime mortgage collapse, and part of the next recovery on more Federal Reserve stimulus—something for everybody. Here are SPY's fifty quarterly closing prices throughout the drama:

TABLE 5. SPY's Fifty Quarterly Adjusted Closing Prices from Q101 to Q213

Year	Q1 ($)	Q2 ($)	Q3 ($)	Q4 ($)
2001	91.94	96.87	82.83	90.97
2002	91.40	79.26	65.80	71.33
2003	68.79	79.53	81.74	91.43
2004	93.25	94.78	92.87	101.21
2005	99.17	100.60	100.60	106.10
2006	111.07	109.37	115.29	122.91
2007	123.73	131.64	134.16	129.24
2008	117.23	114.25	104.15	81.69
2009	72.50	84.30	97.27	103.21
2010	108.81	96.45	107.21	118.75
2011	125.75	125.79	108.41	121.00
2012	136.36	132.48	140.89	140.35
2013	155.09	159.64		

Summarized this way, the stock market isn't so daunting, is it? For all the strong opinions from bulls and bears, vociferous presentations predicting future direction, projected impact of a showdown in Washington or geopolitical outburst overseas, and speculation on the Fed's next move, the only thing that matters is a handful of prices. Some are high, and some are low as the market moves up and down in response to waves of human emotion washing over it. Rather than looking as silly as the z-val "pros" running around guessing loudly what will happen next, we'll react to each quarterly closing price by selling or buying our stock fund to the 3 percent signal line. As we do so, we'll wonder what all the fuss is about.

Let's say we began with $10,000, as in previous examples. The 80/20 starting mix between our stock side and our safe side put $8,000 in SPY and $2,000 in VFIIX. The year-end 2000 price of SPY was $103.09, so our $8,000 owned 77.6 shares. Our $8,000 plus 3 percent put our 3 percent signal line at $8,240 for the first quarter of 2001. The closing price of SPY that quarter was $91.94. Our 77.6 shares times $91.94 were worth only $7,135, which was $1,105 below our signal line at $8,240, so we needed to buy 12 shares of SPY to catch our stock fund up to the 3 percent signal line. SPY paid a dividend of $0.316 that quarter. Multiplied by our 77.6 shares, the dividend added $24.52 worth of new VFIIX shares to our VFIIX balance, plus VFIIX itself paid a dividend of $0.170. Together, the dividends brought our VFIIX balance up to $2,141. Buying 12 shares of SPY at $91.94 used $1,103 from our VFIIX balance, and our stock fund rose to 89.6 shares of SPY worth $8,238—close enough to the $8,240 signal line we wanted.

Observe the magic at work here. This simple plan of making up the difference between what the market delivered and our 3 percent signal line guided us to buy SPY at a price almost 11 percent cheaper than it had been three months prior, when we began our plan at the end of December 2000. Do you think most stock investors were eager to buy after the S&P 500 fell 11 percent in the first quarter of 2001? Not on your life. Peruse the zeitgeist back then.

The New York Times reported on February 22, 2001, "The pessimism gripping United States stock markets deepened yesterday, as investors nervous about weak corporate earnings and higher inflation sent stocks to new lows for the year."

BBC News reported on March 14, 2001, "Stock markets around the world are falling because they fear that the slowdown in the economies of Japan and the United States could become global, hurting company earnings."

The New York Times reported on March 15, 2001, "The stock market fell sharply yesterday, with the Dow Jones Industrial Average falling below 10,000 for the first time in five months . . . The Federal Reserve, which has cut short-term interest rates twice this year, is widely expected to cut rates again next week, but investors appear to be losing faith in the Fed's ability to engineer a quick recovery. . . . The decline 'worries me,' President Bush said."

Businessweek reported in a story headlined, "When Wealth Is Blown Away," on March 25, 2001, "Many terrified—and suddenly poorer—investors now sit paralyzed on the sidelines. . . . [T]he plunge in stocks has them holding onto their wallets for dear life. . . . [which] could lead to more cuts in consumer spending and further depress corporate profits, sending the stock market into a downward spiral. 'It's going to be sharper on the downside than it even was on the upside,' says [one of the many z-val economists offering predictions]."

Following this commentary, SPY *gained* 5.4 percent in the second quarter of 2001.

While the rest of the investment public attempted to navigate such observations, which emphasized freezing in place or selling to prevent further damage, you pulled out your calculator to see that SPY's price at the end of March 2001 put you way below the 3 percent signal line, and you bought the number of low-priced shares needed to catch up. End of involvement. As the z-val crowd pontificated, you spent a grand total of fifteen minutes to outperform them in the very next quarter. Remember, most z-vals lose to the plain index over time. Our 3 percent signal plan beats the index, thereby beating almost every "pro" who manages to get his or her name in the news with what you're coming to see as merely distracting commentary.

How It Performs

Following the same simple procedure at the end of each quarter that we followed at the end of the first quarter of 2001, our 3 percent signal portfolio outperformed the S&P 500. The extreme market swings that characterized the period would have signaled buying amounts that exceeded our cash balance in nineteen quarters— although one did so by only $58, another by only $111, and nine others by less than $800, so eight quarters is more like it—for a total of $30,711 of new cash needed. (We'll explore later the occasional need for extra cash.) Had you followed the plan and added new cash in the nineteen quarters that needed it, you would have ended with a balance of $71,152 instead of SPY's ending balance of $15,489 with all dividends reinvested. Stripping out the $30,711 of new cash required during this time period's extreme sell-offs to keep the buy orders going (about $205 per month over the 12.5-year period), you still grew your initial $10,000 into $40,441. That's 161 percent better than buying and holding the market would have achieved.

In the next table, these results are summarized and compared with those from other plans using the same two stock and bond funds, SPY and Vanguard GNMA. The plans are arranged in descending order by ending total balance. Notice the strong performance of 3Sig when it fully funded all buy signals by adding new cash when its bond balance was insufficient, but also *when it funded none of them* beyond the buying power of its bond fund balance, as shown in the superiority of Plan 4 over Plan 5:

TABLE 6. SPY Investing Plan Comparison

Plan Number	Plan from December 2000 to June 2013	Starting Balance ($)	Total New Cash ($)	Ending Stock Balance ($)	Ending Bond Balance ($)	Ending Total Balance ($)
1	3% signal plan with **SPY** and **Vanguard GNMA**, 80/20 mix, *all* new cash provided	10,000	30,711	60,959	10,193	71,152
2	New cash needed in Plan 1 distributed across 50 equal quarterly buys of **SPY** after initial $10,000 buy (dollar-cost averaging)	10,000	30,711	63,667	0	63,667
3	New cash needed in Plan 1 added to buying and holding **SPY**	40,711	0	63,055	0	63,055
4	3% signal plan with **SPY** and **Vanguard GNMA**, 80/20 mix, *no* new cash provided	10,000	0	13,973	2,336	16,309
5	Buy-and-hold **SPY**	10,000	0	15,489	0	15,489

The top-performing plan was 3Sig, with all buy signals funded. Dollar-cost averaging Plan 1's new cash amount into SPY across all fifty quarters of the time period, as shown in Plan 2, didn't work better. Even investing all the new cash demanded by Plan 1 in SPY at the beginning of the time period produced inferior results, as shown in Plan 3. The final apples-to-apples comparison, between Plans 4 and 5, with no new cash in either case, shows 3Sig beating a plan that just bought and held SPY the whole time.

Dollar-cost averaging is the technique of contributing a fixed amount of money to an investment on a regular schedule, such as monthly or quarterly. Dollar-cost averaging into indexes and buying and holding indexes are the two most popular set-and-forget investment techniques. Each performs much better over time than almost all z-val advice, of course, but 3Sig performs even better than both, and does so more safely by keeping some of its assets in a bond fund. This makes for not only a better raw performance but a better risk-adjusted one, too. Plan 1 beat Plan 2 with 14 percent of its ending balance in safe bonds. Ditto with Plan 4 over Plan 5. We'll look at this advantage more closely later.

Finally, this stronger 3 percent signal performance is after we've been overly generous to dollar-cost averaging plans and buy-and-hold plans. In real life, almost all of them distribute capital across several different funds rather than concentrating on one stock market index, as the examples just given show. When people diversify across several funds and asset classes, they do worse over long time periods than they would have done by just buying and holding a stock index. This is due to what you learned in Chapter 1 (that most managers lose to the market) and also because nonstock funds will underperform stocks over time.

To show that 3Sig is better than just about anything else, we compared it not to run-of-the-mill rivals but to high-performance versions of dollar-cost averaging and buying and holding. It still came out on top.

The Myth of Buy-and-Hold

There's a key point we have to consider here, however, and it's that people *don't* buy and hold through awful times. Like accurate market forecasting and Peter Perfect's track record, buying and holding through thick and thin exists only in theory for almost all investors. Given the fear-inducing headlines and commentary that appear during sell-offs, no wonder people bail out at the worst possible moments and fail to get back in until most of the recovery is gone.

3Sig helps buck these emotional urges by showing in a simple formula when it's time to buy more shares on the cheap or, at the very least, hold on to what you already own. Glance back at Table 5 on page 64 showing all fifty quarterly closing prices for SPY. From the third quarter of 2007 to the first quarter of 2009, the price of SPY fell 46 percent. A theoretical buy-and-hold investor who began the time frame with $10,000 in SPY saw the balance drop from $14,888 in the third quarter of 2007 (Q307) to $8,375 in Q109, a 44 percent loss. The balance fell less than SPY's price fell, due to dividend reinvestment. Imagine the feeling of doing nothing while your account dropped 44 percent on pessimistic commentary.

Everybody believes in buy-and-hold when times are good, but almost nobody does when times are bad. A fully invested portfolio looks most brilliant just before it collapses. The odds are overwhelming that our buy-and-holder watching her balance fall from $14,888 to $13,158, then $12,899, then $11,836, then $9,364, then $8,375 would have pulled the rip cord from a low altitude and sworn off stocks forever—or at least until the bulk of the recovery was over and the z-vals started talking about how much profit the smart money made from the bottom, which, of course, nobody other than Peter actually bought.

This tendency is compounded by the very reason some advisers advocate buy-and-hold investing, which is that the bulk of market gains happen on just a few days. It's true that a person who buys and holds is guaranteed to be in on those days, but because buying and holding is so psychologically difficult to maintain when it maximizes losses at the market's lowest points, it sets the odds of abandoning the technique highest just when it's about to finally pay off. Ironically, then, a strategy that's supposed to guarantee that a person's money will be invested during the tiny subset of days that produce gains actually makes it likely that person will bail out just ahead of such days precisely when holding on is most desirable.

The very commitment to buying and holding is what leaves people invested to the point of greatest pain, when they sell. If they weren't committed to buying and holding, they would give up earlier and spare themselves some of the spiral to the bottom. Anybody can ignore a small loss, and maybe even a medium one. It's the big ones that shake 'em loose. Being fully invested to the bottom of a stock market crash is emotionally excruciating. The final, dominant urge is "Just get me out of here. I don't care what the market does next, I simply don't want to be part of it anymore."

Buy-and-hold is what people say; buy-and-bail is what they do.

Any system that doesn't precondition both the investor and the portfolio for falling prices runs a high risk of exceeding the investor's emotional fortitude and suffering the performance-killing decisions that follow. This aspect of investing is usually relegated to a tiny subsection within presentations on formulas and advice for staying disciplined, but the emotional weakness of human beings is the primary reason we fail at investing. It's not a subpoint at all; it's the main point.

There are two classic mistakes that emotional investors (which is to say, all investors) make: buying the top and selling the bottom. We can't say which is worse, because one leads in the direction of the other, but here we're looking at the problem of crying uncle at the bottom. When we do so, we're engaging in a kind of market timing without even knowing it. The motivation is to stop the pain, but selling as a way to do so assumes that the market will keep going down. If we knew it would go up, we'd stay put and let the rising prices assuage our suffering. We think it will never stop, though, so we get out of the market.

Strategies that leave us deciding with our emotions when to be in and out of the market almost always miss the bulk of the market's performance. Numerous studies have confirmed that the market's rising and falling are unevenly distributed, with most days going nowhere as movement concentrates into a small number of remaining days.

In February 2013, for example, the investment company Fidelity published charts showing that the worst times are actually the best times to invest. It showed four examples of this, each detailing the five-year gain in stocks following the bottom of a bear market: 367 percent after the Great Depression ended in May 1932, 267 percent after the 1970s malaise recession ended in July 1982, 251 percent after the most dramatic Federal Reserve interest rate tightening ended in December 1994, and 111 percent after the Great Recession kicked off by the subprime mortgage crash ended in March 2009.

The same report demonstrated the impact of missing the small number of days when the market staged its biggest moves higher. Had an investor beginning with $10,000 on January 1, 1980, stayed fully invested in the S&P 500 through December 31, 2012, her account would have been worth $332,502. Had she missed the five best days—just *five* days in a thirty-three-year time frame—she would have forgone $117,229 in profits to end up with a balance of $215,273. The same calculation was run removing the ten best days, thirty best days, and fifty best days to create a convincing illustration that missing concentrated up moves inflicts severe performance damage. Remove the fifty best days from this investor's thirty-three-year journey, and the final account balance falls $303,175, to a paltry $29,327. Here's the summary:

TABLE 7. Impact of Missing Goods Days on a $10,000 Investment in the S&P 500 January 1, 1980 to December 31, 2012

Days Missed	Ending Balance ($)
Invested on all days	332,502
Missing best 5 days	215,273
Missing best 10 days	160,340
Missing best 30 days	63,494
Missing best 50 days	29,327

This type of research is usually rebutted by z-vals showing that returns are similarly *improved* by missing the worst days. In both cases (missing the concentrations of the best days and worst days), the conclusion is mathematically obvious. Look how self-evident the answer is when we frame the question this way: "Gee, I wonder what will happen to my performance if I remove some of the very best days. Oh, what do you know? It went down." Conversely: "Hmm, let's see where performance goes when I remove some of the very worst days. How about that? It went up." It doesn't take much imagination to get the picture.

Of course removing the best days will result in lower performance, and of course removing the worst days will result in higher performance. Therefore ... what, exactly? Since none among us knows ahead of time which days will be the best and worst, we're back to coin tossing. There's a 50 percent chance you'll correctly get out of the market ahead of the good days and bad days, and another 50 percent chance you'll reenter ahead of the good days and bad days. This leads most academics to conclude that staying the course is the best way to go because the market rises over time, so the great days will overcome the bad days to net out to the long-term performance of the market.

Wouldn't it be great, though, if we reacted just a little more intelligently to these good days and bad days? If only there were a system that told us when the good days added up to a level where profits should be harvested, or the bad days compounded down to a level where new money should be invested. Oh, wait, there is such a system: 3Sig. It keeps you mostly invested all the time, and guides you to do the right thing when the world goes frothy and it's harder than ever to think straight. Over a lifetime, *mostly* invested in practice trumps *fully* invested in theory.

Outperforming with Less Risk

Even though buy-and-hold is a fantasy, it's often used as the benchmark to judge various investment plans. The common question is "Does the plan earn enough more than buying and holding to make it worthwhile?" With 3Sig, the answer is yes, as you read in "How It Performs" on page 67. It's even worthwhile with a low percentage of capital in stocks, one so low that the plan requires no additional cash.

To have avoided needing any cash infusions in 3Sig during the time period of the example we're considering, we would have had to begin with a conservative 37/63 mixture of stocks and bonds, or $3,719 in SPY and $6,281 in VFIIX. Nobody could have known this at the time, and our plan doesn't require getting the balance perfectly right, but if somebody had been very careful during the dot-com crash when this time frame began and chosen to start with such a cautious allocation, they still would have outperformed buying and holding SPY to the middle of 2013.

This consideration is called "risk-adjusted performance." It takes into account that there's more to an investment story than just raw growth. Sure, somebody somewhere may have doubled his money, but how much risk did he take to do so? Probably quite a bit. Somebody else may have earned far less, but probably faced a lot less risk. This matters because risk tolerance varies among people, and many are willing to accept lower returns for the comfort of lower risk. Thus, if you can outperform the stock market while allocating only a portion of your capital to stocks while some remains safely in bonds, you'll achieve higher risk-adjusted and raw performance than an all-stock portfolio that's buffeted by every market storm.

This is what 3Sig achieved when it began the time frame with only 37 percent of its capital in SPY, and it never needed fresh cash. The buy-and-hold SPY balance ended at $15,489 including all dividends reinvested. If we started our 3 percent signal plan with only $3,719 in SPY we would have ended at $36,155, with $29,508 in SPY and $6,647 in VFIIX. That's 133 percent better than buying and holding SPY—with less exposure to stock risk. We'll look more closely at risk-adjusted performance in the next chapter.

Cash Shortages

You may be concerned about cash shortages that crop up now and then when you have most of your capital in stocks and the market tanks. These shortages give Peter Perfect another opportunity to try tempting you back into the follies of forecasting, so let's pause to address them.

Before we do, remember that our plan puts its safe side into bonds. When the bond fund runs out of funds, I'm calling it a "cash shortage" even though it's technically a "bond fund shortage." Everybody knows that a cash shortage means we need more cash, and indeed that's the case here, too. When the bond fund runs dry, we need to add more cash.

We ran into nineteen quarterly cash shortages when the buy

signal called for more new shares than our bond fund could afford. One of the quarters required less than $100, five required between $100 and $300, and five required between $500 and $800. These eleven delivered modest demands. The other eight required more than $1,000. The biggest shortfall happened in the heart of the sub-prime mortgage collapse, when the three quarters from Q308 to Q109 required respective new cash deposits of $3,054, $6,537, and $3,905. Using a technique you'll learn later, called "30 down, stick around" (in which you stay fully invested in stocks after a big crash), caused another large shortfall, in Q210, when the market hit its first dip in the recovery. Had the plan been selling on the way up, it would have generated enough cash to cover the drop. Since it was fully invested in stocks, however, the bond fund was empty and needed new cash for buying. This was actually a profitable situation because staying fully invested on the way up grew the stock account enormously. All nineteen shortfall quarters added up to $30,711 in new cash needed over the course of these 12.5 years. These were the nineteen shortfall quarters, rounded but with a correct total sum:

TABLE 8. Nineteen Quarterly Cash Shortfalls Using SPY from Q101 to Q213

Quarter	New Cash Needed ($)	Quarter	New Cash Needed ($)
Q301	286	Q206	575
Q202	1,124	Q407	221
Q302	1,907	Q108	2,993
Q103	643	Q208	1,383
Q104	58	Q308	3,054
Q204	204	Q408	6,537
Q304	768	Q109	3,905
Q105	727	Q210	5,162
Q205	273	Q311	779
Q405	111		30,711

Such shortfalls occasionally happen when we are dealing with the stock market because we can't know what it's going to do. If we knew enough to achieve a perfect balance of bonds to stocks, we'd know enough to time the market in the first place and wouldn't need this plan. Nobody can do that, which means we're occasionally going to have to manage cash shortages. As long as you can fund them, they're great opportunities.

This time period was extremely volatile and included two of the biggest stock market crashes ever. Almost nobody saw them coming, and even fewer were well positioned ahead of them. Five of the nineteen quarters requiring new money happened in a row during the subprime mortgage crash, from the first quarter of 2008 to the first quarter of 2009. The last big one, Q210, was also related to the subprime crash because the plan stayed in stocks for the recovery. It's impressive that this plan correctly signaled investors to buy the steep sell-off rather than selling, as many z-vals advised. The recovery that ensued made all those brave buys during the crisis pay off.

Another point is that $30,711 doesn't seem like such a large figure when you realize it came to an average of $204.74 per month during the 12.5-year stretch. People interested enough in their finances to read a book like this are people who save money, which makes me think this additional cash demand would not have been impossible to meet. Regular cash contributions to a plan, such as those into a retirement account, greatly reduce the number of shortfall quarters, but even they can't guarantee eliminating them completely. You'll see this unfold in a detailed example in Chapter 7.

For an apples-to-apples comparison, look at the following excerpt, taken from Table 6 on page 68. Notice how 3Sig's average new cash needed per month of $204.74 stacks up against the same $204.74 per month invested in SPY at the end of every quarter regardless of price, a dollar-cost averaging plan. Three months of $204.74 monthly savings turns into $614.22 going into SPY at the end of each quarter. We'll start the plans with the same $10,000 balance, and we'll allocate our 3Sig portfolio into the same 80/20 mixture of stocks to bonds at the start, and both plans will end up using the same $30,711 in new cash. Here's the result, with all dividends reinvested:

TABLE 9. 3Sig with SPY Beating Dollar-Cost Averaging Its New Cash

Plan from December 2000 to June 2013	Starting Balance ($)	Total New Cash ($)	Ending Stock Balance ($)	Ending Bond Balance ($)	Ending Total Balance ($)
3% signal plan with **SPY** and **Vanguard GNMA**, 80/20 mix, *all* new cash provided	10,000	30,711	60,959	10,193	71,152
New cash needed in above plan distributed across 50 equal quarterly buys of **SPY** after initial $10,000 buy (dollar-cost averaging)	10,000	30,711	63,667	0	63,667

At the end of the 12.5-year period, with each approach starting at the same $10,000 balance and investing the same amount of new cash, buying $614.22 worth of SPY each quarter produced an ending balance of $63,667 while our 3Sig plan produced an ending balance of $71,152 with less risk. Our signal achieved an 11.8 percent improvement even though it finished the period with $10,193 in bonds—14 percent of our capital.

It's possible that your bond fund will drop to zero and that you'll have no extra cash available in your life when 3Sig tells you to buy more stock. In such cases, you can at least understand from the plan's advice that you should not sell into the falling market. This, too, is valuable. When headlines and stories panic people, it's tempting to get out entirely at just the wrong moment. A cool-headed look at what the signal is saying should provide you with confidence to stay put, because you'll come to trust it after many quarters of sound advice. You'll know you should be buying, but you can't, so you'll do the next best thing, which is holding the shares you already own for their eventual recovery. After they recover, you'll resume selling excess profits and rebuilding your bond fund balance with the proceeds. Running out of cash doesn't end the plan; it just pauses it.

Even this worst-case scenario—which isn't terrible—is almost always avoidable with a cash management technique we'll look at later.

Because we're investing in the stock market, where anything can happen, it's impossible to construct a plan that functions perfectly in any environment. We can't predict how high or low prices will go, so we have to come up with a plan that navigates the fluctuation in a way that outperforms the market in almost all time frames. The 3 percent signal is such a plan, but it can issue a buy signal big enough to exceed your bond fund reserves. Such moments usually mean that a very good opportunity is at hand, so we'll strive to keep you ready for this.

In rare cases when you're not ready, you'll shrug and stand by until your stock balance recovers and you can pick up where you left off. No big deal.

Executive Summary of This Chapter

The performance goal with 3Sig is 3 percent per quarter. It rebalances back to this signal line when you either sell a stock profit surplus down to it or buy a shortfall up to it. Key takeaways:

✔ We will use proceeds from a safe bond fund to buy more of our stock fund when the market fails to deliver 3 percent in a quarter, and replenish the bond fund by selling excess profit from the stock fund when the market delivers more than 3 percent in a quarter.

✔ Our quarterly schedule is just right. It maximizes profits while minimizing activity. Frequencies higher than

quarterly ones increase activity without increasing performance.

✔ The 3Sig plan with SPY handily outperformed powerful
alternatives, including dollar-cost averaging and buying
and holding.

✔ Beware the myth of buy-and-hold. It exists only in theory. Everybody believes in buy-and-hold when times are
good, but almost nobody does when times are bad.

✔ The 3Sig plan guides us through this tendency. It tells us
when the market's good days have added up to a level
where profits should be harvested, and when its bad days
have compounded down to a level where new money
should be invested.

✔ Keeping part of the plan in safe bonds also helps to
weather stock storms.

✔ It's possible for our plan to run out of buying power. In
such times, buy signals tell us to stay put for recovery,
which is helpful. However, such moments have been historically rare, suggesting that gradually built savings can
help you take advantage of these exceptional buying opportunities.

CHAPTER FOUR

What Investments to Use

We've discussed several important concepts so far. You've seen that most investors lose to the market. You've discovered that automatically selling higher prices and buying lower prices, whether along a coin toss line or a real price line, nudges your performance up. Then you found 3Sig as a way to know how much to buy and sell each quarter, and saw in the last chapter that 3Sig beat the S&P 500 during the very volatile period from 2001 to 2013.

Now it's time to refine the plan further by exploring what investment provides the best opportunity to beat the S&P 500. There's no rule that says we need to use the index itself when striving to beat it. What if a different market segment works better?

Small Companies for Growth

Along with the rest of the investment industry, we'll continue using the S&P 500 as the benchmark we want to beat. Our 3 percent signal provides us with a way to do so, but we can improve upon its outperformance by running it against not the S&P 500 we're trying to beat, but a different index that beats the S&P 500 over time. This advantage, combined with our 3 percent signal, gives us a double advantage.

We can gain an edge over the large-company S&P 500 by using indexes that track small companies instead. The word *capitalization* and its abbreviation *cap* refer to the size of companies as measured by multiplying their shares of stock outstanding by their market price. When stock investors talk about company size, this is what they mean (as opposed to number of employees or factories or something else). Company size means market cap, and you'll sometimes see it referred to as large cap, medium cap, and small cap. What constitutes large, medium, and small companies changes over time due to earnings growth and stock price fluctuation, but here's the rough breakdown currently: an average large company has a market cap of $60 billion, an average medium company has a market cap of $5 billion, and an average small company has a market cap of $1 billion.

The following table compares the performance of different indexes as achieved in ETFs that follow them. The S&P 500 tracks large-cap stocks; other indexes track other company sizes. Notice the disparity in the average annual returns of these six indexes through October 31, 2013:

TABLE 10. Performance of Different Indexes via ETFs

ETF Symbol	Index	Tracks	1-Year Avg. Annual (%)	3-Year Avg. Annual (%)	5-Year Avg. Annual (%)	10-Year Avg. Annual (%)
DIA	Dow Jones	30 large companies	21.8	14.6	13.7	7.3
SPY	S&P 500	500 large companies	27.1	16.5	15.1	7.4
MDY	S&P Mid-Cap 400	400 medium companies	33.3	17.3	19.4	10.1
IJR	S&P Small-Cap 600	600 small companies	39.4	20.4	18.2	10.5

(continued)

ETF Symbol	Index	Tracks	1-Year Avg. Annual (%)	3-Year Avg. Annual (%)	5-Year Avg. Annual (%)	10-Year Avg. Annual (%)
IWM	Russell 2000	2,000 small companies	36.3	17.7	17.2	9.0
QQQ	Nasdaq 100	100 leading Nasdaq companies	29.3	17.9	21.3	9.7

The medium- and small-company indexes have performed better than their larger-company brethren, and are where we should focus our attention. The simplest way to beat the S&P 500 is to just own the S&P Small-Cap 600 or Russell 2000 or a different small-cap index, but we'll go one better and move our capital into and out of small caps using 3Sig. This puts a base-improvement system to work on a base that's already better than the one we're aiming to beat. Small-company indexes outpace the S&P 500 on their own, and we'll improve their performance even more with 3Sig.

There's another reason that small-cap indexes work well with our plan. They are more volatile than larger-company indexes, which means their prices fluctuate more, and fluctuation is what makes our system work. It's the movement between higher and lower prices that enables us to buy low and sell high by comparing the index to our 3 percent signal line and responding accordingly.

There are several ETFs and mutual funds that target small-company indexes. Most 401(k) plans and other retirement accounts offer securities in each of the large-, medium-, and small-company varieties, making it easy to implement 3Sig just about anywhere you keep your retirement funds.

Three excellent ETFs for targeting small caps are iShares Core S&P Small-Cap, Schwab U.S. Small-Cap, and Vanguard Small-Cap. Respectively, they track the S&P Small-Cap 600 Index, the Dow Jones U.S. Small-Cap Total Stock Market Index, and the CRSP U.S. Small-Cap Index. Each ETF is cheap to own, with an expense ratio of 0.20 percent or less and a portfolio turnover rate of 20 percent or less. The turnover rate of less than 20 percent means that in most years, the funds leave 80 percent of their portfolios untouched. This is good because it minimizes trading costs. Here are their profiles as of October 31, 2013, with the SPDR S&P 500 ETF shown for comparison:

TABLE 11. Comparison of Small-Cap ETFs with SPY Through October 31, 2013

Symbol	Name	Started	Yield (%)	Expense Ratio (%)	1-Year Avg. Annual (%)	3-Year Avg. Annual (%)	5-Year Avg. Annual (%)	10-Year Avg. Annual (%)
IJR	iShares Core S&P Small-Cap	5/2000	1.3	0.16	39.4	20.4	18.2	10.5
SCHA	Schwab U.S. Small-Cap	11/2009	1.6	0.08	37.9	19.1		
VB	Vanguard Small-Cap	1/2004	1.4	0.10	36.4	18.7	19.6	
SPY	SPDR S&P 500	1/1993	1.9	0.09	27.1	16.5	15.1	7.4

As you can see, all three small caps have handily outpaced their large-cap cousin, which happens to be the market measure we're aiming to beat with our 3 percent signal plan.

Index mutual funds are also an option, available against the same indexes at comparable expenses and performances. For example, Vanguard Small-Cap (NAESX) tracks the same CRSP U.S. Small-Cap Index as its ETF equivalent, Vanguard Small-Cap (VB), just shown.

For our plan, we'll use IJR because it's old enough for historical research, is one of the most widely available ETFs targeting small companies and thus makes for a good general example, and is fairly cheap.

However, if you have access to a cheaper alternative, then by all means use it. For example, both SCHA and VB charge lower expense ratios and some retirement plans do, too. These are tiny differences, however, and IJR is very cheap compared with most ETFs. The decision to use a small-cap ETF in the plan is far more important than choosing which small-cap ETF, because they'll all get the job done at a reasonable cost. Wherever you manage your 3 percent signal plan, use the lowest-cost small-company index fund available for your stock account.

Bonds for Safety

Remember that the plan divides its capital between stocks and bonds. The target allocation between the two for most of your working life is 80/20 stocks/bonds, and you'll rebalance back to this periodically when your bond balance becomes too big a part of your portfolio. The rebalance trigger is 30 percent for most of your life.

When you contribute new cash to your account, put it immediately into the bond fund, where it will wait until being deployed later into the stock fund with the plan's quarterly signals.

The reason the plan keeps part of its capital in bonds is for safety. Bonds fluctuate much less than stocks, and they sometimes go up when stocks go down. Plus, bonds pay steady dividends. Constant cash flow from dividends is comforting in addition to providing a big part of investment performance. By keeping a portion of your capital in bonds, you'll preserve purchasing power for the plan's stock market buy signals and you'll earn a decent return on that capital while it waits to buy stocks. If you kept the safe portion of your account in cash, by contrast, it would earn nothing and your overall performance would trail the market over long, rising periods.

Thus, you'll keep a target 20 percent of your account in a bond fund. There are many bond funds to choose from, and a lot are available as ETFs with low expense ratios. This is good news. Your goal wherever you run the plan will be to keep roughly 80 percent of your money in the cheapest small-cap stock index fund available and 20 percent in the cheapest bond index fund available.

The main bond market consists of short-term, intermediate-term, and long-term bonds of the government and corporate variety, as shown here:

TABLE 12. The Bond Market

Total Bond Market					
Short-Term		Intermediate-Term		Long-Term	
Government	Corporate	Government	Corporate	Government	Corporate

Beside this core structure of the market are agency bonds issued by the Government National Mortgage Association (GNMA, or Ginnie Mae), and high-yield bonds that are often referred to as junk bonds. The risk in junk bonds is too high, so we can dispose of them out of hand—not hard to do, given their name. GNMAs, on the other hand, are suitable for our purposes. Like U.S. Treasuries, GNMAs present the highest level of safety because they're backed by the full faith and credit of the U.S. government.

Let's compare Vanguard bond ETFs in each of the main bond market categories, its mortgage-backed bond market ETF, and the Vanguard GNMA mutual fund that was launched in June 1980. The reason we'll include Vanguard GNMA is that it has been around long enough to have been used in 3Sig when our fifty-quarter time frame began at the end of 2000. For you, starting the plan now, one of the cheaper ETF alternatives makes more sense and is available in more accounts. Here they are, with data through October 31, 2013:

TABLE 13. Comparison of Vanguard Bond Funds Through October 31, 2013

Symbol	Name	Started	Yield (%)	Expense Ratio (%)	1-Year Avg. Annual (%)	3-Year Avg. Annual (%)	5-Year Avg. Annual (%)
BND	Vanguard Total Bond Market	4/2007	2.2	0.10	-1.1	2.9	5.9
BSV	Vanguard Short-Term Bond	4/2007	1.1	0.11	0.6	1.5	3.7
BIV	Vanguard Intermediate-Term Bond	4/2007	2.9	0.11	-1.7	3.9	8.5
BLV	Vanguard Long-Term Bond	4/2007	3.9	0.11	-7.3	6.2	10.9
VMBS	Vanguard Mortgage-Backed Securities	4/2009	1.1	0.12	-0.6	2.3	
VFIIX	Vanguard GNMA	6/1980	2.4	0.21	-0.8	2.7	5.4

Vanguard isn't the only company providing low-cost bond index funds, but it dominates the category. Other low-cost alternatives appear regularly and may emerge as worthy considerations as they build track records. For example, Schwab U.S. Aggregate Bond (SCHZ), launched in July 2011, charges just a 0.05 percent expense ratio.

The rough one-year returns reflect the worries of bond investors in 2013 that interest rates would rise. This fear revealed key tradeoffs in the bond market. Long-term bonds offer higher yields and strong long-term performances but are more sensitive to interest rate fluctuation. Our goal in 3Sig is not to become bond trading aficionados, but just to use a reliable, low-cost bond index fund to store the safe allocation of our account. For this purpose, a total bond market fund such as BND or an intermediate-term bond fund such as BIV is best. These are as evergreen as they come, usually near the middle of the pack, very cheap, and do exactly what we expect bond funds to do.

Even in the time frame shown in the table, BND lost just 1.1 percent, which barely qualifies as a sniffle in the stock market. Plus, bond fund price losses are offset by the steady dividends they pay. For instance, in the six months ended in early November 2013, BND lost 2.1 percent in price but paid out more than $1.00 in dividends at a monthly rate of about $0.17 per share. The dividends reduced the six-month loss in BND by 57 percent, to 0.9 percent. Over long periods, the importance of dividends is even clearer. Some 90 percent of the total return of a broad mix of bonds since 1976 came from dividend payments, not price change.

Remember, this book's historical examples use Vanguard GNMA as the bond fund because it was in business back in 2000, when our fifty-quarter time frame began, and I want to use historical data rather than theoretical to show you that 3Sig works regardless of the economic environment. Since April 2007, however, cheaper alternatives to Vanguard GNMA have existed, and you should take advantage of them. You want the cheapest total bond market index fund or intermediate-term bond index fund you can get your hands on, or at least your money in.

The Performance Advantage

It's time to see how much better we can do by using IJR as our stock fund instead of SPY, which we used in the last chapter. We know that IJR's higher volatility and better long-term performance should provide an advantage, but we need to check. We'll run the exact same time frame, the fifty calendar quarters from the beginning of 2001 to the middle of 2013. We'll start with the same amount of money and allocations as before, with 80 percent of our $10,000 beginning in IJR and the other $2,000 in Vanguard GNMA. The only change is that we're going to run 3Sig with IJR instead of SPY to see if using small caps instead of large caps will put us even farther ahead of the S&P 500.

Here are IJR's fifty quarterly closing prices:

TABLE 14. IJR's Fifty Quarterly Adjusted Closing Prices from Q101 to Q213

Year	Q1 ($)	Q2 ($)	Q3 ($)	Q4 ($)
2001	30.40	34.18	28.63	34.42
2002	36.89	34.53	28.13	29.49
2003	27.73	33.31	35.72	40.85
2004	43.48	45.04	44.22	50.00
2005	48.97	50.98	53.61	53.77
2006	60.68	57.87	57.12	61.50
2007	63.28	66.50	65.35	60.92
2008	56.15	56.52	55.90	41.55
2009	34.51	42.24	49.88	52.31
2010	56.95	51.86	56.75	66.08
2011	71.12	71.03	56.89	66.61
2012	74.64	71.94	75.87	77.47
2013	86.58	90.09		

IJR closed the fourth quarter of 2000 at $32.34. Our $8,000 allocated to it bought 247 shares. It paid a $0.04 dividend in the first quarter of 2001 and finished the quarter at $30.40. Our 3 percent signal line from our $8,000 stock balance was the same $8,240 as before. We didn't make it that quarter. Our balance of $7,520 was $720 short, so we needed to buy 23.68 shares. Our bond balance rose from its initial $2,000 to $2,126, thanks to dividends from IJR and itself, plus its own modest price appreciation, but then fell to $1,407 when we bought our new shares of IJR. The end result was that our IJR balance rose to 271.05 shares worth $8,239.92—on the money again.

Here are the same plans we ran with SPY in Table 6 on page 68, but run with IJR instead, in descending order by ending total balance:

TABLE 15. IJR Investing Plan Comparison

Plan Number	Plan from December 2000 to June 2013	Starting Balance ($)	Total New Cash ($)	Ending Stock Balance ($)	Ending Bond Balance ($)	Ending Total Balance ($)
1	New cash needed in Plan 2 added to buying and holding **IJR**	37,249	0	101,648	0	101,648
2	3% signal plan with **IJR** and **Vanguard GNMA**, 80/20 mix, *all* new cash provided	10,000	27,249	69,318	16,403	85,721
3	New cash needed in Plan 2 distributed across 50 equal quarterly buys of **IJR** after initial $10,000 buy (dollar-cost averaging)	10,000	27,249	78,105	0	78,105
4	3% signal plan with **IJR** and **Vanguard GNMA**, 80/20 mix, *no* new cash provided	10,000	0	24,065	5,695	29,760
5	Buy-and-hold **IJR**	10,000	0	27,289	0	27,289

One difference you'll notice right up front is that putting all the new cash required by our plan into an initial giant buy-and-hold of IJR produced the highest ending balance. This did not happen with SPY. It's not a useful discovery, though, for three reasons: First, most people don't have all the money they're ever going to invest over a long time frame available at the beginning of the time frame. Second, nobody knows in advance which investments will best perform with a buy-and-hold approach in the time frame. Third, most people buy and bail rather than buy and hold. For these reasons, the ranking of the other plans is of most interest to us.

Among the other plans, Plan 2, which is the base 3Sig version, produced the highest ending total balance. It used new cash more effectively than the other two plans receiving new cash, even the

dollar-cost averaging of Plan 3. In Plans 4 and 5, which did not receive new cash, 3Sig outpaced buying and holding IJR, delivering an
ending total balance of $29,760 compared with $27,289.

The 3Sig plan's strong performance against the small-cap index
both with additional cash and without is good news, but our real
goal is beating the S&P 500 as represented by SPY. We accomplished
this, too, and by a lot. The following table compares IJR and SPY in
two important plan permutations, 3Sig and dollar-cost averaging
the amount of new cash needed by the signal:

TABLE 16. 3Sig with IJR Beating 3Sig with SPY

Plan Number	Plan from December 2000 to June 2013	Starting Balance ($)	Total New Cash ($)	Ending Stock Balance ($)	Ending Bond Balance ($)	Ending Total Balance ($)
1	3% signal plan with **IJR** and **Vanguard GNMA**, 80/20 mix, *all* new cash provided	10,000	27,249	69,318	16,403	85,721
2	New cash needed in plan 1 distributed across 50 equal quarterly buys of **IJR** after initial $10,000 buy (dollar-cost averaging)	10,000	27,249	78,105	0	78,105
3	3% signal plan with **SPY** and **Vanguard GNMA**, 80/20 mix, *all* new cash provided	10,000	30,711	60,959	10,193	71,152
4	New cash needed in Plan 3 distributed across 50 equal quarterly buys of **SPY** after initial $10,000 buy (dollar-cost averaging)	10,000	30,711	63,667	0	63,667

Using IJR produced a better performance in each permutation
when compared with SPY. In Plan 1 versus Plan 3, 3Sig delivered an
ending balance of $85,721 using IJR but only $71,152 using SPY, a
20.5 percent improvement. Small-cap stocks are the way to go.

We did need new cash again, but less than when we ran the plan with SPY. Using IJR, only eleven quarters ran into a shortfall as compared with nineteen quarters using SPY. Here are the eleven IJR shortfall quarters, rounded but with a correct total sum:

TABLE 17. Eleven Quarterly Cash Shortfalls Using UR from Q101 to Q213

Quarter	New Cash Needed ($)	Quarter	New Cash Needed ($)
Q302	389	Q308	1,083
Q103	927	Q408	7,814
Q304	193	Q109	5,598
Q407	1,529	Q210	5,183
Q108	2,699	Q311	1,232
Q208	600		27,249

Not only did IJR come out ahead of SPY in 3Sig, but it did so with a smaller cash shortage.

In both cases, 3Sig ended the time frame with a good chunk of its capital in safe bonds. This is important. It's beating the market with less risk, delivering both a higher raw performance and a higher risk-adjusted performance.

Look at how Plans 2 and 4, the dollar-cost averaging plans, produced lower ending balances with *all* their capital in stocks via either IJR or SPY, and zero in bonds. Meanwhile, Plans 1 and 3, the 3Sig plans, produced higher ending balances with hefty bond reserves. In IJR the $16,403 bond reserve was 19 percent of the $85,721 total balance. In SPY the $10,193 bond reserve was 14 percent of the $71,152 total balance.

To see why this helps, watch what would happen if the market dropped 20 percent the next quarter, as it did in the fourth quarter of 2008. For simplicity, assume that both IJR and SPY fell this amount and that bonds held steady. Here's how the four plans would look before and after the damage:

TABLE 18. Impact of a 20% Drop on 3Sig and Dollar-Cost Averaging

Plan Number	Plan from December 2000 to June 2013	Ending Bond Balance ($)	Bond Balance After 20% Market Drop ($)	Ending Stock Balance ($)	Stock Balance After 20% Market Drop ($)	Ending Total Balance ($)	Total Balance After 20% Market Drop ($)
1	3% signal plan with **IJR** and **Vanguard GNMA**, 80/20 mix, *all* new cash provided	16,403	16,403	69,318	55,454	85,721	71,857
2	New cash needed in Plan 1 distributed across 50 equal quarterly buys of **IJR** after initial $10,000 buy (dollar-cost averaging)	0	0	78,105	62,484	78,105	62,484
3	3% signal plan with **SPY** and **Vanguard GNMA**, 80/20 mix, *all* new cash provided	10,193	10,193	60,959	48,767	71,152	58,960
4	New cash needed in Plan 3 distributed across 50 equal quarterly buys of **SPY** after initial $10,000 buy (dollar-cost averaging)	0	0	63,667	50,934	63,667	50,934

In one fell swoop of precisely the type that derails most investors, the balances changed dramatically. The dollar-cost averaging plans, with all of their balance in the stock market, suffered the entire 20 percent drop. Plan 2 fell 20 percent, to $62,484 from $78,105, while Plan 4 fell 20 percent, to $50,934 from $63,667. The 3Sig plans, with a good chunk of their capital in bonds, muted the impact of the drop. Plan 1 fell just 16.2 percent, to $71,857 from $85,721, while Plan 3 fell only 17.1 percent, to $58,960 from $71,152.

The bond balance maintained by our signal plan delivers four benefits in bad quarters: First, it lessens the damage of the falling market. Second, it supplies buying power to take advantage of the bargain prices that follow. Third, it provides comfort. Fourth, and perhaps most important, it instills confidence in us to make the right move. What is the right move after prices have fallen hard? To buy, of course, which is what the plan would signal. In these two cases, the plan would have been able to fully fund the IJR buy signal with its bond balance, and 71 percent of it with SPY.

All this is impressive enough, but remember that we're actually understating the performance advantage of the plan over the way most people invest. In the real world, our 3 percent signal plan using IJR outperforms most investment approaches by a much bigger margin than the one shown in these tables. Few investors run their portfolios with the mechanical precision and emotionless rigor assumed in the dollar-cost averaging examples here. Most people second-guess what moves they should make, and they frequently guess wrong. Part of the advantage you gain with 3Sig is the confidence to do what it says and the satisfaction of having taken action as the market moves, which guards you against the perils of personal judgment.

Finally, even if a person never deviates from his dollar-cost averaging plan, he's almost always running it with a diversified group of funds that together underperform the pure stock index allocation used in these examples. If he runs it in a single stock fund only, the high volatility is likely to buck him off the bull. If he runs it in a diversified portfolio, he'll experience less volatility but on the way to lower returns. The 3Sig plan strikes a powerful balance. It beats these higher-performing examples with less risk and more emotional support by offering clear guidance every quarter.

With this in mind, let's compare 3Sig to the messiness of the real world, where Peter Perfect and the z-vals wreak havoc on investors.

Beating the Heroic Holding

The first rebuttal Peter would offer here is that many investments bought and held during the time period we examined would have done better than 3Sig. Just as there's always a bigger fish, always a tougher guy, and always a greener field of grass, so, too, there's always an investment that would have done better.

The problem is that you didn't own it, and neither did Peter. For practical purposes, nobody owned the very best investments at the right times. People talk about them only after the fact, usually with the same wistfulness they reserve for the possibility of having bought a winning lottery ticket. Peter, however, talks about such infinitesimally low-odd possibilities as if they happened every day and will be as easy in the future as he presents them to have been in his what-if fictional version of the past. We'll humor him for a moment.

I like to call these super stocks that got away "heroic holdings." Anybody who held them was a stock market hero, and Peter certainly presents himself that way. In the time frame we've been looking at, the fifty quarters from December 2000 to June 2013, one of the most amazing performers from the list of heroic holdings was Medifast (MED), a nutrition and weight loss company. It ended the fourth quarter of 2000 at just $0.14, and closed the second quarter of 2013 at $25.76, for a gain of 18,300 percent. You'll find few portfolio holdings more heroic than this. Look how much better you would have done putting $10,000 into MED, with no additional purchases along the way, than into these other plans we've been considering:

TABLE 19. Buying and Holding MED vs. 3Sig with IJR and SPY

Plan from December 2000 to June 2013	Starting Balance ($)	Total New Cash ($)	Ending Stock Balance ($)	Ending Bond Balance ($)	Ending Total Balance ($)
Buy Medifast (**MED**) at $0.14 and hold for the entire time period	10,000	0	1,840,000	0	1,840,000
3% signal plan with **IJR** and **Vanguard GNMA**, 80/20 mix, *all* new cash provided	10,000	27,249	69,318	16,403	85,721
3% signal plan with **SPY** and **Vanguard GNMA**, 80/20 mix, *all* new cash provided	10,000	30,711	60,959	10,193	71,152

Case closed! Go out and find the next Medifast. Buy it, hold on for dear life, and sell it at exactly the right moment. You know you can do it. At least we know Peter can.

Suddenly, we see that looking ahead is not as much fun as it is looking back. For every Medifast, there are once-promising stocks that end up like Bear Stearns and Enron, each of which collapsed and disappeared. It's easy to chuckle at investors who owned them, but they weren't acting as recklessly as you might think. A year after achieving second place in its industry on *Fortune*'s Most Admired list, and less than a week after prominent z-val Jim Cramer told viewers of his *Mad Money* television program that "Bear Stearns is fine. . . . Bear Stearns is not in trouble," the company needed an emergency loan from the Federal Reserve Bank of New York, but failed anyway and was sold to JPMorgan Chase for a pittance on March 16, 2008. As for Enron, at the beginning of the fourth quarter of 2001, when it went kaput, thirteen out of sixteen z-val analysts ranked its stock a buy, and two months after it filed for bankruptcy, *The New York Times* thought it "may yet serve as a model for other companies," though presumably without the niggling bankruptcy aspect.

These are just two examples from a list of failed investment

ideas long enough to fill the rest of this book, and each one of them
was bought and owned because the research around it said it
would one day sell for more than it sold for at the time. Peter Perfect
won't ever mention this, of course, and it's Peter's objection to our
3 percent signal we're exploring here, so we'll leave aside how easily people are tricked into buying losers and refocus instead on
one glorious winner, Medifast, and its 18,300 percent gain from
2001 to 2013. What happens in the real world when a lucky z-val
finds himself in possession of a heroic holding such as MED? Let's
find out.

Here are MED's fifty quarterly closing prices during the time
period we've been examining, plus its $0.14 price at the end of 2000:

TABLE 20. MED's Quarterly Closing Prices from Q400 to Q213

Year	Q1 ($)	Q2 ($)	Q3 ($)	Q4 ($)
2000				0.14
2001	0.44	0.33	0.20	0.22
2002	0.83	0.81	1.79	5.32
2003	4.94	11.25	12.35	14.10
2004	8.99	5.31	4.48	3.52
2005	2.87	3.04	4.00	5.24
2006	9.23	17.87	8.68	12.57
2007	7.16	8.95	5.58	4.85
2008	4.23	5.26	6.81	5.52
2009	4.15	11.46	21.72	30.58
2010	25.13	25.91	27.13	28.88
2011	19.75	23.73	16.15	13.72
2012	17.46	19.68	26.15	26.39
2013	22.92	25.76		

There was a lot more drama on the path from $0.14 at the end
of 2000 to $25.76 in mid-2013 than Peter Perfect would mention.

A straight line of profits producing no doubts along the way, this was not.

The z-vals had a field day with MED and its firecracker stock over these years, issuing upgrades and downgrades amid its wide fluctuations. Some were right and some were wrong, which makes sense in a 50 percent environment. Medifast made it into daily market reports when its stock topped the lists of biggest gainers or decliners, such as when it fell 16 percent on September 5, 2006, due to a weak profit outlook after a report showed that the cost of acquiring new clients might be rising.

There were good days, too. On February 16, 2010, Reuters reported, "Shares of Medifast, a maker of diet drinks and weight management products, shot up 17 percent on Tuesday, after Barry Minkow's Fraud Discovery Institute (FDI) ended its investigation of the company saying it wants 'to dedicate its resources to other ongoing investigations.' Medifast's stock had been battered over the past year by the FDI's allegation that the company's Take Shape for Life direct selling subsidiary operated a 'pyramid scheme.'" Between January 8, when the FDI published its report of allegations against Medifast, and February 12, the last trading session before the FDI called off its investigation, shares of MED crashed 38 percent, from $30.91 to $19.04.

Holding through such a plunge, against a backdrop of fraud accusations and the company's being likened to a pyramid scheme, would not have been easy. Peter Perfect leaves out such inconvenient details when telling his heroic stories. We won't.

We'll assume that Peter and other investors in Medifast faced reams of information regarding the company over the fifty quarters just summarized, and that they had to make a decision each quarter on whether to buy, sell, or hold. The period begins with a generous gift on our part, which is granting that Peter bought $10,000 of MED at $0.14 at the end of 2000, which was its lowest price during the entire time frame. Thereafter, we'll toss a coin each quarter. In quarters when Peter owned MED, heads meant he held it and tails

meant he sold it. In quarters when Peter didn't own MED, heads
meant he bought it and tails meant he stayed in cash. This is necessarily simplified because we can't account for partial sale possibilities and other choices Peter might have made, but it will nonetheless
give us an idea for how greatly our 50 percent failure rate can affect
even a winning investment's performance. These are the results of
my coin tosses throughout MED's fifty-quarter history after buying
it at $0.14 in December 2000:

TABLE 21. Coin Toss Path Through MED's Price History

Quarter	MED Price ($)	Coin Toss Result	Action	Cash Balance ($)	MED Balance ($)
Q400	0.14		Buy	0	10,000
Q101	0.44	Tails	Sell	31,429	0
Q201	0.33	Heads	Buy	0	31,429
Q301	0.20	Tails	Sell	19,048	0
Q401	0.22	Tails	Hold	19,048	0
Q102	0.83	Tails	Hold	19,048	0
Q202	0.81	Tails	Hold	19,048	0
Q302	1.79	Heads	Buy	0	19,048
Q402	5.32	Heads	Hold	0	56,611
Q103	4.94	Tails	Sell	52,567	0
Q203	11.25	Heads	Buy	0	52,567
Q303	12.35	Heads	Hold	0	57,707
Q403	14.10	Tails	Sell	65,884	0
Q104	8.99	Tails	Hold	65,884	0
Q204	5.31	Heads	Buy	0	65,884
Q304	4.48	Heads	Hold	0	55,586
Q404	3.52	Tails	Sell	43,675	0
Q105	2.87	Tails	Hold	43,675	0
Q205	3.04	Heads	Buy	0	43,675

Quarter	MED Price ($)	Coin Toss Result	Action	Cash Balance ($)	MED Balance ($)
Q305	4.00	Tails	Sell	57,466	0
Q405	5.24	Tails	Hold	57,466	0
Q106	9.23	Heads	Buy	0	57,466
Q206	17.87	Heads	Hold	0	111,259
Q306	8.68	Tails	Sell	54,042	0
Q406	12.57	Heads	Buy	0	54,042
Q107	7.16	Tails	Sell	30,783	0
Q207	8.95	Tails	Hold	30,783	0
Q307	5.58	Tails	Hold	30,783	0
Q407	4.85	Heads	Buy	0	30,783
Q108	4.23	Tails	Sell	26,848	0
Q208	5.26	Heads	Buy	0	26,848
Q308	6.81	Tails	Sell	34,759	0
Q408	5.52	Tails	Hold	34,759	0
Q109	4.15	Tails	Hold	34,759	0
Q209	11.46	Heads	Buy	0	34,759
Q309	21.72	Tails	Sell	65,878	0
Q409	30.58	Heads	Buy	0	65,878
Q110	25.13	Tails	Sell	54,137	0
Q210	25.91	Heads	Buy	0	54,137
Q310	27.13	Tails	Sell	56,686	0
Q410	28.88	Heads	Buy	0	56,686
Q111	19.75	Heads	Hold	0	38,766
Q211	23.73	Tails	Sell	46,578	0
Q311	16.15	Heads	Buy	0	46,578
Q411	13.72	Tails	Sell	39,570	0
Q112	17.46	Heads	Buy	0	39,570
Q212	19.68	Tails	Sell	44,601	0

(continued)

Quarter	MED Price ($)	Coin Toss Result	Action	Cash Balance ($)	MED Balance ($)
Q312	26.15	Tails	Hold	44,601	0
Q412	26.39	Tails	Hold	44,601	0
Q113	22.92	Tails	Hold	44,601	0
Q213	25.76	Tails	Hold	44,601	0

Well, I'll be. After all the triumph followed by heartache, celebratory dinners followed by sleepless nights, frustration, elation, research, stress, more research, zero validation, bragging, near misses, sulking, and everything else we can list as part of enduring this trading saga with one of the best-performing stocks of this long period, Peter Perfect grew his $10,000 into just $44,601—a far cry from the $1,840,000 he would brag about when telling you, using hindsight, how much a person who bought MED at $0.14 back in December 2000 would have ended up with in June 2013. Perfection is easy to describe in theory, but is unachievable in the real world.

Of course, our look at one possible path through the travails of MED over these years was random, and your own experiment tossing coins to determine each quarterly action will probably produce a different path. The one just given isn't a bad proxy for how our minds might have worked, however, and it included some genuine successes that Peter could have announced to his friends. If anything, this example is too kind to Peter, due to granting the initial $0.14 buy that rocketed his balance up to $31,429 within a single quarter. That kickoff, which we assumed in his favor before even starting our coin tosses, accounted for 91 percent of his gain over the entire period!

The coin tosses began from that excellent base, and they did fairly well. From the third to the fourth quarter of 2002, they grew $19,048 into $56,611. From the third to the fourth quarter of 2003, they grew $57,707 into $65,884. From the first to the second quarter of 2006, they grew $57,466 into $111,259, the high point of this series. Three quarters later, unfortunately, Peter's balance had already dwindled to $30,783. If we don't grant that Peter bought MED at $0.14 in 2000, but instead assume he started the fifty quarters in cash and didn't buy MED until the second quarter of 2001, when it traded at $0.33, the same trail of coin toss results and their associated actions would have guided his ending balance to a mere $14,191. His high point in the series would have become only $35,401 in the second quarter of 2006, which would have deflated to $9,795 three quarters later, an amount below his $10,000 starting balance—pretty distressing.

Although these quarterly moves were generated randomly, we can imagine the mental processes that might have preceded them with a human at the helm. Returning to the rosier scenario where we grant that Peter bought MED at $0.14 in 2000, his immediate 214 percent surge in the first quarter of 2001 would have given him confidence in his abilities, especially after selling at $0.44 and then finding MED at $0.33 a few months later. "Score!" he would have shouted as he bought back in for another run higher. The subsequent 39 percent drop would have been painful, which could explain why he sold and sat in cash for the next year as the price of MED rose 795 percent, from $0.20 to $1.79. Watching that one get away had to have been just as painful, no doubt ruining untold number of holidays and vacations and special events from early autumn 2001 to early autumn 2002, when he finally couldn't take it anymore and bought again. Watching a stock go from $0.20 to $1.79, then *buying*, takes guts. We should admire Peter for this one, especially since it paid off immediately when MED nearly tripled to $5.32 in a single quarter— except that it's hard to admire coin tosses.

We don't know how a person would have actually performed trading MED during these fifty quarters, but we do know that the long-term track record of human beings in the stock market reveals them making the wrong call half the time. This quick example shows how devastating this tendency can be to even the best-performing stocks. It should make you chuckle and smile knowingly when encountering tales of heroic holdings. A reasonable response to stories that begin with "Do you know that if you had just bought this stock ten years ago and held on to it . . ." is to say, "Too bad I didn't buy it then. Neither did you, and even if we had we probably would have sold too soon and bought back in at the wrong times, to say nothing of the inconvenient fact that we didn't know *then* what you're telling me *now* about its overall performance. So, really, Peter, what's the point?"

Having deconstructed Peter's dreamy story of stock market heroism, we'll now add a dose of reality to the comparison table we looked at earlier:

TABLE 22. Hindsight Dreaming in MED vs. Reality

Plan from December 2000 to June 2013	Starting Balance ($)	Total New Cash ($)	Ending Stock Balance ($)	Ending Bond Balance ($)	Ending Total Balance ($)
Buy Medifast (**MED**) at $0.14 and hold for the entire period (hindsight dreaming)	10,000	0	1,840,000	0	1,840,000
3% signal plan with **IJR** and **Vanguard GNMA**, 80/20 mix, all new cash provided	10,000	27,249	69,318	16,403	85,721
3% signal plan with **SPY** and **Vanguard GNMA**, 80/20 mix, all new cash provided	10,000	30,711	60,959	10,193	71,152
Buy Medifast (**MED**) at $0.14 and trade it quarterly with 50% coin toss odds of making the wrong calls (optimistic dose of reality)	10,000	0	44,601	0	44,601
Buy Medifast (**MED**) at $0.33 and trade it quarterly with 50% coin toss odds of making the wrong calls (pessimistic dose of reality)	10,000	0	14,191	0	14,191

Even the highest-performing stocks need to be bought, held, and sold at the right times with the right amounts of money. We get each part correct only half the time, which is bad enough to reduce a potential ending balance of $1.84 million in a heroic holding to just $44,601 in a generous scenario or to $14,191 in a less generous one.

How to Conjure up a Good Track Record

Want to know how to make your investment track record look better than it really is? Newsletter writers and investment advisers do this all the time.

The trick is selective reporting. In our look at the quarterly prices of MED, notice how many impressive gains happened. A z-val reporting his track record could simply include the rising periods that appeared after mentioning the stock and leave out the falling periods and overall performance that would have happened in a typical trading journey peppered with a 50 percent mistake rate.

Toss out enough ideas over the years and you'll soon have a collection of price lines to watch for the inevitable positive result appearing somewhere, even if temporarily. Mention any stock and I can find you a time when it would have produced a positive return. With enough hooks in the water (and no commitment to full disclosure), anybody can look like a stock-picking pro.

Beating Dollar-Cost Averaging

Many investors advocate dollar-cost averaging (DCA) as the best way to approach the stock market. Their objection to 3Sig is that it doesn't provide enough of a performance advantage over DCA to make it worth the extra effort. They're wrong, however, and it's time for the more sophisticated 3Sig strategy to push DCA from the top of the stock market's best practices list.

As you saw earlier, DCA is a good long-term investment plan that cuts out most of the investment industry's noise and focuses on the simple mathematics of having your regularly invested sum of money buy fewer shares when the price is high and more when the price is low, thereby making your average price paid per share lower than the average trading price of the security during the time frame. This table makes the advantage plain:

TABLE 23. The Advantage of Dollar-Cost Averaging

Security Price ($)	Amount Invested ($)	Shares Bought	Total Shares Held	Running Average of Price Paid Per Share ($)	Running Average of Security Trading Price ($)
10	500	50	50	10	10
15	500	33	83	12.05	12.50
5	500	100	183	8.20	10
10	500	50	233	8.58	10
20	500	25	258	9.69	12

Just by automating the regular $500 installment, this investor lowered her average price paid per share to less than the security's average trading price during the period. DCA is popular because of its simplicity. In a head-to-head match with 3Sig on the same security, it can produce a larger ending balance in some time frames that include a long period of rising prices.

The reason for this encapsulates the entire trade-off between DCA and 3Sig. DCA never sells and, therefore, produces no safe bond balance. It is always 100 percent invested. The 3Sig plan does produce a bond balance and is rarely 100 percent invested. In a market that rises over a long period, DCA can pull ahead due to having all its capital invested. The 3Sig plan will sell profits of more than 3 percent quarterly along the path higher, thereby reducing its exposure to the rising stock line.

The Frailty of Full Investment

The problem with DCA is that people don't react well when watching their fully invested plan go into the tank. You read about this in "The Myth of Buy-and-Hold" in Chapter 3, and saw earlier in this chapter, in "The Performance Advantage," how 3Sig muted a 20 percent downturn. Many DCA investors stop sending in regular contributions just when they should be ramping them up or at least keeping them going during periods of low prices. There is no guidance from DCA, just the notion that no matter what's happening in the world, we should send more money. This is emotionally unsatisfying because we are not uninvolved in the world. We read news, we see our portfolios fluctuate in response, and we are prodded into taking action. Uh oh. You know by now that this is where the trouble begins. Our taking action in the stock market means cranking up the 50 percent mistake machine.

The beauty of 3Sig is that it addresses our need to take action by telling us the right action to take. When the market is down, buy. When it's down a lot, buy a lot. When it's up, sell. When it's up a lot, sell a lot. These are not always the correct calls, because the formula cannot know, for instance, whether a market that's up a lot in the last quarter faces two more quarters of going up a lot more. The rational sale after going up a lot in Q4 can turn out to be wrong when the market goes up even more in Q1 and Q2. Over time, however, acting rationally each quarter wins out. In this case, it prevents the oh-so-likely personal judgment call to bet the farm at the top of Q2 because prices have so much upward momentum behind them. That's when the plunge arrives, inflicting maximum damage on your capital because you've just moved it all in, then left the damage to linger after you moved back to cash and now sit grumbling on the sidelines as the market reverses course and marches higher again.

DCA presents this risk because of its fully invested nature and the feeling we have that an automatic monthly or quarterly installment isn't really taking control of our portfolios. "It's just on autopilot," we think. "I need to keep an eye on this plan because it can't adjust to changing conditions." Bingo! It can't, but unfortunately neither can we, with any degree of reliability—unless you consider a 50 percent chance of getting it wrong to be reliable. What happens with DCA in the real world is that people watch their fully invested balance grow over time, but panic when it collapses in a market rout. They pull some or all of it out, then have no guidance, aside from the z-vals, as to when they should move it back in. Thus, the plan is shot. Their regular installments pile up in cash instead of in the investment they're supposed to be buying with the strict discipline that puts average cost reduction to work. Eventually, most people resume directing their regular installments to the investment, but after the best buying opportunity is gone and only until the bottom of the next downturn, when they should buy but instead sell again.

Given this, there's no way for DCA users to know what their account will be worth in the future. Even if they don't fiddle with it, the fully invested stock value fluctuates with the market because there's no system for using a safe account to reset it on a predictable growth path. What will the DCA account be worth at the end of this quarter? Who knows? What will the 3Sig stock fund be worth after rebalancing at the end of this quarter? Three percent more than it was worth at the end of last quarter, which was 3 percent more than the quarter before that.

Better Annual Returns with Value Averaging

In *Value Averaging: The Safe and Easy Strategy for Higher Investment Returns*, Michael Edleson ran dollar-cost averaging and value-averaging strategies through three hundred simulated markets. The two strategies tracked closely, but value averaging won in eighty-four of the first one hundred runs, ninety of the second one hundred runs, and eighty-nine of the third one hundred runs. In comparing annual returns, Edleson found "VA beating out DCA by about a 1.4 percent return on average," as shown in this table adapted from Table 8-1 in the 2006 edition of his book.

TABLE 24. Value Averaging Beating Dollar-Cost Averaging		
Simulation Runs	Dollar-Cost Averaging Annual Rate of Return (%)	Value-Averaging Annual Rate of Return (%)
1st 100	15.74	17.03
2nd 100	13.85	15.35
3rd 100	14.88	16.28

Another issue facing DCA investors is deciding how much to contribute on a regular schedule. In our earlier comparison of DCA with 3Sig, we determined the quarterly contribution by dividing new cash needed by 3Sig during the period by the fifty quarters involved. In the real world, there's no such system available. We couldn't know in advance what would happen in the fifty quarters, so we couldn't know how much additional cash would be needed by 3Sig. Sometimes the amount contributed to a DCA plan is simply a matter of what the investor can afford, making the decision tree a sparse one, but the lack of guidance becomes an issue as an investor acquires more resources over time and as the investment and economy grow. This last part is more significant than you might think.

Say you set a quarterly DCA amount of $300, figuring that $100 per month is an easy number to remember. That's $1,200 per year you're putting into your investment. After five years, you've contributed $6,000. If it had been growing at 10 percent annually, your overall balance would be $7,326. Already, in just five years, at a $300 quarterly pace, you've built up a base account worth enough to make future contributions of $300 less meaningful. As time marches on, they'll become smaller and smaller relative to the size of the account they're supporting. Your income will grow, inflation will push prices higher, and before too long your DCA contribution is not an appropriate size anymore.

In 3Sig, this is never an issue. The plan grows at a percentage rate so that the buy-and-sell guidance it issues remains proportional to the plan size from start to finish. An initial $1,000 stock fund balance needs to grow just $30 this quarter to stay on track. A $300,000 balance built up over many years needs to grow $9,000 this quarter. The plan's formula automatically accounts for this, so that quarterly actions remain meaningful regardless of the account size. Plus, the growth of the balance kicks off cash via sell signals, and this cash goes into the bond fund to support most subsequent buy signals even as they grow over time. You're not handing over $9,000 this quarter, for instance. Some or all of it will be supplied by market growth. If not, proceeds from sales of past market growth will fill in the gap.

With DCA, even if you increase your regular contributions over time to account for a growing income, the installments will pale in comparison to your overall account balance. Let's think very optimistically and say your income quadrupled in the five years after you began contributing $300 quarterly to your DCA plan, so you upped the quarterly amount to $1,200, for an annual amount of $4,800. At the end of the next five years, you've contributed a total of $30,000, and your account value is $41,103, given the same 10 percent annual return the whole time. Back at the five-year mark, when you were sending in just $300 each quarter, those installments were worth only 4 percent of your account value. Now, at the end of ten years, your $1,200 quarterly installments are worth only 3 percent—and $1,200 per quarter isn't chump change. You can see where this is heading. The growth of the money you've contributed in the past always ends up dwarfing your later contributions. This lessens the ability of those contributions to take meaningful action in deep downturns.

Consider this $41,103 you see in your account after ten years of faithful quarterly investing. If the market sells off 40 percent over two quarters, the value of your account is going to drop to $24,662.

The right thing for you to do in DCA is keep sending in your quarterly contributions as the price drops, so you'll buy more shares. However, throwing $1,200 one quarter and then another $1,200 the next, at a problem that's already erased $16,441 from your account value, will feel like fighting a fire with spoonfuls of water. You'll want to take more action, and the action you take might be exactly the one you read about in "The Myth of Buy-and-Hold" earlier: bailing at the bottom. "All I do is keep sending in the same amount of money," you'll think, "but it's never enough to make a difference, and it just evaporates along with the rest of my account. I have to stop this." Then you bail.

With 3Sig, you'll keep your regular quarterly contributions going the same way as with DCA, but you'll benefit from the added buying power of your bond account built up by half of your past contributions and sales proceeds (more on this in the next chapter). This firepower is gratifying in times of crashing prices. Just doing something smart instills in you the confidence to stick with it. You can respond to your own "I have to do something" instinct by replying, "I am doing something: following 3Sig, and it always ends up working. It will this time, too."

More Funds, Worse Performance

Because of these severe drawbacks when DCA and buy-and-hold are used with a single stock fund, they are almost always divided across an assortment of funds and asset classes. Your regular monthly or quarterly contributions would not go into just a small-cap fund, for instance. They would instead go into a large-cap stock fund, a growth and income stock fund, an international stock fund, a bond fund, a Treasury fund, and so on. In your younger years, this allocation might end up something like 40 percent aggressive stocks, 30 percent steady stocks, 20 percent bonds, and 10 percent Treasuries. This type of diversification dilutes performance and will almost always lose to 3Sig's concentration of 80 percent of your assets in small-cap stocks. Keeping 80 percent of your capital in small caps is very aggressive and would be risky except that the other 20 percent of your money and your additional contributions are standing by to purchase market weakness when it appears. Watching this work, you will feel your stress alleviated as you outperform nearly every other stock market approach available.

Thus, 3Sig actually puts more money in the small-cap section of the market than does any real-life DCA plan. Holding out the example of running DCA with 3Sig's new cash through a 100 percent small-cap allocation in a past period is a Peter Perfect trick. Nobody would do so, just as nobody ever buys at the exact bottom or sells at the exact top, as Peter constantly suggests is possible. However, as you saw earlier, 3Sig can come out ahead of even these fictional 100 percent small-cap-focused DCA examples on a raw-return basis, and more so on a risk-adjusted basis.

Dollar-cost averaging is a good investment method, certainly better than risking important financial goals on open-market coin tossing with z-vals. However, it's not as good as 3Sig because: it achieves a lower risk-adjusted performance (and usually a lower absolute performance) in the focused one-fund version due to being always fully invested, it does not satisfy our need to react to market events, it does not provide guidance on increasing or decreasing contributions in response to market prices or the changing value of the portfolio over time, and it almost always ends up diversified across lower-performing asset classes because nobody can handle the stress of full investment in aggressive stocks without the benefit of a clear buy-and-sell formula. Here's how the two plans compare:

TABLE 25. Why 3Sig Is Better than Dollar-Cost Averaging

Dollar-Cost Averaging	3 Percent Signal
Always fully invested, in the case of a focused one-fund version, thus it faces maximum market risk.	Benefits from a bond balance that tempers market risk and offers timely buying power.

Dollar-Cost Averaging	3 Percent Signal
Does not satisfy our need to feel in control of our investments, which leads to our using personal judgment, which can derail the whole plan.	Satisfies our need to feel in control by issuing quarterly signals in response to price movement, which means we're likely to stay the course.
Provides no guidance for changing regular payment amounts in response to market conditions.	Provides complete guidance by signaling whether to buy or sell, and in what proportional quantity.
Grows on a variable schedule that's entirely dependent on market movement.	Grows its stock balance on a predictable 3 percent quarterly schedule, achieved with the help of its bond balance.
Is usually diversified across lower-performing asset classes as the only way to achieve safety and peace of mind because there's no buy or sell guidance issued.	Can concentrate on high-performing small-cap stocks because its buy-and-sell guidance puts their volatility to work in a way that provides peace of mind and higher profits.

30 Down, Stick Around

In the previous section on dollar-cost averaging, and in "The Myth of Buy-and-Hold" in the last chapter, you read that one of the biggest weaknesses of fully invested plans is that they're so painful at the bottom, causing people to sell, thereby locking in losses by missing out on the recovery that follows. The 3Sig plan gets around this by signaling for us to buy the lower prices, or at least hold on if there's no cash available for buying.

For a moment, focus on what would make the fully invested plans work. Staying put, right? If buy-and-hold investors just ignored the market's plunge and truly held on, they'd benefit from the recovery. If dollar-cost averagers kept their plan going and remained fully invested through the bottom, they'd also benefit from the recovery. Our plan strives to put more money to work during extreme sell-offs to benefit more in the recovery. Is there a way we can further tweak it to perform even better when the market rebounds from a deep sell-off?

Yes. I call it "30 down, stick around" to describe that whenever the market loses more than 30 percent, you should stay put in stocks. That is, after a steep stock market sell-off, you'll stick around stocks for the recovery rather than pulling money out by selling on the way up.

We have to define a couple of terms here. The 30 percent drop is calculated from the quarterly closing prices of SPY (not daily or real-time prices) in the previous two years. SPY works well for this purpose because it's an excellent proxy for the general stock market, and it's a rebound in the general market that we're trying to capture. If you use something other than SPY, such as a more focused index or an individual stock, it could drop 30 percent from its high of the past two years without offering good odds for a rebound. If SPY falls 30 percent from its high of the past two years, there's a very good chance that the market is going to rebound powerfully. Since we use quarterly closing prices only, the two-year lookback means you need to glance over just eight prices. A good memory jog is that you should "keep an eye on SPY."

As for how long you'll stick around following a 30 percent drop: four sell signals. They might happen back to back, four quarters in a row, or they might be interspersed with a few buy signals, which you would follow as usual. In case the market is not going to recover quickly, we should put a further time limit on how long you'll remain in stick-around mode, which is two years. Put it together, then, and here's the "30 down, stick around" rule:

- The stick-around mode is triggered when the quarterly closing price of SPY falls 30 percent from its quarterly closing price high within the past two years.

- "Stick around" means you'll ignore the next four sell signals. They might happen in a row, but they might be interspersed with buy signals. Either way, ignore four of them.

- You'll exit stick-around mode and resume the regular plan after you've ignored four sell signals or two years have passed.

It's likely you'll never need the two-year addendum. In back-testing, the plan has always generated four sell signals within two years of a drop greater than 30 percent. The reason we should specify a time limit nonetheless is that it's conceivable the market could fall 30 percent and then flatline for longer than two years. If so, it's not in a dramatic recovery to be held. It's in something else, and the plan needs to revert to its standard mode of harvesting stock market profits for later buying. After the long sideways path, the market might fall again so the plan generates buy signals. You'll want to have harvested some profits to prepare for such a contingency, so you shouldn't let the stick-around phase last longer than two years. Similarly, if the market takes more than two years to fall 30 percent, there's less chance of a sharp recovery.

Now that you know the rule, let's get back to why it boosts performance.

The 3Sig plan instructs us to buy cheaper prices as the market falls, which will eventually pay off. From the bottom of big crashes, the market frequently rises most aggressively immediately afterward, piling up gains that most people miss because they're waiting for signs of safety, which don't usually appear until many of the gains are gone. The 3Sig plan will detect the big quarterly gains during such a phase and signal to sell excess profits beyond its target. By ignoring four such sell signals, you will leave your money in stocks during the most powerful part of the recovery and then resume following the signal as usual.

Let's run through a simple comparison using the crash of 2007–2009 and its subsequent recovery. We'll begin with a $10,000 balance at the end of 2006, investing half in IJR and leaving the other half in cash (not bonds this time) for later purchases. Here's how it went to the bottom of the crash in the first quarter of 2009:

TABLE 26. Running Out of Cash in the Crash of 2007–2009

Quarter	SPY Price ($)	IJR Price ($)	IJR Balance Before Signal ($)	Cash Balance Before Signal ($)	Signal (Shares)	Held After Signal (Shares)	IJR Balance After Signal ($)	Cash Balance After Signal ($)	Total After Signal ($)
Q406	122.91	61.50	0	10,000	Buy 81.30	81.3	5,000	5,000	10,000
Q107	123.73	63.28	5,145	5,000	Buy 0.08	81.38	5,150	4,995	10,145
Q207	131.64	66.50	5,412	4,995	Sell 1.62	79.76	5,304	5,103	10,407
Q307	134.16	65.35	5,212	5,103	Buy 3.84	83.6	5,463	4,852	10,315
Q407	129.24	60.92	5,093	4,852	Buy 8.76	92.36	5,627	4,318	9,945
Q108	117.23	56.15	5,186	4,318	Buy 10.86	103.22	$5,796	$3,708	$9,504
Q208	114.25	56.52	5,834	3,708	Buy 2.40	105.62	$5,970	$3,573	$9,542
Q308	104.15	55.90	5,904	3,573	Buy 4.38	110.00	$6,149	$3,328	$9,477
Q408	81.69	41.55	4,571	3,328	Buy 42.42	152.42	$6,333	$1,565	$7,898
Q109	72.50	34.51	5,260	1,565	Buy 36.60	189.02	$6,523	$302	$6,825

At this point we're at the bottom of the bear market, almost out of cash, with our total account balance down 32 percent, even though our IJR balance has grown 3 percent per quarter religiously, thanks to our following the signal. Unbeknownst to us, the market would now recover. If we had not adhered to the "30 down, stick around" rule but had instead followed the plan's sell signals, our account would have grown in the following two years in the manner shown in Table 27 on the next page.

Notice that the most powerful part of the recovery happened directly off the bottom, as IJR rose 65 percent from $34.51 at the end of Q109 to $56.95 at the end of Q110. During this profitable phase, we sold on the way up, thereby muting our gains. We still did well, growing our total balance 82 percent in these first two years of the recovery, but would have done better if we'd entered a stick-around phase and ignored the first four sell signals after SPY dropped 30 percent.

TABLE 27. Impact of Following All Sell Signals in the Recovery

Quarter	SPY Price ($)	IJR Price ($)	IJR Balance Before Signal ($)	Cash Balance Before Signal ($)	Signal (Shares)	Held After Signal (Shares)	IJR Balance After Signal ($)	Cash Balance After Signal ($)	Total After Signal ($)
Q209	84.30	42.24	7,988	302	Sell 30.05	158.97	6,715	1,566	8,281
Q309	97.27	49.88	7,929	1,566	Sell 20.30	138.67	6,917	2,579	9,496
Q409	103.21	52.31	7,254	2,579	Sell 2.48	136.19	7,124	2,708	9,833
Q110	108.81	56.95	7,756	2,708	Sell 7.34	128.85	7,338	3,126	10,464
Q210	96.45	51.86	6,682	3,126	Buy 16.89	145.74	7,558	2,251	9,809
Q310	107.21	56.75	8,271	2,251	Sell 8.57	137.17	7,784	2,737	10,521
Q410	118.75	66.08	9,064	2,737	Sell 15.84	121.33	8,017	3,784	11,801
Q111	125.75	71.12	8,629	3,784	Sell 5.22	116.11	8,258	4,155	12,413

On the quarterly price schedule—the only one you need to watch—SPY peaked at $134.16 in Q307. The threshold marking the stick-around phase was 30 percent below this, or $93.91. SPY slipped under $93.91 in Q408, triggering the stick-around phase of ignoring the next four sell signals within a two-year period. The next signal, in Q109, was a buy signal and followed as usual because the stick-around phase ignores sell signals only. After a 30-percent market drop, more buy signals means the market is still struggling and should be bought to the extent that cash availability will allow. Why? Because a recovery is on the way and more buying ahead of it will turn into more profit after it.

The first sell signal to be ignored arrived the next quarter, in Q209, and the next three to be ignored arrived back-to-back through Q110. It doesn't always go this way. It's possible to get buy signals mixed in with the sell signals to be ignored, but the "four to ignore" (another handy mnemonic rhyme) came in a row after the subprime mortgage crash bottomed in Q109. Here, then, is how we would have done with the exact same amount of money invested in the exact same recovery by adhering to the stick-around rule:

TABLE 28. Benefit of Ignoring Four Sell Signals in the Recovery

Quarter	SPY Price ($)	IJR Price ($)	IJR Balance Before Signal ($)	Cash Balance Before Signal ($)	Signal (Shares)	Held After Signal (Shares)	IJR Balance After Signal ($)	Cash Balance After Signal ($)	Total After Signal ($)
Q209	84.30	42.24	7,988	302	Ignored sell signal 1	189.02	7,984	302	8,286
Q309	97.27	49.88	9,428	302	Ignored sell signal 2	189.02	9,428	302	9,730
Q409	103.21	52.31	9,888	302	Ignored sell signal 3	189.02	9,888	302	10,190
Q110	108.81	56.95	10,765	302	Ignored sell signal 4	189.02	10,765	302	11,067
Q210	96.45	51.86	9,803	302	Buy 24.78 (but could afford only 5.82)	194.84	10,104	0	10,105
Q310	107.21	56.75	11,057	0	Sell 11.45	183.39	10,407	650	11,057
Q410	118.75	66.08	12,118	650	Sell 21.17	162.22	10,719	2,049	12,768
Q111	125.75	71.12	11,537	2,049	Sell 6.98	154.24	10,970	2,616	13,586

Look how much better we did. Ignoring the first four sell signals after SPY dropped 30 percent put our Q111 ending balance at $13,586 instead of the $12,413 it became without following the stick-around rule. It delivered a 9 percent improvement in this case, even though ignoring the four sell signals left our cash balance too small to afford the full buy signal in Q210.

The reason the rule works is not hard to understand. When the stock market is in a powerful recovery, it's best to leave capital invested in stocks. The highest odds of getting a powerful recovery are in the time frame following a big drop in a small time period, which we're defining as two years. A bear market is usually considered a 20 percent drop, so limiting the stick-around rule to periods following a 30 percent drop makes this a seldom-used but highly beneficial modification to the plan.

You may wonder if this benefit was unique to this time frame, that maybe it wouldn't be as helpful in other time frames. In fact, it has been. In the two decades from 1993 to 2013, the stick-around rule boosted performance over the standard plan that follows all sell signals, even when it caused a shortage of cash in subsequent buy signals, which you saw happen in Q210 in this example. The 30 percent threshold was the ideal level as well, producing the biggest performance boost for the funding shortfalls it caused. Other thresholds (such as when the market drops 25, 35, 40, or 45 percent) didn't work as well.

Using the S&P 500 itself rather than SPY as its proxy shows the rule appearing just four times in the 1950–2013 period: 1970, 1974, 2002, and 2009. The four ignored sell signals in each case left the plan fully invested for S&P 500 gains of 38 percent in the 1970 instance, 62 percent in the 1974, 14 percent in the 2002, and 43 percent in the 2009.

Getting around funding shortfalls with a bottom-buying account, which you'll learn about in the next chapter, further magnifies the stick-around rule's boost. It enables you not only to stick around for the recovery but also to take advantage of the first "buy-the-dip" opportunity that appears on the way higher.

Variations on the Plan

You know now that the plan uses small-cap stocks as its growth vehicle and bonds as its safe vehicle. It's natural to wonder if we could use the exact same strategy aiming for 3 percent growth per quarter but with different vehicles. What if something other than a small-cap stock index could be used just as easily with better results? In researching the plan over many years, I've tried just about every type of investment vehicle the market offers, but nothing has been able to beat 3Sig's base case meaningfully and consistently. Let's run through a few examples.

Other Market Segments

There is no end to the ways we can divide up the stock market. We already looked at separating it by capitalization, or company size, and found that smaller company indexes are better than larger company ones because they're more volatile on their way to a higher return. Another way that people divide the market is by sector and industry. Stock groupings go in the following order from wide to narrow: sector, industry, company. The idea with moving up the list from individual company stocks to industries and sectors is that we'll have a better chance of choosing which entire groups of similar stocks will perform well than which handful of companies or single companies within the groups will beat their peers.

It's easy to test whether specific sectors can outperform the broader market. The S&P 500, for instance, is divided into nine sectors, and there's a SPDR ETF representing each of them. Not a single one beats small-cap stocks over time. There are pockets of time in which certain sectors outperform, but trying to guess which sectors and which times introduces familiar trouble.

The business of picking the next top-performing sector or industry has no better track record than the business of choosing top-performing stocks, and we know what a crapshoot that is. The same questions apply. What qualifies as a bottom? When do you buy it? When do you sell it and move to a different sector or industry? How much of your money do you use? The z-vals are just as bad with sectors and industries as they are with stocks for all the same reasons, so we can dispose of this approach without a second thought.

What about focusing on regions of the world or individual countries? Same problem. If choosing stocks within our own country is difficult, why would it be any easier choosing them in other countries or choosing which entire countries are looking better than others? On top of the now-familiar list of pitfalls, country diversification introduces the joy of currency exchange complexities and geopolitical risks. If there's one thing we know our investment portfolio doesn't need, it's extra layers of complication. We'll set this one aside.

I could go on, but I'm sure you already detect a pattern, which is that various ways of grouping stocks don't get around the basic limitation of our 50 percent error rate in the market. This stock, that stock; this country, that country; this industry, that industry; this sector, that sector—get out your darts and coins. The only array of choices broader than the parts of the market is the range of z-val opinions on those parts, which sport no better odds than yours. Quick reminder: 50 percent.

Even if back-testing revealed that a certain sector beat IJR by a substantial margin, our inability to know whether it could do so again would make it a typical stock market gamble to move our plan from the general market to the winning sector from the last time frame. Maybe that sector will have another strong decade; maybe it won't.

In my testing, however, none of the sectors achieved a substantially better performance than IJR, so we need not even consider the gamble. What's more, almost every brokerage and retirement account includes a small-cap fund option, whereas fewer include sector fund options. This could be the simple deciding factor, and now you know that you're not missing anything if your account offers no sector funds. Just run 3Sig with the cheapest small-cap fund available to you and you'll do well.

Filtered Funds

There's another way to view stock investments that involves setting a filter and buying what it catches through various cycles. This is better than buying fixed market segments because it gets around the problem of such segments moving into and out of favor. Rather than buying technology stocks, for instance, we might set a filter to buy cheap stocks, or fast-growing stocks, or the stocks most widely owned by investors we respect, and so on. The filter remains relevant through changing market seasons because it catches only stocks that match the formula we feed it. The stocks that were cheap a year ago might be a different set than the ones that are cheap now, and filter results will reflect this. Fixed segments won't. The consumer discretionary sector will always contain the consumer discretionary stocks.

The most popular filter method is one that targets either growth or value stocks. A preference for either growth or value is the most basic division among stock investors, even more central to their characters than whether they prefer large or small companies. A growth investor is more concerned with a company's growth rate than with its size or industry, and will typically build a portfolio of growth stocks of various sizes and industries with possibly an emphasis on small ones, as they have more room to grow. Similarly, a value investor will seek cheap companies regardless of size or industry. Growth stocks boast high earnings and sales increases, and their stocks usually exhibit upward price momentum. Value stocks boast bargain prices as measured by ratios of book value to price, earnings to price, and sales to price. Would a focus on either growth or value consistently boost 3Sig's performance?

In short, no. Each of the capitalization indexes we've been considering (which is to say the ones based on company size) is available in both a growth and value subset. We can compare the overall S&P 500 index of large companies to a subset of the companies in it that meet growth-investing criteria and a subset that meet value-investing criteria. We can run this same comparison on the S&P 400 index of medium-size companies and the S&P 600 index of small companies. Doing so reveals results similar to running the plan with sectors. There are pockets of outperformance as growth and value come into and out of favor, but no meaningful long-term edge over the full small-cap segment.

Besides, almost all accounts provide some type of general small-cap fund. Fewer provide small-cap funds with growth or value filters. Even if they do, they're bound to cost more than the base index itself. Given these factors, the easy conclusion is just to stick with the cheapest general small-cap stock index fund available to you.

Individual Stocks

The idea with 3Sig is to provide you with an evergreen approach to the market that you can run with minimal interference in your life for as many years as you want. To qualify as evergreen, the plan should be used with a diverse stock index rather than a specialty index or individual stock. Anything that can come into and out of favor with no guarantee of eventual recovery is not a good choice because it requires our judgment on when to own it and when to step aside, and we know what folly that introduces. This is why our basic plan runs with IJR or another broad small-cap investment. It works pretty well in all environments for a comforting set-and-forget result.

The plan can work with individual stocks, however, and usually much better than any Peter Perfect attempt to time entries and exits. The reason 3Sig works is that it guides us to buy low and sell high around the 3 percent growth line—no judgment required, just a calculator. The Peter Perfect approach relies on faulty human perspective that thinks it knows when to buy and sell, but gets it right only half the time, which is enough to reduce potential perfection to subpar performance on even the highest flying of stocks. You saw this yourself with the heroic holding Medifast earlier in this chapter.

Some companies are so big and successful that they can work with 3Sig over very long periods, if not for the rest of your life. The big, diversified, global companies on the Dow, for instance, are like indexes unto themselves. Owning dividend-paying conglomerates such as ExxonMobil and IBM and Walmart is similar to owning sector funds targeting oil services, information technology, and retail, for example. Therefore, such stocks are worthy candidates for 3Sig. They introduce individual company risk, namely, in that they'll go bankrupt the way GM did in 2009, but it's a low risk. Setbacks for such massive companies are almost always temporary, and the recovery from them provides profit potential. The 3 percent signal will catch this, issuing buy guidance of the right size when the stocks slip under the 3 percent growth line and subsequent sell signals of the right size when they recover back above the line. The deeper they dip, the more you buy; the higher they spike, the more you sell.

Smaller, aggressive companies can work, too. They introduce a higher risk of company-specific trouble and bankruptcy, but might be worth it with a tiny portion of your overall portfolio. You could implement 3Sig using a small-cap fund in your retirement account with the bulk of your nest egg, but keep a play account on the side for individual stock ideas. Some of these you'll probably want to actively trade for kicks, on the off chance that you get the timing right and make a few bucks, thereby creating your own chapter in *Peter Perfect's Big Book of Stock Stories*. You know by now that these fliers aren't to be relied upon for real financial planning, but you might find one that works better with 3Sig than old, reliable IJR. You should not, however, run it in place of your core plan using IJR or an equivalent; you should run it in addition to your core plan. Whatever excess profits it produces are strictly icing on the cake, the product of a dash of luck as much as anything else.

A good way to use individual stocks is in an account that receives shares of your company's stock as part of your compensation. One problem with these types of accounts is that people let them build up until they own many thousands of shares of their employer's stock. This creates a risky situation when the company runs into trouble and the stock drops. Suddenly, the once-large employee stock account gets cut in half. Even worse, the very trouble cutting the stock in half could be bad enough to cost the employee's job. Talk about a double whammy. "Here's your pink slip and your most recent retirement account statement," says the boss. The pink slip tells you to pack up your office before noon and turn in your badge. The account statement says you're half as well off as you thought you were—just as you head to the unemployment office.

A way to avoid this double whammy is to manage your employer stock account with 3Sig so you build up a safe bond buffer and avoid concentrating too much of your well-being in the fortunes of one company.

With these considerations in mind, let's see how we would have fared in a variety of ten individual stocks using our base-case 3 percent signal plan over the fifty quarters from December 2000 to June 2013, compared with our standard IJR and SPY vehicles, sorted in descending order by ending total balance:

TABLE 29. 3Sig with Ten Stocks from December 2000 to June 2013

Plan from December 2000 to June 2013	Starting Balance ($)	Total New Cash ($)	Ending Stock Balance ($)	Ending Bond Balance ($)	Ending Total Balance ($)
3% signal plan with **MED** (Medifast)	10,000	28,168,633	50,972,179	8,786,211	59,758,390
3% signal plan with **AAPL** (Apple)	10,000	171,966	721,646	0	721,646
3% signal plan with **DDS** (Dillard's)	10,000	63,382	564,312	140,797	705,109
3% signal plan with **KSU** (Kansas City Southern)	10,000	35,528	271,739	67,935	339,674
3% signal plan with **PNRA** (Panera)	10,000	31,704	199,755	66,123	265,878
3% signal plan with **SBUX** (Starbucks)	10,000	51,805	196,835	65,717	262,552
3% signal plan with **MCD** (McDonald's)	10,000	9,477	86,946	11,486	98,432

(continued)

Plan from December 2000 to June 2013	Starting Balance ($)	Total New Cash ($)	Ending Stock Balance ($)	Ending Bond Balance ($)	Ending Total Balance ($)
3% signal plan with **IJR** (S&P Small-Cap 600)	10,000	27,249	69,318	16,403	85,721
3% signal plan with **IBM** (Int'l Business Machines)	10,000	15,094	70,620	5,063	75,683
3% signal plan with **SPY** (S&P 500)	10,000	30,711	60,959	10,193	71,152
3% signal plan with **XOM** (ExxonMobil)	10,000	24,914	67,910	0	67,910
3% signal plan with **WMT** (Walmart)	10,000	20,939	50,013	4,196	54,209

What a hodgepodge this turned out to be. Our old friend Medifast continued its entertaining ways, delivering a jaw-dropping ending balance of $59,758,390. Fantastic, except for the quibbling detail of requiring $28,168,633 in new cash to do so. If you had a spare $28 million during this period, then running the plan with MED would have been a good way to turn it into $60 million. I'm guessing few of my readers fall into this category, and would not have been able to fund the requirements for Medifast, Apple, Dillard's, or Starbucks.

Kansas City Southern paid off for those able to afford the $35,528 of new cash it required. Panera was also very good. McDonald's and IBM required less new cash than IJR and SPY. Even so, McDonald's outperformed both index ETFs, delivering an ending balance of $98,432, compared with $85,721 for IJR, and requiring only $9,477 in new cash compared with IJR's $27,249. You may think Apple was an easy choice, but in 2000, when this time frame began, it had not yet invented the iPod, iPhone, or iPad, and was much less easy an investment choice than it might appear to be today.

McDonald's provided the best balance between new cash required and performance delivered. The problem is you didn't know in 2000 that McDonald's was going to do better than Exxon, IBM, and Walmart in the next fifty quarters, and you don't know now which stock is going to do better in the coming fifty quarters.

You certainly can't count on the z-vals for help. Back in September 2000, McDonald's worried that weak foreign currencies would hamper its earnings, which they did, and the z-val covering the stock at Bank of America downgraded it, even though McDonald's said it would keep growing at its planned pace. In April 2002 a *Fortune* article headline began, "Fallen Arches McDonald's Has Had Six Straight Earnings Disappointments," and the story reported that a z-val at Argus Research "not only slapped a sell on the stock in January—she announced that she was dropping coverage this month. Why? Because clients are no longer interested." The Argus z-val said, "McDonald's is not a growth company anymore."

As you can see, it was anything but obvious to have owned McDonald's during the fifty quarters we're looking at. In retrospect, we know that buying the stock like crazy when the z-vals announced that McDonald's was a goner was a great move. There was plenty of time to acquire shares as MCD fell from $30 in April 2002 to $13 in March 2003, which our 3 percent plan signaled to do. From their March 2003 low, shares of MCD recovered dramatically to $100 in January 2012. In this case, the Argus z-val was right to urge selling the shares in January 2002 to avoid the steep drop ahead, but her subsequent decision to stop covering the company due to lack of client interest was precisely wrong. Over the long term it would have been more beneficial to create interest in the stock, to tell clients to begin a buying program in MCD that acquired as many cheap shares as possible in the weak year ahead. Such a plan would have profited handsomely when MCD recovered, as our 3Sig results prove. The z-val tendency, however, is to bad-mouth and ignore stocks in cheap phases and praise them relentlessly in expensive phases, exactly the opposite of what produces profit. The 3 percent signal relies on arithmetic to overcome this media mistake.

Z-vals are no more helpful when it comes to avoiding dangerous stocks, by the way. The June 2, 2008, *Barron's* cover story, "Buy GM,"

was introduced thusly: "General Motors' turnaround could accelerate in coming years, driving handsome gains for bold stockholders."
GM accelerated all right, but into a brick wall. A year later, it was
bankrupt.

Don't get too excited about the winning stocks among the ten
we've just tested, because a lot of what you're seeing is simply that
the best-performing stocks of the time frame did the best in 3Sig as
well—no great mystery. The same way you would have bought
Medifast at $0.14 in 2000 if you'd known then what you know now,
so, too, you would have chosen to run McDonald's in 3Sig rather
than IJR. This is hindsight bias in all its glory.

The more valuable takeaway than any specific stock to use in the
plan is that 3Sig is a good way to own individual stocks if you decide
to dabble in them. Remember how we eviscerated Peter Perfect's
story of Medifast riches back in Chapter 4? He spun a tale of turning
$10,000 into $1.84 million. We ran the stock through 50 percent
odds of taking the wrong action as its price fluctuated dramatically
and found that the optimistic scenario created an ending balance of
just $44,601, and the pessimistic scenario, only $14,191. Owning the
stock with our 3 percent plan and *no new cash provided*, by contrast,
turned $10,000 into $3.47 million with $510,000 of it in safe bonds
at the end of the time frame. This ending balance is 90 percent more
than buying and holding produced, and a sensational seventy-eight
times more than the 50 percent mistake rate of human judgment
produced.

You might like to see this angle on all the stocks we've just covered, so here are the results of the usual plan running the ten stocks
plus IJR and SPY, but with no new cash provided, sorted in descending order by ending total balance:

TABLE 30. 3Sig with Ten Stocks from December 2000 to June 2013, No New Cash

Plan from December 2000 to June 2013	Starting Balance ($)	Total New Cash ($)	Ending Stock Balance ($)	Ending Bond Balance ($)	Ending Total Balance ($)
3% signal plan with **MED** (Medifast)	10,000	0	2,958,948	510,042	3,468,990
3% signal plan with **AAPL** (Apple)	10,000	0	430,358	0	430,358
3% signal plan with **PNRA** (Panera)	10,000	0	96,765	32,031	128,796
3% signal plan with **KSU** (Kansas City Southern)	10,000	0	100,146	25,036	125,182
3% signal plan with **DDS** (Dillard's)	10,000	0	67,775	16,910	84,685
3% signal plan with **SBUX** (Starbucks)	10,000	0	41,316	13,794	55,110
3% signal plan with **MCD** (McDonald's)	10,000	0	34,398	4,544	38,942
3% signal plan with **XOM** (ExxonMobil)	10,000	0	29,878	0	29,878
3% signal plan with **IBM** (Int'l Business Machines)	10,000	0	29,266	2,098	31,364
3% signal plan with **IJR** (S&P Small-Cap 600)	10,000	0	24,065	5,695	29,760
3% signal plan with **WMT** (Walmart)	10,000	0	16,649	1,397	18,046
3% signal plan with **SPY** (S&P 500)	10,000	0	13,973	2,336	16,309

The 3Sig plan is a fine way to manage an individual stock position, but the persistent fly in the ointment is that nobody knows in advance which stocks will do best, or do well—or even survive, for that matter. Remember: stocks can go bankrupt; indexes can't.

I recommend that you manage most if not all your money in the reliable version of the plan, which uses IJR or another small-cap index equivalent. If you're tempted to risk some of your money on individual stock ideas, then do so with the 3 percent plan separately from your core plan. This way, if you end up in the wrong individual stock—as people tend to do—at least the plan will protect you from your own worst instincts and do its best to manage the stock's volatility to a decent profit. If you end up in a winner (such as Medifast, Apple, Panera, Kansas City Southern, or Dillard's in the time frame we've been examining), the plan will help you extract money from its path higher without needing to consider stressful choices.

When Apple Was a Seed

You may think a company as iconic as Apple was an obvious buy back in December 2000. Wrong. Until the summer of that year, Steve Jobs kept the word *interim* before the word *CEO* in his title after returning to Apple's top spot three years earlier. None of today's popular iThings existed yet. Well, the iMac G3 did, but it looked like a TV stuffed in a motorcycle helmet, not like the svelte machines known as iMacs today.

On October 19, 2000, CNET News reported, "Apple Computer's shares fell as much as 9 percent Thursday following Wednesday's worse-than-expected earnings news." Two months later, the z-val at Lehman Brothers said Apple's expected shortfall of 40 percent from earlier projections was "one of the largest misses I've seen in a long time," and especially worrisome because it was not due just to a general economic slowdown but to Apple's own mistakes.

We find it hard to buy even iconic companies at the right times, own them through the troubles, and sell them when everybody is enthusiastic. We think we can, hindsight says we can, Peter Perfect says he did, and the z-vals pretend they can, but it's all subject to the toss of a coin. There wasn't much reason to expect greatness from Apple at the beginning of these fifty quarters. Hundreds of other not-so-promising companies kept their promises to become not so great, and there's little reason to think we would have chosen Apple from among them back then—or will choose the winner of the next fifty quarters now.

Safer Puzzle Pieces

Most of this section has looked at investments other than small-cap stocks to use on the growth side of 3Sig, in search of higher returns. We found some that could work, and I'm sure there are others, but this book's base case strikes about as good a balance between risk and reward as the plan can deliver.

You may be less interested in boosting the reward side and more interested in decreasing the risk side. If so, you'll be pleased to know there are ways to do so. The simplest is to increase your allocation to bonds. Even if you're in your younger working years, you might decide you'd rather forgo stronger overall performance in favor of a more peaceful journey. Moving your target bond allocation up to 30, 40, or even 50 percent would accomplish this. I urge you to think carefully, however, as the plan's base 80/20 allocation between stocks and bonds is pretty safe, and nearly guaranteed to come out ahead of a higher bond allocation in the end.

Beyond this, a more drastic dose of safety is easy to achieve by substituting cash for bonds. This would get around interest rate risk. Using cash instead of bonds makes the safe side as safe as it can be, with zero fluctuation. It won't grow as much as the bond side over time because the steady stream of bond dividends is hard to get from money market interest rates, but it will certainly offer peace of mind. Here, too, consider carefully because the plan run with bonds performs much better than the plan run with cash, and bond indexes are quite safe.

Finally, you could swap in a total stock market index fund instead of the plan's small-cap index fund. This would neutralize the chance that small caps will underperform over an extended period. With a tiny 0.05 percent expense ratio, the Vanguard Total Stock Market ETF (VTI) covers 100 percent of the investable U.S. stock market, all company sizes and flavors. Running 3Sig with VTI on the growth side and the Vanguard Total Bond Market ETF (BND) on the safe side would be about as evergreen an arrangement as you could assemble.

I still recommend the book's base-case plan running a small-cap stock index on the growth side, a bond index on the safe side, and an 80/20 stock/bond target allocation for most of your working years. If, however, you want more comfort, the plan can accommodate safer puzzle pieces and still keep you out of the clutches of Peter Perfect and the z-vals.

Executive Summary of This Chapter

Our goal is to beat the S&P 500 index of large-company stocks, but there's no rule saying we can't use a different index to do so. We'll use small-company stocks for most of our capital, and bonds for the safe portion of our plan. The higher volatility of small-company stocks improves our plan's performance, and automated reliance on the bond fund keeps us better committed to staying the course than would a fully invested dollar-cost averaging plan. Key takeaways:

✔ Small-company stocks outperform their larger-company peers with more volatility, which our plan transforms into extra profit with signals to buy low and sell high. The higher performance and extra profit extraction provide us with a double advantage.

✔ The only real competitor to our 3 percent signal plan is dollar-cost averaging, which invests more money on a fixed schedule no matter what's happening in the market.

✔ A weakness of dollar-cost averaging is that it's always fully invested with no mechanism for reacting to market movement. This is not emotionally comforting to investors in terrible times, and many panic as their balance collapses, then sell at the wrong moment.

✔ The emotional stress caused by dollar-cost averaging when it's used on a single stock fund leads most people to divide it across many funds. Doing so underperforms a focus on small-company stocks, which is a key part of 3Sig.

✔ The 3 percent signal's automated buy/sell guidance in response to market movement provides investors with emotional comfort to stay the course and benefit from the high performance of small-company stocks.

✔ These advantages enable 3Sig to outperform dollar-cost averaging even when it's used on the same funds, and to greatly outperform it when it's used on other funds, the vast majority of which underperform the market indexes used in our plan.

✔ After an extreme sell-off, defined as a 30 percent drop in SPY on a quarterly closing price basis in the previous two years, our plan will temporarily stay put in its stock fund by ignoring the next four sell signals. This is the "30 down, stick around" rule.

✔ The "30 down, stick around" rule takes advantage of historically high odds for an extreme sell-off to be followed

by a strong recovery, during which we want as much
profit as possible by staying fully invested in stocks.

✔ Other permutations of the plan are possible, such as using sector funds, growth and value funds, individual
stocks, or cash instead of bonds, but nothing delivers
more compelling performance than the base case using
an 80/20 mix of small-cap stocks and bonds.

CHAPTER FIVE
Managing Money in the Plan

I n previous chapters, you learned why we struggle in the stock market, how to nudge performance by automatically buying low and selling high, that 3 percent per quarter is the best signal line showing us to buy or sell, and that small-cap stock and bond indexes are the ideal investments to use in the plan. Next, we're going to get a handle on cash management.

No matter where you run your 3 percent signal plan, you're likely to contribute more cash periodically to your bond fund. In an individual retirement account, you'll probably contribute on a monthly basis. In an employer retirement account, cash usually flows in from every paycheck. In a nonretirement brokerage account, you might set up a regular cash transfer schedule from your bank and send extra cash whenever you're lucky enough to find some.

If the market rises over a long enough period without many setbacks causing 3Sig to buy, your selling proceeds and cash contributions could combine to grow your bond balance until it's too big relative to your stock balance. You want most of your money to work for you by rising with the stock market over time, so an unduly large bond balance should be avoided. Then again, the stock market occasionally plunges so deeply that what looked like an oversize bond balance can suddenly come in handy for buying the lower lows. You need to strike a balance, so to speak.

In this chapter, we'll look at how to invest a large cash balance gradually, techniques for managing your plan's bond balance, the usefulness of a bottom-buying account, and how to adjust your bond balance as you grow older and more risk averse.

Starting with a Large Cash Balance

Managing a large cash balance is tricky. The last thing you want to do is plow it all into the stock market at a key top and watch a third of it evaporate in the months ahead, but you probably also know that you should put the money to work earning more than a low interest rate.

Historically, it's been better to put large sums into the market straightaway, but we are emotional creatures and remember the exact wrong moments for doing so from past news cycles. The magazine covers in the wake of 1987's Black Monday, the talking-head panic during the 1997 Asian Contagion, the I-told-you-so lectures from z-vals in the dot-com crash of 2000, the constant updating of how much wealth was lost during the subprime mortgage collapse of 2008—these and the stress of other financial calamities are seared into our collective consciousness, and we are determined to avoid such money pain if at all possible. Even though the odds of right now being a perfectly wrong moment for investing a large sum of cash are low, your mind tells you that it might be. Thus, cash tends to waste away on the sidelines and miss out on market performance.

To get around this, I suggest breaking up a large cash balance into four equal sizes that you'll invest in 3Sig across the next four buy orders. They won't necessarily happen back to back, so the four quarterly buy signals might span a few years. Whenever they happen, though, you'll add to the signaled order size the extra amount of cash you want to invest. This also works well for transitioning your existing portfolio balance to 3Sig, in which case you would sell a quarter of it with each buy signal, then add the proceeds to your buy order.

For example, if you're dividing $100,000 into four equal amounts that you want to put into the plan, you would add $25,000 to each of the next four buy signals. If the plan signals a buy with $3,000 at the end of next quarter based on your current invested balance, you would add $25,000 to it, for a total of $28,000 invested. If the fund you're using closed the quarter at a price of, say, $88, you would buy 318 shares with $28,000, instead of the 34 shares the plan signaled you to buy with $3,000. After your additional funds go into the plan, it would then calculate the next quarter's 3 percent signal line from the larger investment balance.

After four quarterly buys in this manner, your large cash balance will be working in the plan. If the market goes through rough patches while you're gradually moving your cash balance into it, you can feel good about buying in at lower prices. If it just keeps marching higher before you get all your cash into it, you can feel good that you already moved a portion of your cash in. I'm a big fan of gradual moves as a way of mollifying disappointment in the uncertain environment of stocks.

Purists may scoff at this approach, and would probably cite statistics showing that stocks rise much more often than they fall. What they perpetually ignore is that people are not dispassionate machines making rational choices at every turn. Emotions figure in, in a big way, and moving gradually provides a good compromise between head and heart. It puts your large cash balance to work in a manner that you can comfortably watch happen.

Your Living, Breathing Bond Balance

Both the stock side and the bond side of 3Sig fluctuate in value. The stock side is affected by the market's daily gyrations and by your quarterly buys and sells. The bond side is affected by your deposits, possible occasional withdrawals, and the same quarterly buys and sells that affect the stock side. It may come as a surprise, but you're actually more involved with the bond side than the stock side. It's part of every quarterly trade and is the only side you'll interact with between trades, usually by depositing more cash. All new cash to the plan goes into your bond fund first, and is later incorporated into the stock fund through a quarterly growth target adjustment you'll learn about in the next section.

Due to this activity, your bond balance will vary from month to month and quarter to quarter. Like a lung breathing air in and out, your bond fund will breath money in and out. Also like a lung, this is its normal function. There's no reason for alarm as it moves from inhaling money and becoming bigger, to exhaling it and becoming smaller. Again, like a lung, however, it should stay neither too big nor too small for long.

Most of the examples in this book begin with an 80/20 mixture of stocks to bonds, and it's a good ratio to keep in mind. It provides enough buying power in the bond account to handle a big setback in the market, but keeps the bulk of your capital growing with the market's upward tendency over time. A 5/95 stock-to-bond mix, or a 25/75 mix, or a 50/50 mix, would leave you missing out on too many gains; while a 95/5 mix would leave you without enough bond balance to buy many of the market's downturns. Somewhere between these extremes is where you want your balance, and 80/20 does nicely in most environments—not *all* environments, as you know by now, but most. We'll consider the 80/20 stock/bond ratio to be our base mixture, back to which we want to rebalance periodically, at opportune times flagged by 3Sig.

If you're like most people, you'll run the 3 percent plan in a retirement account. Once you see how well it works, you'll probably end up using it in your nonretirement accounts, too, but we'll discuss cash management here as it relates to your retirement account. The natural direction for the bond side of your retirement is up, due to regular contributions. The stock/bond interaction will stay fairly balanced over time, with occasional deviations from the mean when the market enters prolonged bull and bear phases, but even these are eventually corrected with a reversion to the mean that resets the plan back toward its 80/20 base. Now and then, however, you'll need to intervene to get it back there more quickly.

There are two techniques you'll use to keep your growing retirement bond balance flowing into the stock side of your 3 percent signal plan. Left alone, the plan will issue signals that keep only the initially invested stock balance growing at 3 percent per month. If you don't adjust something as your bond balance grows, the plan's trading signals will steadily become smaller and smaller relative to your overall account balance, and leave too much of your capital uninvolved in the system. We can't have that, so we turn now to the two ways of drawing fresh cash into the plan and keeping the plan's mixture of stocks to bonds correct.

The Modified Growth Target

Remember, all new cash into your plan goes first into the bond fund. You do not divide contributions between the stock and bond funds as you make them. Instead, you'll adjust your quarterly stock fund growth target to incorporate half of the new cash that flowed into your bond fund during the quarter. With 3Sig, every dime of new cash lands initially in your bond fund.

The first way of involving this new cash in the plan is to adjust your quarterly signals higher to account for the growing bond balance. This works best in cases where the pace of new cash contributions to your bond fund is constant, such as 6 percent of pay plus a 50 percent employer match for a total of 9 percent of your salary. If you make $6,000 per month and are paid every two weeks, then 9 percent will become a rate of $270 every other week, or $540 per month. That's $6,480 per year into your retirement bond fund. If you began the plan with a $10,000 balance in your retirement account, the $6,480 per year in new deposits would represent 65 percent of your starting balance in just the first year. This high rate of new cash flow into the plan needs to be incorporated into the system.

The $540 per month in this example is $1,620 per quarter. In the first quarter of the plan, the 3 percent growth target on $8,000 invested (the 80 percent stock allocation of your $10,000 total starting balance) is a quarterly gain of only $240 to $8,240. Your new cash contribution is nearly seven times greater than the plan's growth goal for the quarter. To incorporate all that cash, you'd need a growth target of not 3 percent, but 23 percent! That's $8,000 plus $240 to reach the 3 percent signal line and $1,620 from you, for a total of $9,860.

Remember, though, that we're striving for an 80/20 stock/bond mixture, so you should not move all your cash contribution into stocks every quarter. Some of your new cash should end up in the market, but some should stay in bonds to help with future buying opportunities. Should we divide new cash along the same 80/20 mixture as our overall portfolio, so that 80 percent is earmarked for the stock side and 20 percent remains in bonds? You would think so, but in fact it's better to divide new contributions right down the middle, allocating half to the stock fund growth target while keeping half in bonds.

This is because the stock market tends to rise, and our 3 percent target on the stock side naturally pulls the stock fund balance higher. To help the bond fund stay near its 20 percent base allocation, it's best to leave half of new contributions in it. Easy enough. Divide your quarterly contribution to the bond fund in half, making $1,620 into $810 in this case, and build the $810 into your growth target. In the first quarter of the plan (when you started with $8,000 on the stock side of your account), the quarterly balance goal would have been $9,050 after your new cash was built in. Here's the formula that tells us so:

stock balance ($8,000) + 3% growth ($240)
+ 50% new cash ($810) = goal ($9,050)

It would take 13 percent growth in the quarter to achieve your modified goal. This almost never happens, so in the beginning of your plan, when the balances are low, you'll need to buy more shares of the stock side almost every quarter. This is no problem, because you already supplied your bond fund with the buying power needed for the additional growth target. The "50% new cash" portion of the formula is based on your quarterly contribution, after all, which is in the account and ready to buy. For most people, the situation wouldn't be this extreme, either. First, few people earn $6,000 per month when first starting their retirement plan. Second, by the time they do earn $6,000 per month, their retirement plan balance is high enough that monthly contributions don't introduce such a big distortion.

A big distortion is a good predicament, though, because it means you're directing a lot of fresh cash into the plan. This is a problem most of us would welcome. If you find yourself facing it, keep quiet. Nobody likes to hear a person moaning at the Christmas party about the hardship of managing copious amounts of cash gushing into their retirement account. Besides, if you keep working the cash into the plan using this method, it won't take long until your retirement balance has grown enough to bring the new cash flow down to a more modest relative size.

Let's take this example through a few years, assuming your salary stays constant in the time frame. We'll see how the plan would progress with 50 percent ($810) of each quarterly cash contribution ($1,620) staying in the bond fund balance, while 50 percent ($810) goes into the stock balance at the end of each quarter, with the stock balance growing at exactly 3 percent per quarter so there are no trades triggered by 3Sig. You won't go three years without a buy or sell signal in real life, but we'll assume it here just to illustrate how the plan absorbs new cash:

TABLE 31. How 3Sig Absorbs Half of Quarterly Cash Contributions

Quarter	Retirement Account Bond Balance ($)	Retirement Account Stock Balance ($)	Quarterly Cash Contribution ($)	Stock Balance Goal ($): 3% Growth + 50% of Quarterly Cash ($810)
Q1	2,000	8,000	1,620	9,050
Q2	2,810	9,050	1,620	10,132
Q3	3,620	10,132	1,620	11,245
Q4	4,430	11,245	1,620	12,393
Q1	5,240	12,393	1,620	13,575
Q2	6,050	13,575	1,620	14,792
Q3	6,860	14,792	1,620	16,046
Q4	7,670	16,046	1,620	17,337
Q1	8,480	17,337	1,620	18,667
Q2	9,290	18,667	1,620	20,037
Q3	10,100	20,037	1,620	21,448
Q4	10,910	21,448	1,620	22,902

At the end of the three years, your bond account balance of $10,910 is 34 percent of your total retirement account balance of $32,358. Don't be confused by the $22,902 in the last column of the last row, which is your stock balance *goal* for the quarter. At the beginning of the quarter, your bond balance plus your stock balance came to a total balance of $32,358. Divide the bond balance of $10,910 by the total balance to get 0.34 or 34 percent.

At the end of this three years, our base mixture of 80/20 stocks/bonds had become 66/34—pretty far off. The reason the mixture departed from our base is that the stock balance grew at only 3 percent per quarter on top of the new cash contribution while the bond balance received just as much new cash as the stock side. Since bonds began at only $2,000 and stocks at $8,000, the half of each quarterly contribution left in bonds made that side grow disproportionally more than the stock side. In the first Q2, for instance, $810 represented 41 percent of the previous quarter's bond balance, but only 10 percent of the previous quarter's stock balance. Of course, bonds as a percentage of the total grew more quickly on an equal share of the quarterly contribution.

In real life, the market will be fluctuating and won't return precisely 3 percent in a quarter. You'll be buying and selling along the way. The buying will use up your bond allocation, so it won't just grow continually as a percentage of the total. The selling will add to your bond fund, growing it more. You might think we should tweak our cash contribution so that slightly more goes into the stock side and slightly less remains on the bond side to prevent the 80/20 base mixture from getting out of whack, but it's not worth it given the ebb and flow of the zero-validity environment. We can't know in advance which imbalance the market will produce, or when.

Luckily, imbalances are no problem for us. Now that you know how to incorporate new cash into the plan, it's time to see how to handle departures from the 80/20 base mixture.

The Adjusted Order Size

Most fluctuation around the 80/20 stock/bond mixture is fine. It might move to 75/25, then to 85/15, and back again in most environments. Every once in a while, though, it will get outside a reasonable fluctuation zone and need your intervention to regain its base 80/20 posture.

The reasonable fluctuation zone is anywhere between 70/30 and 90/10. This is subject to interpretation, but the twenty-point range is a good one for giving the market room to wiggle. After each quarter's action, divide your bond balance by your total balance to see the bond balance percentage. If it's lower than 10 percent, it's a good idea to add cash, as we'll discuss later. If it's higher than 30 percent, it's a good idea to adjust an upcoming signal order size to rebalance back to the 20 percent base level.

For instance, if your bond balance is $10,000 and your total balance is $50,000, your bond percentage is exactly 20 percent and your stock balance exactly 80 percent of the total—spot on. If the balance later becomes $15,000 bonds and $70,000 total, your bond percentage is 21 percent. If it becomes $20,000 bonds and $80,000 total, your bond percentage is 25 percent. If it becomes $30,000 bonds and $90,000 total, your bond percentage is 33 percent. At this point, you have too much money in bonds and need to get more into the stock market. To do so, you would wait for a buy signal then increase its size to put more of your ample bond balance to work on the stock side. How much more? Let's have a look.

Putting Excess Cash to Work

If you're like most people taking a casual glance at this plan, you would assume that the bigger the buy signal, the more additional money you want to use. The reason is that a bigger buy signal indicates a better bargain in the market. We want our stock fund to go up 3 percent in a quarter. If it goes up only 2 percent, that's a slight bargain for a purchase. If it goes up 1 percent, that's a better bargain. If it *falls* 5 percent, that's an even better bargain. Hence, the bigger the buy signal, the better the bargain and thus the better the time to put more of your money to work.

With this idea in mind, I structured the original version of this plan around an elegant system of deploying extra bond balance by increasing buy orders by 10 percent for every rounded percentage point below the 3 percent signal in the market's quarterly shortfall. If the market gained only 2 percent in a quarter, that's 1 percentage point less than the 3 percent growth target, so you would have increased your order size by 10 percent. This progression ramped up your strategic deployment of excess bond balance as the market bargain increased, which seems to be just what you want. You would keep this plan in place until your account's bond balance came back down to 20 percent, at which time you would resume the standard 3 percent signal order size.

With Excess Cash, Size Matters

We looked earlier at dividing a large cash balance into four quarterly buys to spread the amount over price and time as a way to get around our fear of moving into stocks just before a crash. Now I argue that it's better to rebalance the plan's bond allocation from 30 percent back down to the target 20 percent in one fell swoop rather than a series of magnified orders. Why the difference? Because our emotions attached to the two cash collections are different.

When your 3Sig bond balance gets to 30 percent, you're going to follow the next buy signal to add in the excess balance to return your bond allocation back down to 20 percent. This extra buying power will have been generated by the plan itself in previous sell signals, and will be a relatively small portion of your overall capital, so you'll feel less nervous about using it in a bigger order. Seeing the plan in action will have instilled confidence in you that its signals work, so following its buy signal to move in extra money generated by its previous sell signals won't create undue stress.

A large initial cash balance or windfall from outside the plan is a different beast. First, it's probably a much bigger portion of your capital than the plan's excess bond buffer. Second, you're emotionally attached to a pile of cash that lands in your lap, keenly aware that it would be a colossal waste to vaporize it in a badly timed foray into stocks. Moving it in gradually across four quarterly buy signals helps you put this money to work prudently while mitigating the stress of doing anything other than admiring it.

As clever as this approach seemed to be, I discovered later that it's unnecessarily complicated. In fact, the plan works better when you wait for bonds to reach the 30 percent line, then use the next buy signal to move all the excess down to the 20 percent line into stocks—regardless of the size of the buy signal. This is counterintuitive but true, and harkens back to the trade-off between bond and stock allocations that we looked at in the "Beating Dollar-Cost Averaging" section of Chapter 4.

The reason it's better to move your excess bond balance in all at once on a buy order rather than fine-tuning order size is that the market doesn't deliver deep drops frequently enough to draw in large bond balances quickly. They end up lingering over several cycles. Since the market's tendency is to rise, putting extra cash in at the first opportunity works better in most environments. Notice that you will use only enough extra bond balance to bring your allocation down to the 20 percent base level. This, combined with letting excess bond balance accumulate up to 30 percent of your account, guards against depleting bonds to an amount so small that you can't fund future quarterly buy signals.

Don't think you won't need it. People naturally expect market movement in one direction to be followed by movement in the other, a tendency sometimes described as the rubber band snapping back. If stocks go down 8 percent this quarter, the thinking goes that the rubber band is stretched too far in the down direction and is tensed for a snapback in the up direction. The farther stocks go down, the more extreme the stretch, so the better the eventual snapback should be, right? Yes, but the key is *eventual*, and you know by now that not a soul on earth can tell you when eventually begins. A quick jaunt through recent market history is all it takes to illustrate this point.

The following is a table of quarters from 2003 through 2012 that returned less than 3 percent in the Vanguard 500 Index Fund, which tracks the S&P 500. There were twenty-two such quarters, of which only nine were followed by quarters returning more than 3 percent while the remaining thirteen underperforming quarters were followed by another underperforming quarter. The thirteen of twenty-two quarters comprise 59 percent of the time. Well over half the quarters signaling to buy into the stock side of your portfolio were followed by at least one more quarter issuing another buy signal. The table highlights the nine losing quarters that were followed by winning quarters. Note that the sequence down the left column does not always list back-to-back quarters:

TABLE 32. The S&P 500's Underperforming Quarters from 2003 to 2012

Quarter Returning Less Than 3% Growth	This Quarter's Performance (%)	The Following Quarter's Performance (%)
Q103	−3.2	15.4
Q303	2.6	12.1
Q104	1.7	1.7
Q204	1.7	−1.9
Q304	−1.9	9.2
Q105	−2.2	1.3
Q205	1.3	3.6
Q405	2.1	4.2
Q206	−1.5	5.6
Q107	0.6	6.2
Q307	2.1	−3.4
Q407	−3.4	−9.5
Q108	−9.5	−2.8
Q208	−2.8	−8.4
Q308	−8.4	−21.9
Q408	−21.9	−11.0
Q109	−11.0	16.0
Q210	−11.5	11.3
Q211	0.1	−13.9
Q311	−13.9	11.8
Q212	−2.8	6.3
Q412	−0.4	10.6

The table shows why you shouldn't get greedy and use a current buy signal to plow your whole bond balance into stocks. A drop this quarter might be a one-off, as in Q304, but it might be the starting gun for a new trend, as in Q407. If you'd moved all of your bond balance into stocks in Q407, you would have been unable to take advantage of the much cheaper prices to come in the five quarters ahead. That was such an unusually bad phase that almost every way of managing bond balance into the downturn ran the bond fund dry and needed extra cash from outside the plan, but pacing buy orders by following 3Sig and the guidelines just given for deploying excess bond balance would have prolonged the plan's internal purchasing power. It will do well enough in most cases that a regularly funded account, such as your retirement, will not run dry.

Even in unusually awful times, though, this modified order approach is pretty good, because you'll prevent it from magnifying buy orders beyond returning an excessive bond balance to its 20 percent range. Once you get bonds back to 20 percent, you'll return to standard order sizes.

Eliminating a Cash Shortage

So far we've discussed what to do in the joyful case of finding yourself with too much cash in your bond fund. What about the less joyful case of finding yourself with too little cash there?

The same way the market's tendency to rise led us to skip adjusting orders in the last section and move all excess bond balance in at the first buy signal, so it leads us to avoid selling extra stock shares beyond the plan's signal. The stock market's upward bias means that all of our rebalancing efforts should focus on keeping as much of our money at work as possible while retaining a reasonable amount of buying power for downturns. We're defining that reasonable amount as the base 20 percent bond allocation, and rebalancing back to it once it hits 30 percent on the upside. On the downside, we'll use a 10 percent bond balance as a signal that we're starting to run dangerously low, and should add more cash.

More cash isn't always available, in which case you should purse your lips and wait for a market recovery to replenish the bond side of your account by selling some of your stock fund into strength. The market will often recover in time to prevent your bond fund from bottoming out—but not always. The plan's bond balance will sometimes go to zero, as it did in the subprime mortgage crash. If there's no outside reserve to draw upon, you'll have no choice but to skip buy signals until your empty bond fund is recharged to a bigger allocation by regular cash contributions and sell signals.

You may need to get comfortable, as it can take several quarters or years for the market to restore your account's base mixture, which is fine. The worst that happens is that you stay at or near zero bond balance for an extended period during which you become a garden-variety buy-and-hold investor. Like anybody holding through the downdraft, you'll sit tight for the eventual recovery. True, you won't take advantage of the recovery by putting more cash to work at lower prices, but nor will you puke at the bottom and sell at the worst possible time, like so many z-val adherents. You'll just wait. When the worm turns and stocks rise for a while, ensuing sell signals will raise cash that goes into your bond fund.

The best course of action to take when your plan runs low on bond balance is to deposit more cash. There's just no way around it. This keeps the plan working as intended, enabling you to take advantage of strong buy signals. You run out of bond balance only when the market has been falling for an extended period or deeply in a short period. In each case, it's exactly the right time to buy as the z-vals get depressed and gnash their teeth publicly about everything wrong with stocks. "Fascinating," you'll mumble as you reach for the BUY button. You can behave this way only if you have buying power in your bond fund.

There's one rare exception to this basic truth, which we'll cover next.

Keep a Bottom-Buying Account

Most of the time your plan will have enough bond balance to fund buy orders, thanks to your regular cash contributions and sell orders issued by 3Sig after strong stock market quarters. For the rare cases when you run out, however, there's another layer of safety you should put in place: a "bottom-buying" account. It's where you should accumulate extra cash for the express purpose of being able to reach for the BUY button when all about you are panicking to sell on the error-prone advice of z-val commentators.

You're contributing to your account's bond fund regularly, earmarking half the contributions for the stock fund's growth target and retaining the other half in the bond fund. Because of this, and because the stock market rises more often than it falls, your most common challenge will be deploying excess balance from your bond fund, not suffering too little. Every once in a while, however, the black knight makes his move and the market crashes big time. Given a little extra cash in such an event, you can make the crash work for you rather than against. You already possess the tool that tells you when you're facing such a moment, 3Sig. Now you need to be sure you have the firepower to take advantage of it.

You can take your time funding the bottom-buying account because you'll almost never need it. In Chapter 7, you'll meet a fictional investor named Mark who ran 3Sig in his company retirement account over the fifty quarters we've been looking at from December 2000 to June 2013, during which time he made typical contributions as his income grew from $54,000 to $81,000 per year. Only three of the fifty quarters demanded more money from Mark, and this was a time frame containing one of the worst stock market dives in history. Put differently, the plan's sell signals and Mark's contributions funded 3Sig 94 percent of the time and needed outside help only 6 percent of the time. An all-clear rate of 94 percent is comforting. It suggests you'll have plenty of time to squirrel away a few nuts in your bottom-buying account so that even rare stock market swoons work for you rather than against.

You don't have to put money in it every month or every quarter, but whenever you come across a little extra and can resist recarpeting the den or whitening every tooth in the family, pad the bottom-buying account. These sporadic deposits add up. If you can manage a regular contribution, so much the better. The savings can serve double duty as a rainy day fund and a bottom-buying account.

Some good funding sources to consider are part of periodic bonuses you might receive from your company, part of occasional profit surges from your business, gifts, tax refunds, property sales, and so on. Such nonregular sources of income are good candidates to supply your bottom-buying account, which can be any type of safe fund at a brokerage firm or bank.

Another good option is to redirect a percentage of increased income to the account. You'll probably apportion growing income to other goals, anyway (including your retirement account, of course), and you could make it a natural part of the procedure to add your bottom-buying account to the list of items needing to be funded. Maybe you give it 5 percent of income growth or something similarly modest. Almost all the time, the bottom-buying fund just sits there doing nothing but reassuring you that there's even more cash tucked away somewhere in the event of an emergency, whether of the stock market or the regular life variety. I'm a big fan of hidden cash pools.

How Much to Set Aside

How much should be in the bottom-buying account? Whatever you can manage, but I like the simplicity of making it a second 20 percent. You're already maintaining a 20 percent bond balance in 3Sig, rebalancing down to it when the balance gets too big and adding to it when it gets too small. Seeing that you also have a bottom-buying balance of the same size is an easy goal to keep in mind.

Admittedly, it's not simple putting it together, because the sums involved can be large. Then again, there's plenty of time, and in the beginning the balances will be more manageable. In our example of starting with $8,000 in stocks and $2,000 in bonds, your fully funded bottom-buying account would hold another $2,000. Over time, you'll grow your retirement account to a balance of $20,000 with $4,000 in bonds, and your fully funded bottom-buying account would hold another $4,000. On it goes at a pace that's not impossible to picture.

For example, 3Sig begun with $8,000 in stocks and $2,000 in bonds at the end of 2000, receiving a $300 quarterly contribution, reached $20,000 in the fourth quarter of 2003 and $30,000 in the first quarter of 2006. That was three years during which to add another $2,000 to the bottom-buying fund so it matched the bond fund's $4,000 target balance, then another two years for the next $2,000. When the subprime mortgage crash exhausted your 3 percent signal plan's bond balance in the fourth quarter of 2008 and left it unable to buy the big drops of the next two quarters, you probably would have added another $1,000 to your bottom-buying fund during the intervening two years, for a total of $7,000 ready to go. That would have covered 80 percent of what the plan needed during the fourth quarter of 2008, which isn't bad. What were most people doing then? Selling as fast their fingers could click.

Keep in mind that the buy signals of those two quarters were among the most extreme ever issued by the plan, as they were among the worst quarterly drops in market history. IJR fell 26 percent in the fourth quarter of 2008, and 17 percent in the first quarter of 2009. Being able to handle half those buying signals is pretty good. Needing to do so is pretty rare.

Thus, while it's not easy to create an additional "just in case" fund of extra cash, it's doable and could be well worth it. Besides, what's the risk? That you have extra cash in the event of an emergency? Nothing wrong with that, even beyond the slim chance that 3Sig will one day tap you on the shoulder and whisper, "Time to buy the bottom." In the case of the subprime slide, you would have been glad you did. By the end of 2009, shares of IJR bought on the plan's fourth quarter of 2008 signal had gained 26 percent, while those bought on its first quarter of 2009 signal had gained 52 percent. Bottom-buying, indeed.

Maximum Danger Point

If the market ever goes so far south that your 3 percent plan ex-hausts its bond balance and everything in your bottom-buying ac-count, and then whatever else you can scrape together, but the plan is still signaling for you to buy more, you've reached the maximum danger point.

This is not for the reason you might expect. It's not the point of maximum danger because the market is going to vaporize your life-time savings. Quite the opposite. It's the point at which you're most vulnerable to doing precisely the wrong thing, bailing at the bottom. Because you've thrown everything you have at your account to no avail, it seems that the wheels are coming off the cart and the stock market will never, ever recover.

This is the dilemma facing buy-and-holders and dollar-cost av-eragers, too, as you read earlier. Avoiding it in almost all circum-stances, even as we seek higher returns through concentrated investing in small-cap stocks with a proven formula, is why 3Sig is better. However, no matter how well you prepare, it's possible for stocks to derail badly enough to wreck your buying power. If you ever enter a downturn with at least 20 percent of your 3 percent signal plan in bonds, and have a good-size bottom-buying account set up, and the market still burns through it all, you're dealing with one seriously Godzilla-size belly flop. You know what, though? They're out there. All we can say about the biggest ones we've seen—and we've seen some real doozies—is that they're the biggest *so far*. Give the banksters and the politicos a few more goes at it, and they'll surely unleash even bigger ones someday.

If and when you're in the teeth of the thing, shaken and bashed to the price floor, out of money, trying to find my phone number so you can call me up and say, "Thanks a lot, pal. This isn't quite going the way you said it would," turn to the signal. What is it telling you? To buy. You can't buy, so what's the next best thing to do? Hold. In this moment, you're doing nothing better than any buy-and-hold investor except that you have an advantage they don't, which is the signal. You might not be able to buy while it's flashing, but you know that it's going to be right eventually and the reason it's going to be right is that today's low prices will become higher prices tomorrow. Even when you can't follow the signal, it will give you the confidence you need to stand pat for the recovery.

Emotional preparation is the key to navigating some of life's hardships, and this is one of them. If you know that your second-guessing engine is going to hit overdrive at this maximum danger point of exhausting your cash, you won't be surprised when it does. "I was aware of this possibility," you'll be able to tell yourself. "I knew it could happen to me, and now that it has, I'm just experiencing the predictable emotion of wanting to escape the pain. I know that's the wrong move, though. I know the market will recover. I know that I should tune out the news and focus on the proven signal, which is telling me to buy, but I'll just hold since I'm out of cash. I know this is the maximum danger point, because if I blow it here, if I bail at the bottom, I could give up many years of progress in one emotional and irrational move."

If you're adequately prepared cash-wise, this will either never happen or happen very rarely, but we can't rule it out. If and when it does happen to you, gird your loins, watch that signal, and keep your money fully invested in the small-cap index. It will pay off eventually. If it's any comfort, know that my money will be right there along with yours, marking time until the recovery.

Adjusting Your Bond Balance as You Grow Older

For most of your working years, the base 80/20 ratio of stocks to bonds will serve you well. As you grow older, however, you'll want to adjust the proportion of stocks lower and bonds higher to build more safety into the mix. The plan makes it easy to do so, and you still need only the two funds. We don't want to leave anything to chance or judgment, so here's my recommended schedule for adjusting the base ratio, along with the level from which you should rebalance back down to the target bond allocation, as you read about in "Putting Excess Cash to Work," earlier in this chapter:

TABLE 33. 3Sig Target Allocation Schedule

Years to Retirement	Stock Allocation (%)	Bond Allocation (%)	Rebalance When Bonds Reach (%)
More than 10	80	20	30
5 to 10	70	30	40
0 to 5	60	40	50
Retirement	50	50	55
Retirement + 5	40	60	65
Retirement + 10	30	70	75
Retirement + 15	20	80	85

This is overly simplistic to a lot of financial planners, who would prefer showing you exhaustive studies of decimalized breakdowns, as if the precision in the numbers made life less unpredictable. I once saw a recommendation for a fifty-year-old to put 41 percent in U.S. stocks, 17 percent in international stocks, 33 percent in U.S. bonds, 8 percent in international bonds, and 1 percent in Treasury Inflation-Protected Securities (TIPS). Somebody would need to have a lot of extra time on their hands to keep on top of an allocation like that. You can probably think of better things to do.

The 3 percent signal plan includes the safety measures financial planners are trying to achieve with additional asset-class allocations. The only distinction among asset classes that matters is volatility, and you should see it as a light switch, either on or off. In 3Sig, the stock side is volatile, the bond side is not. For most of your working years, keeping 80 percent of your capital in the most volatile, highest-performing major asset class, small-cap stocks, will produce the best performance. The 20 percent bond position provides you with buying power to boost performance even more after market sell-offs, and emotional comfort from taking advantage of volatility rather than fearing it.

Once you're within ten years of retiring, you'll decrease your stock exposure to 70 percent and boost bonds to 30 percent, with a new rebalancing demarcation of 40 percent bonds. If your bond balance reaches 40 percent during this phase, you'll take advantage of the next buy signal to move in the excess and reset your target allocation at 70/30 stocks/bonds. Within five years of retirement, you'll adjust the target allocation to 60/40, with a 50 percent bond rebalancing demarcation line. After you enter retirement, you'll decrease stock exposure by ten percentage points each five years until stopping at a 20/80 stock/bond mixture once you're fifteen years into retirement. Because the bond allocations are so high during the retirement years, the rebalance demarcation line moves up only 5 percent each time. Thus, at fifteen years into retirement, with a 20/80 stock/bond allocation, the rebalance happens at 25 percent bonds.

The 3Sig plan is best used as a working-years capital growth engine. The addition of new money from your income, plus the recovery potential inherent in the many years until you retire, provide it with the fuel and room to breathe that it needs. Closer to retirement and into retirement, capital growth becomes less important than capital preservation and income. The rising bond allocation addresses the need to preserve your capital and also provides income.

You might even conclude that 3Sig did its job for you over your working years, but now that you're retired, you want to retire from the plan, too. If so, you could stop running 3Sig and adopt a traditional split of your retirement capital with maybe a third in a large-cap stock index that pays dividends, a third in a bond index, and a third divided between Treasuries and cash. A mixture like that can sit through anything, neither growing much nor losing much, which is acceptable in retirement.

Either way, whether you keep 3Sig going with a larger bond portion for income in retirement or stop the plan in favor of a conservative portfolio mixture in retirement, you'll merely be deciding how to handle the large asset base created by the plan's 80/20 stock/bond mixture run during the majority of your working years. As long as you don't suddenly lose your mind and start trading on z-val advice, you should be fine.

Pulling It All Together

With the addition of these money management techniques to your 3Sig plan, you have a nearly unassailable way to grow your retirement without any interference from z-vals or Peter Perfect.

You'll build your regular contributions into your growth target, earmarking half the total to the stock side and leaving the other half on the bond side. This will put half your new money to work in stocks at the end of every quarter, providing you with much of the benefit of dollar-cost averaging, and you'll also keep half in bonds for future buying power. When the market goes up for an extended period of time or in a bubbly manner, telling you to sell and pushing your bond balance to more than 30 percent of your account value, you'll automatically rebalance it back to 20 percent at the first buying opportunity. When the market goes down and puts shares of your stock fund on sale, you'll be able to take advantage of it by buying more shares with the bond balance you set aside, in almost all cases. On rare occasions, the plan might exhaust its bond balance in an extreme downturn, in which case you'll turn to whatever you've stashed away in your bottom-buying account to take advantage of the unusually cheap prices. If you ever exhaust even that account, you'll follow the signal to remain in place for the recovery.

The 3 percent signal puts your cash contributions to work in good times and bad, high-volume inflection points and low-volume plods ahead. Watching the machinery at work every quarter assures you that you're on top of things, that you need not "dive in and take control" amid tempestuous headlines fanning the wrong flames.

Most of the time, your bond balance will stay at around 20 percent of your account, achieving the base stock-to-bond ratio of 80/20. If it ever reaches 30 percent, you'll move the excess into stocks at the next buy signal. When that arrives, and the z-gang talks about the market having a disappointing quarter and looking ready to move lower, you'll take advantage of this with a buy order and remain agnostic as to where the market will go next. You have no idea, and neither do they.

The modified growth target that incorporates your contributions into the plan, and the rebalancing technique that keeps your bond balance correct, are flexible enough to handle whatever life throws your way. When your salary grows and your quarterly contributions increase, you'll just up the amount you build into your growth target. Temporarily between jobs, with no quarterly contribution? No problem, just drop the contribution to zero. Get a windfall of cash that you want to add to the plan? Dump it in the bond fund. If it takes the bond percentage to 30 percent, let the plan signal when to put that windfall to work in stocks while also moving your mixture back to the base 80/20 ratio. As you get older, you'll adjust this ratio to a lower percentage in stocks and a higher percentage in bonds.

Where do the z-vals fit in? Nowhere. You'll run circles around them using only these techniques and a calculator, just four times per year, while they froth at the mouth daily in the creation of their one reliable product: noise.

Executive Summary of This Chapter

Contributing more cash periodically is common for long-term investment plans. The 3Sig plan handles incoming cash in unique ways. Large balances should be invested gradually. Smaller, regular contributions will initially go into your bond fund, but half their value will be added to the 3 percent growth target, to draw new capital into the plan. A "bottom-buying" account outside the plan can power signals during rare buying opportunities that require more capital than you have in your bond fund. Key takeaways:

✔ To avoid the shock of investing a large cash balance just before a market drop, divide the cash into four equal batches and distribute them over the next four quarterly buy signals.

✔ Our base plan's target allocation is 80 percent stocks and 20 percent bonds, which will fluctuate with the market. When the bond allocation exceeds 30 percent, rebalance it back to the 80/20 target.

✔ The stock market rises over time, so you need to leave some of your cash contributions in your bond fund to maintain a proper allocation and buying power.

✔ The best division of cash contributions is 50 percent. All new cash goes into your bond fund, but you'll add half of its value to the growth target to draw new capital into stocks. The growth target formula is: stock balance + 3% growth + 50% of new cash.

✔ For most of your working life, the reasonable fluctuation zone around the base 80/20 stock/bond target allocation is between 70/30 and 90/10. As you grow older, you'll adjust stocks lower and bonds higher, and move the rebalance trigger up.

✔ When your bond allocation hits its rebalance trigger after a quarterly action (30 percent when the stock/bond target mix is 80/20), use the next buy signal to move the excess bond balance into your stock fund to regain the target ratio.

✔ To react intelligently in rare moments of extremely good buying opportunity, keep a bottom-buying account of savings outside the plan. It can be funded at a leisurely pace because it will almost never be needed.

✔ If you ever exhaust your bond balance and bottom-buying account, you're vulnerable to doing precisely the wrong thing: bailing at the bottom. The plan can still help you by issuing buy signals that encourage you to hold on for the eventual recovery.

CHAPTER SIX

The Plan in Action

You now have enough information to begin running 3Sig.

You read in Chapter 2 that a retirement account is the best place to run it because it enables you to follow profitable quarterly sell signals without worrying about taxes, and we'll confirm that here. However, you can run 3Sig in any type of retirement or nonretirement account you have. Just as there are many types of kitchens stocked with a variety of ingredients, so there are many types of accounts stocked with a variety of investment options. Just as you can cook the same dish with close results in any kitchen, so you can run the same 3Sig plan with results close enough for comfort in any account. What's the key to preparing the same dish anywhere? Similar ingredients and the correct equipment. What's the key to running 3Sig anywhere? Similar investment options and the ability to trade them quarterly. Since the "ingredients" of the plan are simple (just a stock fund and a bond fund), 3Sig will work in whatever account or accounts you have. If you don't have one yet, it's a cinch to open one. In short, anybody can put 3Sig to work with their money right away.

In this chapter, we'll outline the quarterly procedure you'll follow no matter where you manage the plan, learn why it's important to keep costs low and how using index funds in our plan automatically does so, consider taxes, then look at how the plan works in typical brokerage accounts and employer retirement accounts.

The Quarterly Procedure

It's time for brass tacks. In this section, you'll peruse an overview of the five-step quarterly procedure, then learn the steps in more detail. Because the procedure is easy, and you'll repeat it four times per year, it won't take long for you to know it by heart.

At the end of each quarter, you'll check the balance of IJR or another stock fund you're using. If it's grown more than 3 percent plus half of your quarterly cash contributions, you'll sell the excess and put it into your bond fund. If it's right on target at the correct balance, you'll hold. If it's below target, you'll sell enough from your bond fund to buy the stock fund up to the quarter's target balance. Two infrequent situations you'll watch for are whether your bond balance reaches 30 percent of your account and whether the market has dropped 30 percent from its quarterly closing peak.

In brief, the five steps involved in this procedure are:

1.   Determine the quarter's signal line by multiplying last quarter's ending stock fund balance by 1.03, for 3 percent growth, then adding half your quarterly contributions to the result.

2.   Subtract the current stock balance from the signal line. If the result is positive, buy. If it's close to zero, hold. If it's negative, sell. Determine how many shares to buy or sell by dividing the result by the current price of the stock fund. Rounding to a whole share amount is fine.

3.   If the signal is a buy, first sell an appropriate amount of your bond fund to pay for the stock fund buy order. If

the signal is a sell, move the proceeds into your bond fund.

4. If the signal is a sell, verify that your bond fund allocation is still below the rebalance trigger, which is 30 percent for most of your life. If it's 30 percent or higher, make a note to move the excess balance into your stock fund on the next quarterly buy signal to reinstate the bond fund to its target allocation, which is 20 percent for most of your life.

5. Check whether SPY has slipped more than 30 percent from its quarterly closing price high in the previous two years. If it has, enter the "30 down, stick around" phase of ignoring the next four sell signals. This is a rare occurrence but important to get right.

Now, here are the same five steps in more detail:

1. Determine the current quarter's signal line by multiplying last quarter's ending stock fund balance by 1.03, then adding half your quarterly contributions to the result. For example, if last quarter's ending stock balance was $12,845 and you contributed $660 in the current quarter, this would be the calculation:

$12,845 x 1.03 = $13,230	This is 3% growth for the quarter.
$660 / 2 = $330	This is half your quarterly contributions.
$13,230 + $330 = *$13,560*	This is the *signal line* for the quarter.

The signal line will become the stock fund's ending balance after this quarter's action, and is the amount you'll want to grow 3 percent in the next quarter.

2. Subtract the current stock balance from the signal line. If the result is positive, buy. If it's close to zero, hold. If

it's negative, sell. Determine how many shares to buy
or sell by dividing the result by the current price of
the stock fund. Continuing with the signal line from
Step 1, here's the calculation with a current balance of
$12,976 and the stock fund price at $49.17:

$13,560 - $12,976 = $584	Buy $584 worth of the stock fund.
$584 / $49.17 = 11.88	Buy 11.88 shares at $49.17.

Here's the calculation with a current balance of $14,110
and the stock fund price at $53.47:

$13,560 - $14,110 = -$550	Sell $550 worth of the stock fund.
-$550 / $53.47 = -10.29	Sell 10.29 shares at $53.47.

In real life, it's fine to round the numbers to a more convenient whole share amount. For example, it would be
easier to place an order to buy 12 shares than the 11.88
figure produced in the first calculation, and easier to sell
10 shares than the 10.29 figure of the second calculation.
Such small deviations won't make a practical difference
over many years of running the plan, and even the small
differences they make net out to neutral in most time
frames because some share amounts round up while
others round down. Also, fractional share differences
will exert a steadily decreasing influence on your plan as
its balance grows over time. So round away!

3. If the quarterly signal is a buy, divide the amount by
    the current price of your bond fund to see how many
    shares of it to sell in order to pay for the stock fund
    buy. In the Step 2 example of buying $584 of the stock
    fund, here's the calculation with the bond fund price
    at $11.83:

$584 / $11.83 = 49.37	Sell 49.37 shares of the bond fund at $11.83.

If the quarterly signal is a sell, be sure to move the proceeds of the sale into your bond fund right away. With fast order execution these days, you can sell the stock fund shares and move the proceeds into your bond fund in just a few moments, getting everything done during the same log-in session.

4.   If the quarterly signal is a sell, check your bond fund allocation to be sure it's below the rebalance trigger, which is 30 percent for most of your life. Divide your bond fund balance by your whole account balance. If the result is under 0.30, do nothing. If it's 0.30 or higher, make a note to move all of the excess balance into your stock fund on the next quarterly buy signal so your bond allocation is reinstated to its target, which is 20 percent for most of your life. After the sell signal in Step 2, here's the calculation with a bond fund balance of $2,416 and an overall account balance of $15,976:

$2,416 / $15,976 = 0.15   The bond fund balance is at a safe
                                 15% allocation.

If the bond balance had been $4,793 or higher, the 30 percent trigger line in this quarter, you would have made a note to move the excess into the stock fund on the next buy signal.

5.   Finally, make sure SPY hasn't slipped more than 30 percent from its quarterly closing price high of the previous two years. If it has, enter the "30 down, stick around" phase of ignoring the next four sell signals.

This type of big drop is usually obvious, because such sell-offs dominate news. It's a rare investor who manages to disconnect so completely from current events that he'll peruse quarterly closing prices and happen upon an unexpected 30 percent drop. "Oh, look honey, apparently we're in a severe bear market" is not on the top ten list of comments to a spouse after quarterly account check-ins. Also, even if you ever withdrew this thoroughly from news, you would still notice your bond allocation dropping with each quarterly buy signal on the way down, alerting you to trouble in progress.

So, you'll probably be well aware that the stock market is suffering and just look back over recent quarters to see if it's suffered enough to trigger the "30 down, stick around" phase. This is an infrequent occurrence, but an important one to get right, because an enormous amount of gains depends on your buying to the bottom of a bear market and then riding its ensuing recovery with every ounce of your capital. Getting just one of these moments right will greatly improve your ending balance. Getting two of them right could change your life.

Thus, it's worth making a habit to "keep an eye on SPY" to see if it's down enough to trigger the valuable stick-around phase.

To help you with this procedure, I've created online tools that you can use for free. You'll find them, along with other resources related to this book, at jasonkelly.com/3sig.

Little Expenses Are a Big Deal

The financial industry pioneered the concept of fine print. You won't find anybody better at obfuscating important details in hard-to-see places than the legal gremlins at a financial outfit. They know that little expense differences turn into a lot of money over time, so they do their best to make sure you don't notice them. Why? Because a penny saved for you is a penny lost for them. The same financial alchemists who brought you sneaky credit card fees and the sub-prime mortgage crisis are happy to rip you off in retirement as well.

The 3Sig plan helps you avoid the bulk of these unnecessary fees by keeping you out of the most expensive z-val-managed investments in favor of the cheapest index funds available to you. Aside from the performance advantage of 3Sig, its technique of allocating your capital to low-priced index funds will save you tens of thousands of dollars over your lifetime, possibly more than $100,000. In the spirit of a penny saved being a penny earned, you should consider the sum of these forgone fees as comprising part of the strategy's performance advantage. The best part about saving money by avoiding fees is that it's a guaranteed benefit, unlike performance, which comes and goes at the whim of the market. Fees are a certainty; performance is not.

To ensure you appreciate the magnitude of the savings benefit you'll achieve by following 3Sig in cheap index funds, let's delve into how little expenses are a big deal.

In *A Look at 401(k) Plan Fees*, the U.S. Department of Labor revealed how much profit an employee loses by paying high expenses in a retirement account. Its example assumes you're a worker thirty-five years away from retirement with $25,000 in your 401(k). If your investment returns for the thirty-five years average 7 percent while your expenses reduce this by 0.5 percent, your account balance will reach $227,000 by the time you retire, even if you contribute nothing more to it. Crank fees up to 1.5 percent, however, and your account balance will reach just $163,000. The seemingly insignificant percentage point difference in expenses reduced your retirement account balance by 28 percent. Is it worth keeping your account as cheap as possible? You'd better believe it.

To revel in the joy of avoiding high fees, peruse the impact of rising annual operating expenses on an initial investment of $25,000 at a 10 percent annual rate of return for thirty years in the next table. The money that drains away in fees would have itself earned an investment return if it had stayed in the account. Thus, there's also an opportunity cost associated with high expenses, because we miss the chance to have made a bigger profit by investing the lost funds. We can estimate this opportunity cost by calculating the future value of the money paid in fees over the years at the same annual rate of return, accounting for a time delay due to fees being collected gradually. Adding this perspective to the mix reveals the following startling result:

TABLE 34. Impact of Rising Expenses on an Investment

Initial Amount ($)	Annual Rate of Return (%)	Years Held	End Value Before Fee ($)	Annual Fee %	End Value Minus Fee and Opportunity Cost ($)	Amount Lost to Fee ($)	Opportunity Cost ($)	% by Which End Value Is Reduced
25,000	10	30	436,235	0.10	423,336	4,430	8,469	3.0
25,000	10	30	436,235	0.20	410,806	8,679	16,750	5.8
25,000	10	30	436,235	0.50	375,329	20,390	40,516	14.0
25,000	10	30	436,235	1.00	322,683	36,792	76,760	26.0
25,000	10	30	436,235	1.50	277,209	49,838	109,188	36.5

This table shines a harsh light on the impact of rising expenses. A seemingly innocuous 1.5 percent annual fee adds up to $49,838 paid over thirty years on a $25,000 investment growing at 10 percent annually. Keeping that amount in the investment would have added another $109,188 to the value of the account at the end of thirty years. The fees paid and the opportunity missed come to a total of $159,026 erased from the fee-less growth balance of $436,235. The fee and its associated opportunity cost reduced the investment's potential value by a whopping 36.5 percent.

Morningstar's director of mutual fund research, Russel Kinnel, ran a study in 2010 examining the predictive power of the firm's rating system and fund expense ratios. Kinnel asked at the beginning of his report, "How often did it pay to heed expense ratios? Every time." You know that z-val managers lose to indexes, and you know that their actively managed funds charge higher expense ratios than do index funds, so a low expense ratio provides two green lights: you'll directly boost your bottom line by paying less in fees, and you'll probably avoid the detrimental meddling of z-val managers because the lower the management fee, the less they're interested in being involved.

Given this, the results of Kinnel's study confirmed what should have been a foregone conclusion, and emphasized the need to seek out the lowest-priced funds available. In every asset class and every single period, low-cost funds beat their high-cost rivals, showing the expense ratio to be a strong predictor of performance. The higher the expense, the greater the odds of bad results. This turns on its head the notion that "you get what you pay for." In the arena of mutual funds, the more you pay, the more you suffer. In the 2005 group of domestic equity funds, 48 percent of those in the cheapest quintile survived and outperformed versus only 24 percent in the most expensive quintile. The cheapest funds were twice as likely to succeed as the pricey ones.

Kinnel concluded his report with direct advice: "Investors should make expense ratios a primary test in fund selection. They are still the most dependable predictor of performance. Start by focusing on funds in the cheapest or two cheapest quintiles, and you'll be on the path to success."

Later, when we look into specific retirement plans, you'll see me searching out the lowest-priced small-cap stock index fund and bond index fund option in each. You'll do the same in your own account. After reading this section, you know why. Lowering expenses reduces the drain of profit from your investment over time. Also, by focusing on low-priced index funds, you eliminate the damaging influence of z-val investment managers and their 50 percent mistake rates.

There's nothing but upside to keeping expenses down, so 3Sig does so by directing your assets into the lowest-cost funds available in your account.

Tax Considerations

This is rarely a popular section in any financial book, but at least it's preferable to the only other certainty in life. Plus, tax considerations related to 3Sig are not complicated, so we'll dispense with them posthaste.

Because 3Sig takes action four times per year, once at the end of each quarter, it can produce some unpleasant tax consequences in a nonretirement account. Every stock fund sale in the plan is at a profit, because it sells only when IJR or another fund you're using in it is trading above a 3 percent profit for the quarter. Selling IJR at a profit when you've owned it for less than a year will trigger a short-term capital gain tax liability. This is worse than the long-term variety, which is charged on sales of assets held for more than a year, because the short-term capital gain tax rate is the same as your ordinary income tax rate. Long-term capital gains are given special tax treatment as a way to reward nonspeculative wealth accumulation. They're taxed at zero if you're in the 10 percent or 15 percent tax bracket, and at only 15 percent if you're in the 25 percent tax bracket or higher. Most investors find themselves in the latter category, so long-term gains are taxed at 15 percent while short-term gains are taxed at 25 percent or more.

This means that 3Sig's quarterly sales could cost you the higher short-term tax bite if you run the plan in a nonretirement account. Luckily, most people keep the bulk of their lifetime savings in retirement accounts, which are tax-free or tax-deferred, thereby avoiding the issue of capital gains taxes entirely. You can buy and sell as much as you want in a retirement account without caring about taxes until you begin withdrawing from it, in the case of a traditional individual retirement account (IRA). Then, when you take withdrawals, you pay only income tax on them at your regular rate. This rate usually decreases in retirement because your income drops, enabling you to pay less tax on your retirement account withdrawals than you paid on income during your working years. In a Roth IRA, you contribute after-tax dollars and then the gains on those contributions are tax-free as long as you don't withdraw them before age fifty-nine and a half and your account has been open at least five years. Such qualified Roth IRA withdrawals don't incur any tax liability whatsoever. A traditional IRA is a tax-*deferred* account, while a Roth IRA is a tax-*free* account.

These structures mean you can run 3Sig in either of them without worrying about capital gains taxes on your quarterly trading activity. What a fine coincidence, because a retirement account is precisely where most people will want to run the plan.

Outside of retirement accounts, you're stalked by the short-term capital gains tax monster that charges your regular income tax rate on profitable sales of assets you've held for one year or less. Even so, you can fare pretty well in 3Sig outside retirement accounts by keeping track of when you bought various lots of IJR and specifying that you want to sell lots you've owned for more than a year when the plan signals a sale. Almost all brokerage firms offer this capability, but 3Sig involves so little trading that it's easy to track on your own, too. For example, your plan might create this short history:

TABLE 35. 3Sig Sample Trading History

Quarter	Action	Price ($)
Q1 last year	Buy 12 shares	93.71
Q2 last year	Buy 17 shares	95.24
Q3 last year	Buy 65 shares	93.32
Q4 last year	**Sell 73 shares**	101.71

(continued)

Quarter	Action	Price ($)
Q1 this year	Buy 65 shares	99.65
Q2 this year	Buy 20 shares	101.09
Q3 this year	**Sell 9 shares**	104.80
Q4 this year	Buy 17 shares	106.62

In Q4 of last year you had to sell 73 shares. If you did so with any of the shares you bought in the previous three quarters of that year or in the last quarter of the year before, you had to pay short-term capital gains. However, if you sold shares you bought before Q4 of the prior year, you paid only 15 percent in long-term capital gains. Similarly, in Q3 of this year, you needed to sell some of the shares you bought prior to Q3 of last year in order to avoid the short-term capital gains tax. As you can see, it was easy to do so. You bought 17 shares in Q2 of last year, more than enough to supply the 9 shares you needed to sell in Q3 of this year.

Once you've been at the plan a while, you'll have plenty of older blocks of IJR from which to choose when it comes time to sell, making it easy to avoid short-term capital gains tax. Also, you sell profits only beyond a fairly generous 3 percent quarterly pace, which limits both the frequency and the amount you'll sell, thus keeping taxable profits modest. Nonetheless, even the 15 percent long-term capital gains tax paid infrequently on modest profits becomes a hindrance over time, so it's best to run the plan in a tax-advantaged account.

Individual Retirement Accounts

We need to clear up a possible misconception.

There's nothing offbeat or small-time about IRAs, what with fifty million Americans having one, but they're sometimes looked upon as second-tier retirement plans, the type you settle for if you can't get a gold-plated employer or government plan. This is wrong.

I want to set the record straight here and make sure that you, if you're an IRA holder, know that your account is a perfect place to run 3Sig.

When I discuss running the signal in a retirement account, people without an employer retirement plan, such as a 401(k), sometimes look despondent. "I don't have a real retirement account," a friend once told me. "Just an IRA."

This strikes me as an odd comment, because everybody knows an IRA *is* a retirement account. Just look at what the letters stand for: individual retirement account. What people like my friend seem to mean when they say an IRA is not a real retirement account is that it doesn't include company matching, as many employer plans do. This is true in many cases, and the company match is a fantastic benefit of some employer plans, but the lack of a company match does not make IRAs and other nonemployer retirement accounts any less tax-advantaged than a 401(k), which is the main distinction between a retirement account and a nonretirement account. It's the tax treatment, not the company match, that makes a retirement account.

Besides, I have news from the matching department. There are IRA varieties set up by employers that do include a match. I'll list a few in a moment. In such cases, the IRA offers only advantages over larger corporate retirement plans because it includes the same employer matching benefit plus a better list of securities to buy in the account.

Even if you have an IRA without company matching, it will offer a broad range of choices for your money, a lot of which are cheaper than the limited set of choices in some 401(k)s, for example. Because any major brokerage firm can offer you an IRA, you can trade just about every market security in it. In some 401(k)s, employees are limited to just a handful of mutual funds from the same company, which might be ripping off participants. You'll read more on this later.

So, don't despair if the only retirement account you have is an IRA. There's nothing wrong with that. It's an excellent place to run 3Sig. The plan works like a charm in any IRA, including:

- a traditional or Roth IRA set up at a bank or broker, which can trade almost anything. These are usually run on your own without any involvement by a company or other party;

- a simplified employee pension IRA (SEP-IRA), an IRA established by an employer for the firm's employees (see, even an IRA can involve employers: an employer can contribute up to 25 percent of the employee's wages); or

- a savings incentive match plan for employees IRA (SIM-PLE IRA), which is set up by an employer for employees, as the name conveys, and includes matching.

There's just no reason to feel bad if your only retirement account is an IRA, even if it's the traditional IRA with no employer involvement. You can use it to run 3Sig without tax consequences, and will be able to scour the entire market of securities for the lowest-priced funds to use in it. You won't get lost in the abundance, however, because our plan requires just two funds in order to work as advertised. Still, it's good to know an IRA includes the ability to buy a cheaper alternative if you happen to find one. You're not locked into a preset list.

With the benefits of an IRA in mind, we'll move on to looking at how to run it, along with your nonretirement money, in a brokerage account.

Typical Brokerage Accounts

The brokerage industry has been around a long time, so there are many good choices for your regular accounts and retirement accounts such as the traditional IRAs and Roth IRAs we looked at in the previous two sections. We'll cover company retirement accounts, such as 401(k)s, in the next section. The following brokerage firms offer both regular accounts and retirement accounts, with access to IJR and other small-cap vehicles in both:

E*Trade	etrade.com
Fidelity	fidelity.com
Firstrade	firstrade.com
Schwab	schwab.com
Scottrade	scottrade.com
ShareBuilder	sharebuilder.com
TD Ameritrade	tdameritrade.com
TradeKing	tradeking.com
Vanguard	vanguard.com

Opening a new account is simple at any of them, and they also make it easy to roll over an old retirement account from a former employer to a traditional IRA. This can offer advantages over your old plan, such as freedom from restrictions that may have limited your usage of the funds in your former workplace plan and the ability to use the funds penalty-free for a first-time home purchase or qualified educational expenses. Probably the best improvement, however, is access to a much wider variety of investment options, including IJR but also other ETFs and a slew of mutual funds, stocks, bonds, CDs, and so on.

Brokerage pricing has come down in recent years. There are no account fees involved anymore, and the cost of online trades is less than $10 almost everywhere. Best of all, many ETFs (including our friend IJR) can be traded without commission at several brokers. That's right. You can open an account in which it's completely free to buy and sell IJR each quarter. There's usually a requirement to hold the ETF for at least thirty days after purchase, but 3Sig automatically does this, so it's not a concern. At Schwab, you get commission-free access to its IJR equivalent, Schwab Small-Cap Core (SCHA), boasting a tiny 0.08 percent expense ratio. At Vanguard, you get commission-free access to its IJR equivalent, Vanguard

Small-Cap (VB), boasting an almost-as-tiny 0.10 percent expense ratio. At many other brokers, you get commission-free access to IJR itself, boasting a still-very-cheap expense ratio of 0.16 percent.

In short, you'll have trouble going wrong. Any of the brokers just shown will get you up to speed in the right type of account with cheap or free access to IJR or a good alternative. Visit their sites to compare current offers and decide which is best for you.

Putting Cash into Your Account

It all starts with cash. Unless you're rolling over an existing account from somewhere, you'll need to fund your new brokerage account with cash. We've used $10,000 as a starting balance in this book's examples, but you can start with any amount.

To move cash into your brokerage account, log in and find your way to what is usually called the "Accounts" area, then to what is called "Deposits and Withdrawals" or "Transfer Money" or something similar. There, you can link your bank account to your brokerage account and initiate a one-time transfer or recurring transfers.

Buying and Selling

All the brokerage accounts make it easy to buy and sell investments, which makes sense, since that's their job. When you're ready to begin 3Sig, find your way to the "Trade" area of your broker's site, then the "Stocks/ETFs" section where you'll specify the symbol you want to buy, the quantity, the type of order, and so on.

Let's say you started your account with $10,000 in cash and will begin your plan with $2,000 of it in a bond fund and $8,000 of it in IJR after it closed the previous day at $96.26. Dividing your $8,000 by $96.26 shows that you need to buy 83.11 shares, but you decide that 83 is close enough and easier to track, and that a limit order to buy at $96 is fine, too. So, you'll place a limit order to buy 83 shares of IJR at a price of $96. If and when it fills at that price, it will use

$7,968 of your cash. Not sure what a limit order is? Then the next section is for you.

Market and Limit Orders

With a little help from *The Neatest Little Guide to Stock Market Investing*, let's review the difference between market and limit orders.

A market order "instructs your broker to buy a security at the current ask price. That's it. Your buy price is whatever the thing is trading for when the order reaches the floor. With today's fast communications, that price is going to be fairly close to where it was when you placed the order, if not the exact same price." In the example with IJR just given, if you placed a market order for 83 shares and it opened the next day at $96.09, you would probably buy it at $96.09 exactly. If your order didn't fill at that exact price, then it would fill fairly close to it, maybe at $96.05 or $96.15.

Next, we're going to cover limit orders, but before we do, I want to pause and mention that the simplicity of market orders makes them a perfectly acceptable way to go in 3Sig. You can try to get better prices with limit orders, and they can work out, but given 3Sig's quarterly pace and long time horizon, the pennies of improvement provided by limit orders is often not worth the trouble. Add to this the chance that whatever benefit a limit order achieves in one quarter will be erased by a limit order in another quarter, and the appeal of market orders grows even stronger. Nonetheless, limit orders are a valid approach to buying and selling, so we'll see how they work in the plan.

A limit order tells your broker "to buy or sell a security at a price you specify or better. That means if you say to sell a stock at $10, your broker will sell either at $10 or at a higher price. If you say to buy a stock at $20, your broker will buy either at $20 or at a lower price." In the IJR example just given, you told the broker to buy IJR at $96 or lower and to keep the order in place until you canceled it. "When you place a limit order, it is either a day order or a good-till-cancelled (GTC) order. A day order expires at the end of the current trading day regardless of whether or not its conditions were met." A GTC order remains open until its conditions are met, which might never happen, or until it reaches the end of its time in force. Different brokers default to different times in force for GTC orders. Fidelity defaults to a six-month duration, TD Ameritrade to a four-month duration, and other brokers may use different durations. The maximum is six months.

At the end of each quarter, you'll look at your balance and IJR's closing price to determine whether you're above or below the 3 percent growth target, and how many shares to sell or buy to reset to the target. If your limit order to buy 83 shares of IJR at $96 filled at $96 exactly, then your stock balance would be $7,968 and the 3 percent growth target for this quarter would be $8,207. That's $7,968 plus 3 percent, or times 1.03, to get $8,207. You can figure your IJR price target for the quarter easily, too: $96 plus 3 percent, or $96 times 1.03, to get $98.88. If IJR is trading at less than $98.88, so your balance is under $8,207, you'll buy more of it. If it's right at $98.88 and your balance is $8,207, you'll stand pat. If it's more than $98.88, so your balance is over $8,207, you'll sell some of it.

We'll say it came in short this quarter, at $97.74, making your 83 shares of IJR worth only $8,112. That's $95 short of the goal, so you will need to buy $95 worth of IJR at $97.74. Technically, you needed just 0.97 shares of IJR, but in real life you would almost certainly buy a single share with a market order to keep things simple and accurate enough. If you picked it up at $97.75 the next day, you'd then own 84 shares worth $8,211, close enough to the $8,207 for us to call the quarter a wrap. The goal for the next quarter is another 3 percent growth on top of the new $8,211 balance, or $8,457.

Let's say it was a great quarter, with all sorts of cheering from z-vals and talk of technological breakthroughs, with optimistic charts and raised target prices. However, at the close of the quarter, you dutifully ignored the chatter as always and looked only at the numbers. IJR closed the quarter at $109.48, making your 84 shares worth $9,196—much more than the $8,457 goal. Great! You sell the excess profit this quarter, which amounted to $739. That came to 6.8 shares, which you would most likely have rounded up to 7 shares.

Right about here in the quarterly procedure, I can imagine you putting down your pencil and pausing to think. "You know," you'll say to yourself, "it sure felt good riding this thing up to $109, and it's still going strong. Maybe I should skip this quarter's sale." It happens to the best of us. You probably expect me to launch into a lecture on the importance of sticking to the plan and ignoring your meddling nature, and so on. Rest easy. Remember, one of this plan's strengths is that it acknowledges your emotions while issuing rational signals, and it can handle a desire to prod the numbers now and then. It's natural to see a market going up and your own profits mounting, and wanting to let the climb run as long as possible. The good news for you—as you sit there thinking about how nice it would be to make even more money on the rising rocket you know as IJR—is that there's a way to stick with the 3Sig plan while also satisfying your desire to meddle. We'll cover it next.

Trailing Stops and Other Trading Tactics

Just as you can buy with a market or limit order, you can also sell with a market or limit order. The market order sells IJR at its current price, period. If you place the order after hours, then it will fill at the open the next day, usually pretty close to where it ended the previous trading day. In this case, you would return to the "Trade" area of your broker's site and fill in the form to sell 7 shares of IJR with a market order. If it filled at $109.50, you'd own 7 fewer shares of IJR for a new total of 77 and your cash fund would increase by $767 (the 7 shares you sold times their $109.50 sale price). You'd move this cash into your bond fund. Your new IJR balance would be $8,432, and your goal for the next quarter would be 3 percent more than this, or $8,685.

What if, though, you were right about the market being on a

tear and having a lot higher to go before taking a breather? You'd feel bad if two weeks after you sold IJR at $109.50 it traded at $114.50, for example. Your 7 shares sold would have fetched an extra $35 had you waited. That's not exactly champagne worthy, but it won't take long in the plan before you've moved from dealing with just 7 shares on a quarterly sale, to 70, and eventually 700. At such high levels, the $35 profit missed would amount to $350 and $3,500, respectively.

One way to avoid the disappointment of selling too low while still sticking with the plan is to use a trailing stop order. Here's how I explained trailing stops in *The Neatest Little Guide to Stock Market Investing*:

> You want to own the stock as long as its uptrend continues, and that's the specialty of trailing stops. They "trail" behind the price as it rises upward, but lock into place when the price begins to fall. You specify in your order the distance from the price at which the stop order to sell kicks in. As with all stop orders, this one can be a market to sell immediately or a limit to sell at a specified price. When you set the distance from the price, you do so with either a dollar amount or a percentage distance. I prefer the latter. The bigger the dollar amount or the wider the percentage, the less likely the order is to trigger—but the more loss you're willing to accept before you sell. A typical order might be a 10 percent trailing stop.

In this case, you knew the plan called for you to sell 7 shares of IJR and that you technically should have done so at the market price, but you saw the market rising powerfully and wanted to try getting as much out of the uptrend as possible. Instead of placing a market order to sell, you could have placed a trailing stop order to sell the 7 shares. If you used a 10 percent trailing stop, you would risk losing all the quarterly profit as IJR fell 10 percent, to $98.53, from its quarterly closing price of $109.48. That's no good, of course, and with every quarter in the plan seeking just a 3 percent profit, you need to use what are called "tighter" stops, such as 1 percent or 2 percent.

Let's say you saw the big outperformance for the quarter and decided you could afford to lose up to 2 percent from IJR's quarterly closing price while seeking an even higher sale price. After placing this order, the biggest risk would be that IJR fell immediately by 2 percent, to $107.29 from $109.48, reducing the profit from your sale of 7 shares to $751 instead of the $767 you would have achieved with a market order that filled at $109.50. The better case—and the one you believe will happen as evidenced by your choosing to place a trailing stop order instead of a market order—would be that IJR continue rising. Each rise would ratchet up the trailing sell-stop price to a higher level that locked in more profit.

We'll think positively and say the better case unfolded this quarter. After you placed your 2 percent trailing stop order, IJR rose from its quarterly close of $109.48 to the following higher prices and their new 2 percent trailing stop prices:

TABLE 36. Rising Prices and 2% Trailing Stops for IJR

IJR High Price ($)	2% Trailing Stop Price ($)
111	108.78
113	110.74
115	112.70
120	117.60
130	127.40

This would have been a quarter to remember, with IJR rising 19 percent, to $130 from $109.48, and it does happen. In the second quarter of 2003, IJR rose 20 percent. In the fourth quarter of that same year, it rose 14 percent. In the second and third quarters of 2009, the start of the bounce-back from the subprime mortgage crash, it rose 22 percent and 18 percent, respectively. It rose 16 percent in the fourth quarter of 2010 and 17 percent in the fourth quarter of 2011. Big quarters exist, sometimes back to back. If you suspect you're at the beginning of one, you might want to risk a little profit by betting on even higher prices with a trailing stop order. Of course, you know by now that what you suspect has a 50 percent chance of being wrong, but we'll leave that aside for the moment.

The table shows that each tick higher in IJR pulls the trailing stop up with it, always at the distance you specify, which is 2 percent in this case. If IJR slips back to the last price locked in by the trailing stop, you'll sell there. This frequently happens even if the market is ultimately heading higher after the pullback. In the table's price history, it's possible that IJR would have fallen back to $112.70 after touching $115. Your sell order would have filled, and then IJR would have gone on to greater glory at $120 and $130 without your 7 shares along for the ride.

This happens *all the time* in the stock market. As useful as trailing stop orders can be, they are not magical. The market specializes in going barely far enough in the direction you least want it to go, just to trigger the orders you'd rather it not trigger if the trend is a short one, and then reversing right away to cause you the maximum amount of frustration. Investors say the market will do whatever frustrates the greatest number of people. You wouldn't be too upset if your trailing stop triggered at $112.70 while IJR was en route to $102, but you would feel pretty lousy if it filled at $112.70 and IJR bottomed at $112.68. Too bad the latter way is how it often goes.

For instance, back in the amazing second quarter of 2009, when IJR gained 22 percent overall, it fell 3.7 percent on April 7. That one day would have triggered a trailing stop of 4 percent or less placed after the previous day's closing price because IJR fell 4 percent to its low of the day on April 7, and a 3 percent stop is about as loose a one as you're likely to use in 3Sig. What's worse, IJR rebounded 8 percent in the following two days—yes, 8 percent in two days. In this case,

3Sig would have spared you the pain of stopping out in the one-day downward blip ahead of the breathtaking two-day spike because it signaled a big buy at the end of the first quarter, not a sell. This was exactly the right call.

A time that could have caused maximum frustration for a tight sell stop was the third quarter of 2009, just after the 22 percent charge higher in the second quarter. Had you felt strongly that the market would keep going up, you might have set a 2 percent trailing stop on IJR in response to the plan's big sell signal. On the first day of the quarter, July 1, IJR topped out at $45.50, and your 2 percent trailing stop locked in a trigger of $44.59. Guess where IJR opened the next day? At exactly $44.59, triggering your order to sell. Three weeks later, it traded at more than $48 and finished the quarter at $52.34, for a 17.8 percent gain. Maximum frustration! Welcome to the wiggling worm of the market.

This is the rub with stop-loss orders. If you set them too tightly, they trigger easily and stop you out of a position that might well have been just moving around on its way higher. If you set them too loosely, you lose a lot before the sale protects you from further losses. In our 3 percent signal plan, trailing stops can be a good way to satisfy your emotional need to try squeezing as much as possible from a strong move higher, but they rarely help much. Why? Because the tiny 3 percent profit margin we're working with on a quarterly schedule makes tight stops the most obvious type to use. Most trailing stops should specify a range of 5 to 10 percent to avoid triggering on random market noise, and such loose stops are best used on long-held positions that have appreciated 50 or 100 or 1,000 percent. When you're up tenfold over five years, you can afford a 10 percent slip before selling. When you're gunning for a 3 percent gain in a quarter and happen to exceed it by a bit, you can't. Thus, tight trailing stops in 3Sig are usually better for emotions than for performance.

Does this render them worthless? No. If they make you feel more in control of your investment as you stick generally to the plan, and you crave such a feeling in the zero-validity environment, then they provide you with comfort while doing little harm. The worst that happens with a tight stop is that you give back some of your previous quarter's gains. In the course of your life, that's a blip and a cheap price to pay for a market lesson learned. The 3Sig plan protects you against making too big a mistake because it limits the number of shares you'll sell in any given quarter. Even if the worst-case scenario unfolds on your trailing stop order, it will unfold on only a fraction of your shares rather than all of them. In this example, you sold just 7 of your 84 shares of IJR. No matter what price you sold those 7 shares at, your remaining 77 shares continued benefiting from IJR's rising price.

Should you decide to use a trailing stop when selling, be sure to adjust the number of shares you're selling so that even the worst-case scenario will keep your plan on track. To make this easier to understand, we'll use an example with more shares in our portfolio. Instead of 84 shares and selling 7, we'll assume 8,400 shares and selling 675. With the new higher share amount, your goal for the quarter was $845,733. When IJR closed the quarter at $109.48, your 8,400 shares were worth $919,632, for a $73,899 surplus. Dividing that by the closing price of $109.48 showed you needing to sell 675 shares. If a market order to do so filled at $109.50, you'd then own 7,725 shares worth $845,889—close enough to the $845,733 goal.

You decide, however, to try your luck with a trailing stop. You place the order to sell 675 shares with a 2 percent trailing stop. From the quarterly closing price of $109.48, the initial stop trigger would be at $107.29. If the worst-case scenario unfolds, as it so often does in the zero-validity environment, then you would sell 675 shares at $107.29, and be left with 7,725 shares worth only $828,815—a full $16,918 below the $845,733 goal. No good!

The way to avoid this problem is to adjust the number of shares to the worst-case scenario price. At $107.29, your 8,400 shares would be worth $901,236 for a $55,503 surplus. Dividing that by $107.29 would reveal you need to sell only 517 shares. You would place a

2 percent trailing stop on that quantity instead of the 675 shares you would have sold at the quarterly closing price. Now, even if the worst-case scenario unfolds and you sell 517 shares at $107.29, you will be left with 7,883 shares worth $845,767—close enough to the $845,733 goal.

What about a better scenario unfolding? That happens, too, and is the one you believed would happen in this example. If the sun shines on your little corner of the market, and IJR rises, without a 2 percent hiccup, to $120, then finally slips 2 percent to $117.60, you sell 517 shares at $117.60, to add $60,799 to your bond account. You would still own 7,883 shares of IJR worth $927,041—a giant $81,308 more than was necessary for the quarter, and nobody's complaining.

For a moment in this scenario, go ahead and consider yourself a virtuoso investor, a master of markets, to have awaited more profits in your 517 shares before selling, and to have done so while never risking the integrity of the 3Sig plan. The not risking the integrity of the plan is the part that revealed your true competence in this case. Getting the higher price was just lucky, but setting the order in such a way that bad luck could inflict no damage—that took skill. Don't feel the need to mention this while crowing about the high sale price, though. The z-vals never do.

What about quarters when you buy? Is it worth trying for a better price then? It can be. If you're supposed to buy a certain number of IJR shares after it closed the quarter below the target, you might set a limit order a little below where it's trading if you think it'll drop even more. As long as you don't set the limit too far under its quarterly close, this usually works. It's one way to put the market's inherent volatility in your favor. The same force that causes so many tight trailing stops to fill even when the general trend is higher can help your tight buying limit order fill in the same situation.

For example, if IJR closed the quarter at $98.45 and you're supposed to buy 320 shares, you might set a limit order to buy at $97. The same way you adjusted the sell order to the worst-case scenario, you can adjust this buy order to the price at which it will fill rather than the current market price. If you were supposed to buy 320 shares at \$98.45, you would need to buy 325 shares at \$97 to use the same amount of cash.

The risk is that IJR never reaches your \$97 before embarking to higher prices. Oops. In that case, your cash that was supposed to be put to work would instead sit idle while IJR appreciated. This is why a tight limit order to buy is the best idea. Anything under 2 percent stands a good chance of filling, with the chance increasing as the distance decreases. With IJR at \$98.45, for instance, a limit order to buy at \$98 would have a very good chance of filling. It's only 0.5 percent below the last closing price, and such volatility happens regularly. It wouldn't require much of a share quantity adjustment, either: 321 instead of 320.

If your head is spinning by now and you're thinking, "The heck with it, I'd rather not adjust prices and quantities each quarter," just stick with market orders and let the plan dictate what you do. Generally what happens is that people who begin 3Sig thinking they're going to outsmart it with trailing stops to sell and loose limit orders to buy experience the worst-case scenario enough times to finally wonder why they're bothering, and then just go with market orders to sell and tight limit orders to buy. There's no better investment instructor than the market itself, so this process is understandable. Knowing the fifty-fifty odds of failure intellectually is one thing; feeling them in your bones and bank is quite another.

It bears repeating that 3Sig keeps a safety net under your experiments. Go ahead and try whatever limit orders and distances you want to try. The worst that will go wrong is that you'll mess up with a small portion of your stock balance, either giving up all the quarterly profit in a selling quarter or completely missing the buy price in a buying quarter, and then shake your head, mutter something like "I'll be darned, it really didn't go the way I thought it would," and fix it in later quarters. As life challenges go, this is nothing.

Employer Retirement Accounts

Many employers provide or "sponsor" retirement plans. These are sometimes called "defined contribution plans" because you decide what percentage of your salary you want to contribute to the plan, and then your employer automatically deducts the money from each paycheck and puts it into your retirement account. Some employers provide matching funds, usually at a fraction of the amount that the employee contributes, such as 50 percent. This is free money and should be maxed out by everybody regardless of the investment strategy they pursue. The most common employer retirement plans are 401(k)s for employees of corporations, 403(b)s for employees of most nonprofit groups and parts of the public education system, 457s for certain nonprofit groups and state and municipal employees, and the Thrift Savings Plan (TSP) for federal employees.

With more than fifty-five million American workers actively participating in 401(k) plans, they're the type you hear about most often. However, all the plans are similar beyond the distinct groups who use them, which makes it easy for us to discuss running 3Sig in any one of them.

In a section of its website called "Smart 401(k) Investing," the Financial Industry Regulatory Authority (FINRA) explains the investments available in most places. Your plan will offer at least three investment choices but possibly more than a hundred, with the average one carrying between eight and twelve alternatives. The investments are frequently just mutual funds, but some plans behave like brokerage accounts, enabling you to trade the full range of stocks, bonds, funds, annuities, and so on. Many employers offer matching contributions, which employees might be able to invest as they see fit. If the employer chooses how to invest its contributions, it often does so by issuing shares of company stock. FINRA mentions how easy it is to go wrong in an employer retirement account. The more choices available, the harder it is to assemble the right mixture for your goals and risk tolerance. It's up to you to get it right.

This is a prime example of giving people enough rope to hang themselves, and it applies to IRAs as well, because they put the full market of choices in front of people who might not know the difference between shares of stock and soup stock. People working in fields unrelated to finance, who may have no interest in finance whatsoever, are expected to employ a wide range of financial instruments to shepherd their savings through complex markets toward retirement. No wonder many end up taking on too much risk and suffering in severe sell-offs such as the subprime mortgage crash of 2008, or taking on too little risk and reaching the end of their careers with only a piddling balance after a lifetime of labor.

This is where society has gone, though: from the good old days of traditional pension plans in which your employer contributed all the money, made all the investment decisions, took on all the investment risk, and handled all the administrative details for you, to the current moment, with a plan funded mostly by you and managed by you, for better or worse. It's too often for worse, which is what inspired me to write this book.

What's needed by people tossed unwittingly into the world of financial folly on self-directed accounts is a simple plan that works everywhere and can be run even by people uninterested in the vagaries of the stock market. The longer I'm in this business, the more I think this group should include everybody. With scandals in all directions, z-vals running wild, Peter Perfect whispering on every corner, and asset prices becoming more manipulated over time, the stock market is a life-wrecker for anybody unprepared. Unfortunately, most participants in employer retirement plans *are* unprepared, through no fault of their own. They didn't set out to become financiers, and it's beyond me why society thinks everybody should—d'oh, except that it's obvious when we ask, "Who benefits?"—the z-val fee collectors.

Happily for overwhelmed retirement investors everywhere, 3Sig is ready to help. Whether you face a tiny list of investment options or the wide-open market of choices, the plan will work. All it needs is a bond fund and a stock fund, preferably of the small-cap variety, but even a general stock index fund will do in a pinch.

The conundrum for both IRA and employer plan retirement investors is that the best way to save money is to sift through a broad range of investment options for the lowest-cost one, but the broader the range, the more overwhelmed people feel. The result is that too many people end up either overdiversified in a sea of choices and just muddle along through the years with no performance edge, or forced into expensive choices on a short list of options. The 3Sig plan is indifferent to the number of choices. Once you put it to work with the least expensive bond fund and stock fund available in your plan, you won't need to care about all the other options offered by the plan anymore. The investment industry doesn't want you to know this, but I do. If your plan offers few choices, all expensive, we'll do the best we can.

Let's look at some real-life plans to see how easily anybody can start using 3Sig in their employer retirement account. You'll notice similarities to your own employer plan, which will make it a cinch to apply the methods right away and leave market stress behind for good.

Private Sector

Before we get into 401(k) plans, I'm going to tell you about the trouble I encountered when asking companies for specific details on their programs—and why they're loath to reveal them. It will make you wiser to the ways of the world, particularly the world of finance, and will reinforce the shrewdness of using cheap index funds and 3Sig to deny the charlatans too big a slice of your money.

Guarding 401(k) Details

At dinner one night, a friend told me he was frustrated with his go-nowhere 401(k) and wanted to try a new approach.

"Why don't you run 3Sig?" I suggested. He said his 401(k) didn't include IJR among its options, so he assumed the plan couldn't work for him.

"Sure it could," I replied. "Show me your 401(k) brochure and I'll tell you which fund will work best as a substitute for IJR."

The next week, he delivered his company's 401(k) materials. It took me all of two minutes to find the lowest-cost bond fund for his safe balance and the lowest-cost substitute for IJR. In the process of finding and circling these choices with my friend, I noticed his face light up as if a giant golden finger had descended from the heavens to show him how to set up an effective plan inside his company account. "That's it?" he asked. "Just those two?"

"Just those two," I confirmed.

He looked relieved. I could tell what a weight the languishing retirement account had been on him. He'd taken hits in the downturns and not participated enough in the upturns. He'd tried the general allocations suggested in the company brochure, but they produced humdrum performance. He tried focusing on "hot" funds after reading articles in the investment media. As usual, these appeared just ahead of crashes. My friend had fallen prey to Peter Perfect and the z-vals attached to his 401(k). He would no longer do so, and the calm that came over him made me smile.

This experience gave me the idea to look over a collection of real-life 401(k) plans and other employer plans to show how easy it is to implement 3Sig in them, then share them with you here so you could find situations similar to yours and get started right away by following these other examples. I figured I might as well begin with my friend's company. He had taken back the brochure I marked up for him, so I asked him a few days later if he could get me a copy of his company's 401(k) materials to keep.

"To write about our plan in your book?" he asked. I said yes. He paused. "I'm not sure. I need to check with HR. They're pretty nervous about this kind of exposure." I tried another friend, who agreed to provide a copy of his company's materials, but with this caveat:

"We have a very risk-averse senior management team." He explained that the team would not look kindly upon the public perusing details of its benefits package. I ran into this again and again and again.

401(k)s Come at a Price

A public policy organization called Demos published an eighteen-page report, *The Retirement Savings Drain: The Hidden & Excessive Costs of 401(k)s*, in May 2012. Analyst Robert Hiltonsmith introduced the topic by asking, "Do you know how much you pay for your retirement plan? If you're like many Americans saving for retirement in a 401(k), the answer is 'no.' An AARP survey found that 65 percent of 401(k) account-holders had no idea they were even paying fees, and 83 percent, or 5 out of every 6, lacked even basic knowledge about the many fees and expenses that everyone with a 401(k) pays." Key findings of the report include:

- A two-earner household with each partner earning the median income for their gender during their working years will pay an average of $154,794 in 401(k) fees and lost returns.

- Over time, the typical mutual fund earns a 7 percent return, before fees, matching the average return of the stock market. However, expenses eat up more than a third of the total returns, reducing performance to just 4.5 percent.

- The median expense ratio for 401(k) plans with fewer than one hundred participants was 1.29 percent, while for plans with more than ten thousand participants, it was 0.43 percent.

Given the report's findings, no wonder Hiltonsmith concludes that "the 401(k) system is a very bad deal for workers."

I switched tracks, contacting companies directly to see if I could receive waivers to write about their plans. "We don't release any benefit details," they said, across the board. The various representatives told me to refer to their companies as "a leading Internet technology firm," or "a major oilfield services company," or "a midsize retailer in the United States." Some of them are famous giants you do business with regularly, others are little-known outfits. Not a single one granted me permission to use its name while discussing the particulars of its employee retirement plan. In fact, not one would provide details. One even dismissed me thusly: "If you want to know the plan, get a job here."

That brought me full circle back to where I'd started. Using my e-mail list of readers and other contacts, I requested materials from thousands of employees. A boatload of brochures and reports poured in, often with notes asking me to "make sense of this mess" and "point me in the right direction." Almost all the material came with a warning never to use the company name. Along with the recipe for Coke, the Google search algorithm, and the eleven herbs and spices that flavor KFC's chicken, 401(k) details are among corporate America's best-kept secrets.

This struck me as bizarre. Wouldn't companies want the world to see the fine retirement plans they offered employees? Then I processed and cross-compared the many plans delivered to me, and the reason for the secrecy became clear as day.

It was a sad discovery, one shedding light on why American workers find it harder to get ahead with each passing year, and why employers lock down details. Many plans are terrible, charging employees far too much for the limited set of options into which they're forced to direct their retirement savings. It's a great business for the investment firms running the plans, because the employees have nowhere else to go. In some cases, *every* option available to them will result in paying too much to achieve too little. This is the key lesson to keep in mind when examining your specific plan. Costs matter. Companies know this, and don't want to show the world how much their plan charges employees to invest for retirement. Why don't they work harder to lower these costs? Because participants bear them all. A 401(k)'s expense structure means nothing to the sponsoring company because it doesn't pay any of it. Its employees do.

My purpose here is not to publicly compare Company A's plan with Company B's. The specifics are irrelevant to everybody except employees of Companies A and B. All that matters are general trends indicating what to look for in your own plan to start 3Sig, which will save you money while achieving a better performance. Despite all the secrecy, there are only minor differences from place to place. Let's identify them by looking at four plans, working our way from a big aerospace firm to a small nutritional supplement company.

Aerospace and Defense Corporation

This maker of aircraft, satellites, and missile technology employs more than 175,000 people. Its 401(k) plan manages $14 billion in assets. Participants can "direct the investment of their account balance at any time," according to the plan's disclosure document. There are no restrictions on when they can change their allocations or place trades. They do so by logging on to a website.

The 401(k) offers fourteen funds in the usual categories: bonds, stocks, real estate, and the employer's stock fund, plus nine so-called age-based or target date funds. The latter are popular ways to reduce some of the stress of investing for retirement by leaving the asset allocation up to a fund manager, based on the age of the investor or number of years to retirement, which are usually closely related. Most people in their twenties are about forty years away from retirement, while most people in their fifties are about ten years away. Age-based funds allocate a greater percentage of assets into stocks when a worker is younger and less as the worker gets older. Many of them specify the target year of retirement, such as 2040, and are therefore called "target date funds." The idea is that if you're going to retire in about 2040, you'll just save your money in a 2040 target date fund and rest assured that its asset mixture will adjust properly as you get closer to 2040. This company offers nine such funds. In 2013, their target dates ranged from current retirement to 2050.

Nestled among the 401(k)'s other offerings is a Russell 2000

Small-Cap Index Fund, which is the one that should be used on the stock side of 3Sig. This particular one is cheap, too, with an expense ratio of just 0.07 percent, much lower than the expenses of the funds managed by z-vals, and as usual, the cheaper, unmanaged index fund has performed better. This fund is an excellent choice for 3Sig. At the end of 2012, here's how the funds in the plan that had at least a ten-year track record compared on an average annual performance basis, along with their expense ratios:

TABLE 37. Comparing Funds in the Aerospace and
Defense Corporation's 401(K)

Investment	1 Year (%)	5 Years (%)	10 Years (%)	Expense (%)
Science and Technology Fund	16.0	3.4	7.7	0.67
Stable Value Fund	2.7	3.4	4.2	0.29
Russell 2000 Small-Cap *Index* Fund	16.5	3.8	9.7	0.07
International *Index* Fund	18.1	-3.3	8.4	0.13
S&P 500 *Index* Fund	16.0	1.7	7.1	0.05
Balanced *Index* Fund	12.0	3.1	6.2	0.08
Bond Market *Index* Fund	4.1	6.0	5.2	0.06

Notice the stock index funds beating the supposedly high-performing Science and Technology Fund. With a name like that, one expects shoot-the-lights-out performance from the Who's Who stocks of the future, but no such luck. The nonspecialized, plain vanilla, unmanaged, available-just-about-anywhere Russell 2000 Small-Cap Index Fund outperformed the sci-tech fund in every time frame—while charging ten times less. Without a doubt, the small-cap index fund is your huckleberry.

For the safe side of 3Sig, the Bond Market Index Fund is just dandy, at a diminutive 0.06 percent expense.

As for the age-based funds, their fees are pretty steep, with expense ratios ranging from 0.33 percent in the current retirement fund to 0.42 percent in the 2050 fund. Most such funds just combine index products and charge an extra fee for the service. Since 3Sig utilizes the cheap index funds directly and nudges performance higher with its quarterly buys and sells, it's a better way to go than the age-based funds. As you read earlier, it's a simple procedure to reduce your stock exposure in 3Sig as you near retirement. No need to pay up for it.

All told, employees of this company can feel good about their plan because it includes low-priced index fund options. The small-cap one will work splendidly with 3Sig while charging only 0.07 percent to do so. Too bad industry data suggest that if this company's employees are typical 401(k) participants, most of them have chosen more expensive options.

Oilfield Services Company

This oilfield services giant employs more than a hundred thousand people. Its 401(k) manages $4.5 billion in assets.

Like the aerospace corporation's 401(k) in the previous section, this company's plan offers target date funds as a way for participants to get around some of the stress of picking and choosing investments. They were introduced in June 2013 to "provide a single retirement portfolio for those participants who prefer to invest in one investment option that is professionally managed on their behalf," according to the spring 2013 edition of the company's employee retirement journal. The three asset categories in the target date portfolios are growth, income, and inflation sensitive.

In addition to the age-based portfolios, the 401(k) offers a selection of other investment options, including the plan's Stable Value Strategy, Large-Cap Equity Strategy, Inflation Sensitive Strategy, and individual stock funds covering the basics: large caps via the S&P 500, mid caps, small caps, and non-U.S. stocks. Notice that second-to-last one? That's usually the one we want, the small-cap fund, but this plan's small-cap fund is an actively managed one rather than an index type. As ever, the index has done far better

than the z-val-managed one offered by this plan, and is cheaper. As
of March 31, 2013, the most recent data in the literature I received,
here's how a small-cap index fund stacked up against this plan's
Small-Cap Equity Fund on annualized performance and expense:

TABLE 38. Comparing Funds in the Oilfield Services Company's 401(K)

Investment	1 Year (%)	3 Years (%)	5 Years (%)	10 Years (%)	Expense (%)
Small-Cap Equity Fund	13.1	11.6	9.2	10.5	0.87
Russell 2000 Small-Cap *Index* Fund	16.3	13.5	8.2	11.5	≤ 0.16

The unmanaged index handily beat this plan's actively managed small-cap fund in three of the four time frames. Evidently, too
many of the Small-Cap Equity Fund's coin tosses have gone wrong.
'Twas ever thus. What's worse, the z-val-managed fund charges an
annual expense ratio of 0.87 percent (more than five times higher
than IJR's 0.16 percent) for the service of losing to the index three
quarters of the time. As if this weren't enough, remember that IJR's
0.16 percent is at the *high* end of the cheap ways to own the small-
cap index. This plan's z-val small-cap fund is thirty-two times more
expensive than its peer in the federal government's TSP plan, which
you'll read about later. Actively managed funds are rip-offs, pure
and simple.

If I were employed by this company, I would request the addition of a plain old small-cap index fund option such as IJR or one of
its cheaper peers. It would cut the z-vals out of the loop and enable
me to own the better-performing raw index at a lower fee. In the
meantime, I would use the plan's mid-cap stock index fund with
3Sig. In the following table, again with data through March 31, 2013,
look at how the plan's S&P 500 large-cap index and its mid-cap
index have compared with their z-val-managed alternatives on
annualized performance and expense:

TABLE 39. Index Funds Winning in the Oilfield Services Company's 401(K)

Investment	1 Year (%)	3 Years (%)	5 Years (%)	10 Years (%)	Expense (%)
Large-Cap Growth Equity Fund	7.9	12.8	5.3	7.8	0.51
S&P 500 Large-Cap *Index* Fund	13.8	12.5	5.7	8.4	0.13
Small-Cap Equity Fund	13.1	11.6	9.2	10.5	0.87
Mid-Cap Equity *Index* Fund	17.7	14.9	9.7	NA	0.15

This is an easy choice. The mid-cap equity index fund has out-performed every other fund, including the z-val-managed small-cap equity fund, and did so with a low 0.15 percent expense ratio, just a tad more than the S&P 500 index fund's 0.13 percent. The mid-cap index fund is the best choice for 3Sig in this 401(k). Employees can keep the safe side of their plan in the bond index fund at a low 0.15 percent expense ratio. In 2008, the bond fund gained 5.4 percent while the S&P 500 lost 37 percent and the Russell 2000 lost 34 percent.

Sporting Goods Retailer

This company operates some five hundred sporting goods stores in the United States and employs around fifteen thousand people. Its 401(k), with $75 million in assets, offers age-based portfolios managed by Wells Fargo at net expense ratios of between 0.60 and 0.70 percent—way too much.

The plan also offers an array of domestic stock investment choices, including a small-cap vehicle that works well in 3Sig: Van-guard Small-Cap Index Fund, with an expense ratio of 0.28 percent. Naturally, there's a z-val option, too, with an expense ratio of 1.48 percent to bamboozle all the poor souls who don't know any better than to pay five times more for subpar performance, which is what the z-val route has delivered. At the end of July 2013, here's how the two small-cap choices compared by trailing total returns, and expenses:

TABLE 40. Comparing Funds in the Sporting Goods Retailer's 401(K)

Investment	1 Year (%)	3 Years (%)	5 Years (%)	10 Years (%)	Expense (%)
Z-val Small-Cap Fund	25.6	15.1	5.5	11.0	1.48
Vanguard Small-Cap *Index* Fund	33.3	21.8	10.5	11.2	0.28

Believe it or not, some people are paying a 1.48 percent expense ratio to suffer the inferior z-val performance when they could pay 0.28 percent to ride the superior index performance.

In all plans, let's go with the inexpensive, superior choice, shall we? One should always lock in the lowest fee possible. A good rule of thumb is to avoid any fund charging more than 0.75 percent. With index funds, the expense is usually less than 0.30 percent, and frequently much less.

While this plan does offer a reasonably cheap small-cap index option, it's not as cheap as it should be. We know from other plans and even the retail brokerage market, that expense ratios under 0.20 percent and even 0.10 percent are available. For a company with fifteen thousand employees, there's no excuse for not shopping around to find a cheaper 401(k) program for its workers. If I were one of those workers, I would demand it.

In the meantime, participants in this plan should choose the small-cap index fund for their 3 percent signal plan. For the safe side of the plan, they can use the Vanguard Intermediate-Term Bond Index Fund, which returned an annualized 6.6 percent over the three years ended June 30, 2013. Its expense ratio is 0.22 percent.

Nutritional Supplement Company

This maker of nutritional supplements employs three hundred fifty people and markets its products through a multilevel network of two hundred fifty thousand independent sales associates. It's been highly ranked in small-company surveys by both *Businessweek* and *Forbes*. Its 401(k) manages less than $10 million in assets.

Unfortunately, it offers employees only overpriced mediocrity. From its balanced funds to its age-based funds to its stock market funds, the z-vals are in control. Fees are exorbitant, performance in need of refurbishment. Employees probably need their company's own nutritional products just to combat the stress this 401(k) plan must induce.

Even the index fund choices are too expensive, with fees above 0.40 percent. The age-based funds charge about 1.00 percent, and most of the other funds charge more than 1.00 percent. At the end of July 2013, here's how the plan's index funds compared with their z-val equivalents on trailing total returns, and expense:

TABLE 41. Comparing Funds in the Nutritional Supplement Company's 401(K)

Investment	1 Year (%)	3 Years (%)	5 Years (%)	10 Years (%)	Expense (%)
Large-Cap Equity Income Fund	18.8	14.4	8.3	8.1	1.21
S&P 500 Large-Cap *Index* Fund	24.8	17.6	8.2	7.5	0.42
Mid-Cap Value Fund	16.9	10.5	5.9	9.4	1.00
S&P 400 Mid-Cap *Index* Fund	32.3	18.7	10.1	10.5	0.43
Small-Cap Blend Fund	23.1	15.1	7.8	10.2	1.16
Russell 2000 Small-Cap *Index* Fund	34.2	19.9	10.4	10.4	0.44

This table should be committed to the memory of every 401(k) investor in America. The index funds beat their z-val equivalents in ten out of twelve time-frame comparisons. In the two where the index fund lost (the five-year and ten-year time frames of the large-cap category), it did so by a small amount that was more than offset by the giant difference in expense ratios. On top of all this, the best fund of the whole bunch was the one our plan prefers, the Russell 2000 Small-Cap Index Fund, which returned more than every other fund in every time frame except the ten-year, when it lost to the mid-cap index fund by 0.1 percent. This is a compelling confirmation to stick with the small-cap index whenever possible.

While this plan does include a small-cap index fund that will work with 3Sig, it charges too much for it. Employees should contact management about finding a way to reduce the expense ratios of index fund offerings by a factor of three or more. There's just no reason to pay 0.44 percent for an index fund. It's not even managed, after all. It uses the exact same index owned by every other index fund, but charges much more to do so.

As for the safe side of our plan, this company's employees have no good choices. The money market fund pays nothing, but charges 0.48 percent anyway. The two standard bond funds charge 0.85 and 0.89 percent, and the inflation-adjusted bond fund charges 0.73 percent. The best bet is probably the 0.85 percent expense bond fund, as it provides the highest performance and lowest risk, but it's overpriced.

There's nowhere for this company's employees to hide from high fees. Every choice in the 401(k) eats up too much profit over the years. Nonetheless, the small-cap index fund is the best choice and will work with 3Sig.

Smaller Plans Are More Expensive

As we progressed through the previous four examples spanning an aerospace and defense corporation with 175,000 employees to a nutritional supplement company with 350 employees, the quality of the 401(k) plans decreased. The smaller the company you work for, the higher the risk that you'll be stuck in a 401(k) plan that's too expensive. This is not a perfect correlation, but it's strong enough to warrant your attention. Look at these key stats for the four plans we've just reviewed:

TABLE 42. Bigger Companies Offer Cheaper Funds

Company	Employees	401(k) Assets ($)	Small-Cap Index Fund Expense (%)
Aerospace and Defense	175,000	14.0 billion	0.07
Oilfield Services	100,000	4.5 billion	0.15 (mid-cap)
Sporting Goods	15,000	75 million	0.28
Nutritional Supplements	350	<10 million	0.44

The biggest of the four companies offers a very cheap small-cap index fund, the second biggest offers a mid-cap fund at twice the expense of the bigger company's small-cap fund but still pretty low, the third-biggest company's small-cap fund nearly doubles the expense ratio again, and the smallest of the companies offers an index fund that charges so much that it's almost as bad as some z-val alternatives.

In many cases, smaller firms lack the resources to insist on lower fees. When the aerospace company meets with a 401(k) plan management firm and says it has 175,000 employees with $14 billion to invest, it can drive a hard bargain on expense ratios. When the nutritional supplement company tries meeting with a plan management firm, it might have trouble getting a space on the firm's calendar. "How much you got?" the plan manager receptionist probably asks, pencil poised above the meeting schedule. "Did you say *less* than ten *million* dollars? I see. Hmm. Maybe we can fit you in toward the end of next month." In this environment, what odds does the little nutrition outfit stand of dickering down a 0.44 percent expense ratio to less than 0.10 percent? Slim, to be sure. Add in the fact that the company has little incentive to work hard doing so because it doesn't pay the fees itself but just passes them along to employees, and it's no wonder so many private-sector retirement plans are bad for participants.

This representative sampling of four companies across the size spectrum is not statistically significant, but it does match the findings of larger studies. In the sidebar on page 189, you read that the public policy organization Demos reported in May 2012 that the median expense ratio for 401(k) plans with fewer than one hundred participants was 1.29 percent, while for plans with more than ten thousand participants, it was 0.43 percent.

The Society for Human Resource Management (SHRM) publishes the *401k Averages Book* (without parentheses around the *k* for some reason), which is packed with findings detailing fees for a range of plans, from tiny ones with twenty-five participants to giant ones with thousands of participants. It compares the fees of small plans with average account balances of $10,000 to large plans with $50,000. The thirteenth edition displayed data through the end of September 2012 across 154 charts. Among its key findings:

- Small plan average investment expenses (the expense ratios charge by mutual funds for assets held within the plan) were 1.37 percent.

- Large plan average investment expenses were 1.00 percent.

- The average target date fund expense for a small plan was 1.37 percent, while the balanced fund average was 1.45 percent.

- The average target date fund expense for a large plan was 0.98 percent, while the balanced fund average was 1.12 percent.

The smaller your plan, the more alert you need to be to high expenses. Luckily, implementing 3Sig works the same way regardless of your plan's size. You simply find the cheapest small-cap index fund option available. If no index option is available, then you go with the cheapest z-val-managed small-cap fund until you can convince your company to get on the ball and add low-cost index funds to its 401(k). Ditto with the bond fund.

It's easy to see why 3Sig's focus on the cheapest index funds for your retirement assets will save you a bundle. Among the four plans we looked at, the most expensive small-cap index fund's expense ratio was 0.44 percent, and the cheapest was 0.07 percent, both far cheaper than the 1.00 percent and 1.37 percent averages across all funds reported in the *401k Averages Book*.

Government

Some parts of government, such as the military, maintain traditional pension plans that entail no investment management but just provide a defined benefit based on time in service, earnings history, and related factors. Other government plans, however, operate like 401(k)s and require investor involvement to achieve optimal performance. They're excellent places to run 3Sig because their expenses are extremely low. Everybody in government who is eligible to participate, including military personnel, should take advantage of them.

You read in the previous section that the larger a retirement plan, the lower its costs tend to be. Thus, it will come as no surprise that the biggest plan of them all, the federal government's, offers some of the cheapest index funds anywhere. It's called the Thrift Savings Plan. In this section, we'll look at it and a plan offered by Ohio State University.

Thrift Savings Plan (TSP)

The investment retirement program for federal employees is called the Thrift Savings Plan (TSP), which is a defined contribution plan similar to 401(k)s in the private sector. It accepts contributions of the traditional variety, in which workers defer paying taxes on deposits and earnings until withdrawal; and also of the Roth variety, which go into the retirement account after paying income taxes but are then tax-free at withdrawal. At the end of 2012, the TSP managed $330 billion for about 4.6 million enrollees.

As with many private-sector plans, the TSP offers target date portfolios. It calls them "L Funds," the *L* standing for "lifecycle." It also offers five individual investment funds that are also named with a single letter, which track the following:

C Fund	Standard & Poor's 500 Stock Index
F Fund	Barclays Capital U.S. Aggregate Bond Index
G Fund	Short-Term U.S. Treasuries
I Fund	Morgan Stanley Capital International EAFE Stock Index
S Fund	Dow Jones U.S. Completion Total Stock Market

On this list, it's trickier to find the best stock fund suited for 3Sig because none of the funds uses the phrase "small cap" or something similar. The correct choice is the "S Fund," which tracks the Dow Jones U.S. Completion Total Stock Market Index. It's a subset of the Dow Jones U.S. Total Stock Market Index that excludes components of the S&P 500. The S&P 500 is an index of large companies, as you know, and the Dow Jones U.S. Completion index skips all of them to focus on small- and medium-size companies. The S Fund is as close as the TSP comes to a small-cap index, and will do just fine for our purposes. It's easy to remember what the fund tracks if we think of the *S* as standing for "small."

For all the criticism that government receives, we should pause and admire that its TSP plan presents no way for employees to accidentally choose an overpriced z-val option for their retirement money. Every one of the five individual funds is based on either Treasuries or an index, and they're all super cheap, charging less than 0.030 percent for the past several years—only 0.027 percent in 2012. This low fee also applied to the age-based L Funds that combine the individual funds in various allocations depending on proximity to retirement, but tack on no extra service fee for doing so.

Government employees can proceed confidently with 3Sig using the S Fund. The plan will manage risk and reward, while the nearly free fund keeps expenses negligible while tapping the profit potential of smaller-company volatility. Here's how the S Fund's performance compared with the C and I Funds, and IJR, in 2003 (to show a big upside year) and then 2008 through 2012:

TABLE 43. TSP Fund Performance vs. IJR

Investment	2003 (%)	2008 (%)	2009 (%)	2010 (%)	2011 (%)	2012 (%)	Expense (%)
C Fund	28.5	–37.0	26.7	15.1	2.1	16.1	0.027
I Fund	37.9	–42.4	30.0	7.9	–11.8	18.6	0.027
S Fund	42.9	–38.3	34.9	29.1	–3.4	18.6	0.027
iShares Core S&P Small-Cap (IJR)	38.5	–31.5	25.8	26.6	0.8	16.3	0.160

As you can see, the S Fund is an excellent choice, beating IJR in four of these six sample years while charging an extremely low expense ratio to do so. This sample shows it falling lower than IJR, then rising higher, which is ideal for 3Sig, because the plan uses such volatility to put more money to work at the lower prices, then harvests bigger profits at the higher prices.

The government is rightfully proud of its low-cost retirement plan for employees. In the January/February 2013 issue of its TSP newsletter *Highlights*, it boasted that the Thrift Savings Plan's low expenses more than fulfilled the mandate for low administrative cost set down by Congress when it created the program in 1986. The

2012 expense ratio of 0.027 percent "is just 27¢ for every $1,000 in your account. Such low fees are very rare in defined-contribution plans, where the average fee is $8.30/$1,000 account, and in 10 percent of plans, you'd pay more than $13.80." Its source for this claim is a 2011 study by the Investment Company Institute.

It warned against moving funds out of the TSP and into a private employer retirement account after leaving government service: "Financial service companies are in the profit-making business and would like to get their hands on a share of your savings, which could mean much higher costs for you. The TSP, on the other hand, is not in the business of turning a profit." It's a plan run by federal employees for employees intended to help prepare for retirement at the lowest possible cost. According to our brief tour of the plan here, it's succeeding admirably.

TSP enrollees would use the G Fund for their bond allocation in 3Sig. It's a safe choice, and happens to be the default fund. It's outpaced inflation over the years, too, and performed much better than the near-zero money market yields that followed the subprime mortgage crash. In the go-go year of 2003, the G Fund returned 4.1 percent. In the swan-diving year of 2008, it returned 3.8 percent.

Members of the Armed Forces: Attention!

While the military offers a defined pension plan, it probably won't do so forever, and you probably won't qualify to participate even if it does. In a 2011 report to the secretary of defense, "Modernizing the Military Retirement System," the Defense Business Board wrote that the current pension plan needs to change because it's an "unfair" holdout from an era when life spans were shorter, the military paid less than civilian jobs, second careers were less common, and military skills did not transfer well to the private sector.

Now, a full "83 percent of those serving in the military will receive no retirement benefit. Military personnel serving 5, 10, or 15 years will depart from service with no benefit or pension. This cohort includes the majority of troops who have engaged and will engage in combat." It takes twenty years of military service to qualify for the retirement pension, and only 17 percent of the modern volunteer force gets there.

The good news is that military personnel can participate in the TSP—and should. Starting a TSP account while serving is smart because you can take it with you into civilian life later. In a sense, then, you can use 3Sig in the TSP to create your own portable government retirement benefit while serving in the armed forces.

The Ohio State University Alternative Retirement Plan (ARP)

The Ohio State University, in Columbus, Ohio, was founded in 1870. With 500,000 alumni, 65,000 students, 23,000 staff members, and 7,000 faculty members, it ranks among the largest institutions of higher education in America.

Faculty and staff members of OSU must participate in either the university's Alternative Retirement Plan (ARP) or the Ohio Public Employees Retirement System (OPERS). Except for contributions to Medicare, they do not participate in the federal Social Security system. The ARP is a defined contribution plan, like a 401(k), in which participants manage their own investments. The OPERS is a defined benefit plan, a traditional pension that requires no participant money management. There's also a hybrid option called the OPERS Combined Plan, which puts employee contributions into a self-directed investment account and university contributions into the formula-based pension. The 3Sig plan can be run in any self-directed account, so we'll look at the ARP option here.

OSU faculty members contribute 11 percent of their pretax salary to the ARP, staff members contribute 10 percent, and the university kicks in additional contributions in an amount determined by the employee's salary.

The management of investments happens through an ARP provider. There were nine of them in June 2013, including Fidelity Investments, and Teachers Insurance and Annuity Association–College Retirement Equities Fund (TIAA-CREF). The array of choices offered by each of these two covers the basic asset classes: annuities, bonds, money market, real estate, stocks, and target date funds. Among the myriad z-val-managed, overpriced stock fund choices, I found two fairly low-cost index fund candidates for 3Sig. It takes some digging, but they're in there.

At Fidelity, participants can choose the Spartan Small-Cap Index Fund–Fidelity Advantage Class, which tracks the Russell 2000 at an expense ratio of 0.19 percent. With "Spartan" in the name, you'd think this fund would be dirt-cheap, but it's not. It's better than the z-val alternatives on the list, though, some of which levy expenses higher than 1.00 percent. Another yellow flag on this Spartan fund is that it charges a 1.50 percent fee when you redeem shares held for less than ninety days, so participants using it need to be sure to sell only shares they've owned for at least ninety days. This is easy to do in 3Sig, due to its quarterly schedule, but it needs to be monitored so sales don't inadvertently happen at the eighty-nine-day mark, for example. For the safe portion of 3Sig, the Spartan Short-Term Treasury Bond Index Fund–Fidelity Advantage Class provides fairly steady performance that usually beats the money market while charging a 0.10 percent expense ratio.

At TIAA-CREF, participants can choose the Vanguard Small-Cap Value Index Fund, which tracks the CRSP U.S. Small-Cap Value Index at an expense ratio of 0.34 percent. However, the actual expense ratio of the fund is 0.24 percent, onto which this plan tacks an additional 0.10 percent for a total of 0.34 percent, so it makes sense to go the cheaper route at Fidelity instead. People might also consider opening an account directly at Vanguard, where a balance of $10,000 or more provides access to the company's affordable Admiral Shares. The expense ratio of Vanguard Small-Cap Value Index Admiral Shares is just 0.10 percent, less than a third of what the same fund costs via the ARP plan at TIAA-CREF. Unfortunately, Vanguard is not an ARP provider, so an account there for OSU employees would have to be an IRA in addition to (not as a way of running) the ARP plan.

I couldn't find anything cheaper than Fidelity's Spartan Small-Cap Index Fund among any of the ARP providers. I found an assortment of beautifully designed brochures, but their content was typical investment industry boilerplate, and their funds were either the z-val variety or overpriced index variety.

My perusal of the Ohio State University's ARP confirmed that no matter where you keep your retirement funds, you must remain on guard against the multitude of bad options put before you by investment industry apparatchiks. There's almost always a way to avoid their traps, park your money in low-cost funds, and serenely run it with 3Sig, but don't expect them to help you find it.

Public Employee Plans

There are many different retirement plans for public employees, depending on where they work. Most offer a defined benefit traditional pension option and a defined contribution option similar to a 401(k). The defined contribution options usually look something like the Alternative Retirement Plan of the Ohio State University. In fact, the same handful of investment companies appears on the list of providers nearly everywhere you turn: Fidelity, ING, T. Rowe Price, Vanguard, and so on.

In each case, employees directing their own retirements should search through the list of offered funds to find the cheapest small-cap index choice available for the stock portion of 3Sig and the cheapest bond fund for the safe portion of the plan. That's all there is to it, anywhere you keep your retirement account.

Target Date Funds in 3Sig

Target date funds are becoming popular, which is good news for many retirement investors. Prior to the rising popularity of these premixed, automated portfolios that determine asset allocations based on how many years until a person retires, many plans defaulted to a safe fund such as the TSP's G Fund. In too many cases, the retirement accounts would remain mostly or even entirely in such low-risk, low-return funds for a long time, if not the entire time, until retirement. Such an account will not grow enough to meet retirement goals, in most cases.

The target date portfolios are an improvement over low-risk funds for people who will just choose one option and never check in again, which is a surprisingly large number of people. Without even knowing it, they might actually do better than many active investors following z-val advice and other sources of befuddlement, simply by contributing more money every paycheck and doing nothing when markets tank. Lazy investors, rejoice!

However, for those willing to work just a tad more than zero, 3Sig on a small-cap fund will almost always outperform target date portfolios. The reason is that target date portfolios combine asset classes in a way that dilutes stock exposure by combining it with assets such as bonds and government securities. As investors get closer to retirement, these allocations are gradually adjusted from emphasizing stocks to emphasizing safer assets. The 3Sig plan also mixes assets, but just two: the safe fund, which could be government securities or bonds, and the stock fund, which should be a small-cap variety but could be another type.

We could lean in favor of target date funds if there were reliable patterns behind their asset allocation, but there aren't. In 2011, Morningstar reviewed thirty-six target date funds with a target date of 2020 and found that their stock allocations ranged from 35 percent to 80 percent, with an average of 61 percent. This shows what might be the biggest problem with target date funds, which is that they're frequently underallocated to stocks when considering Social

Security and other benefits a person may receive in retirement. Social Security is currently solvent, and we're promised it always will be, so let's assume as much. Lower-income earners who elect to receive Social Security payments in their early sixties will tap an asset with a capitalized value of about $300,000. For higher-income earners who defer payments until they're seventy years old, the value is about $500,000. This safe $300,000 to $500,000 asset should be a major consideration when deciding how much of the capital in 401(k)s and other retirement accounts is best invested in stocks. For the majority of most people's lives, almost all of it, because the risk of stocks is partially offset by the safety of Social Security benefits.

The 3Sig plan's focus on small-cap stocks usually produces more volatility than broad-based stock funds, the lower lows and higher highs that are the hallmark of small-company stock behavior. The 3 percent signal automatically puts the lower lows to work by buying them, then takes advantage of the higher highs by selling them. Doing this with most of your money in small caps comes out ahead of doing it with all your money in a mixed fund, such as an age-based portfolio. For example, here's how a few retirement target portfolios managed by Wells Fargo performed from 2008 to 2012, compared with IJR:

TABLE 44. Wells Fargo Target Date Funds vs. IJR

Investment	2008 (%)	2009 (%)	2010 (%)	2011 (%)	2012 (%)	Expense (%)
Wells Fargo Advantage Dow Jones Target 2015 Fund (WFSCX)	−16.4	16.0	10.4	3.1	7.3	0.49
Wells Fargo Advantage Dow Jones Target 2030 Fund (WFOOX)	−31.4	28.0	15.0	−1.4	12.3	0.51
Wells Fargo Advantage Dow Jones Target 2045 Fund (WFQPX)	−35.5	33.2	17.1	−4.1	15.0	0.52
iShares Core S&P Small-Cap (IJR)	−31.5	25.8	26.6	0.8	16.3	0.16

The table shows Wells Fargo doing a good job of dialing down risk and volatility as the target retirement date moves closer. In the 2008 waterfall, the Target 2015 Fund lost only 16.4 percent compared with 31.4 percent in the 2030 and 35.5 percent in the 2045. IJR lost 31.5 percent that year. Similarly, the 2015 fund gained less in up years. It achieved a steadier path by taking on less investment risk, which is what one would expect with retirement just a few years away.

Notice that the 2045 fund was quite volatile, even more so than IJR in 2008 and 2009, when it dropped 35.5 percent then gained 33.2 percent, respectively, compared with only 31.5 percent and 25.8 percent for IJR. In those two years, the Target 2045 Fund would have been a good vehicle for 3Sig because of the lower low and higher high. Generally, the farther away the retirement target date, the more the target date fund will behave like IJR, because a greater percentage of it will be allocated to riskier stocks.

Could you use a target date fund with 3Sig? Sure. The beauty of our plan is that it doesn't care what the fund owns. All we need is a fluctuating price that moves above and below our 3 percent signal line, and the more movement, the better (within reason). Small-cap index funds are usually the best way to go because they're volatile, require no human judgment, always recover, and are cheap. However, there's no reason a different fund couldn't be used instead of a small-cap index fund. As far as the plan is concerned, you could use a fund that owned anything: a pool of sporting bets, nonfat dry milk futures, works of art, baseball cards and other artifacts, maybe Ming Dynasty ceramics. As long as the fund fluctuates in price and eventually recovers, it can work with 3Sig. Thus, certainly a target date retirement fund can work.

Then again, why bother? While you *can* use anything, you might as well go with a small-cap index fund if it's available. Notice the much cheaper expense ratio in IJR than in any of the Wells Fargo funds. In most 401(k)s, the target date funds charge even more than the roughly 0.50 percent that Wells Fargo charges in these. In June 2013, Morningstar found the asset-weighted average expense ratio in target date funds to be 0.91 percent.

For 3Sig, it's smarter to choose the lowest-priced small-cap index fund available than it is to choose a higher-priced fund of any variety. The performance of the small-cap index will eventually beat nearly every alternative, and charge less on the path to doing so. In this four-year comparison, for instance, Target 2045 finished with a net gain of only 11 percent, while IJR posted a 28 percent gain—and charged 69 percent less. As you read at the beginning of this chapter, such expense differences matter a lot.

While target date funds offer a way for investors to put their retirement on autopilot, 3Sig's minimal effort, lower prices, and superior performance make it a better alternative for investors willing to check in quarterly. As evidenced by your reading this book, you're such an investor, and back on page 153 you learned how to adjust the plan's allocations on your own as you near retirement, sparing yourself the high expense of paying an age-based fund to do it for you.

The Plan Works Where You Work

You work where you work, and your retirement money is kept where it's kept. Maybe you're one of the lucky people in a top-shelf plan bursting with cheap index funds, maybe one of the unlucky with his money stuck in a list of overpriced options, wondering if it's too late to apply for a job at the Post Office just for access to the TSP. Either way, you'll better your future by running 3Sig with whatever's available to you.

We've looked at a variety of retirement accounts, from IRAs at brokerages, to 401(k)s offered by companies, to government plans. Some offer matching, some do not. Some are good, some are not, but no matter where you work, regardless of how good or bad your retirement plan is, you can run 3Sig in it. A self-directed retirement account is just a tax-advantaged place where you can save your money in a variety of investments. Whatever you do for a living, wherever you keep your retirement funds, this is how it works.

Your plan might not be exactly like any of the ones we've reviewed here, but it's probably close. Your job is to look through your plan's list of investment choices to locate the cheapest small-cap index fund available for the stock portion of 3Sig and the cheapest bond index fund for the safe portion. If there's no small-cap index, then try a mid-cap. If that's not there, go with the cheapest stock index fund of any variety you can find. Index funds are cheaper and perform better than their actively managed peers. So, you'll use the lowest-priced small-cap or mid-cap index fund in your plan, but you can get by with a general stock index fund if necessary.

You can run 3Sig wherever you're saving for retirement. Don't think you can't.

Executive Summary of This Chapter

You're ready to begin 3Sig. A retirement account is the best place to do so because the tax advantages enable you to follow profitable sell signals without worrying about taxes. However, 3Sig also works well in a regular brokerage account. The plan's simple quarterly procedure is the same everywhere. No matter where you keep your money, choose the cheapest small-cap stock index fund and bond index fund available, and you'll be ready to run 3Sig. Key takeaways:

✔ There are just five steps in the quarterly procedure, and you'll come to know them by heart after following the plan for a while.

✔ Morningstar found that low expense ratios in funds are "the most dependable predictor of performance." It advises focusing on the cheapest funds available. The 3Sig plan delivers these low-cost benefits because it uses the cheapest small-cap stock index fund and cheapest bond index fund available in your account.

✔ A tax-advantaged retirement account is the best place to run 3Sig because profitable stock fund sell signals there will trigger no tax consequences.

✔ To avoid short-term capital gains tax in nonretirement accounts, sell shares you've owned for more than a year. The plan's quarterly schedule makes tracking easy.

✔ Employer retirement accounts, such as 401(k)s, are fine for the plan. Most offer many bad choices, however, making it necessary to search carefully for the cheapest small-cap stock index fund and bond index fund available in your plan. The larger the company, the larger the 401(k), thus the better the odds of finding good low-expense funds for the plan. If you work at a small company, be extra careful.

✔ Target date funds are popular because they simplify investing for retirement by automatically adjusting asset allocations as retirement nears. However, they're more expensive than 3Sig and usually underperform it.

✔ Wherever you work, wherever you keep your money, you can run the plan.

CHAPTER SEVEN
The Life of the Plan

You know everything you need to know to put 3Sig to work in your accounts right now. You might still hesitate, though. It's nothing like the advice you've read and heard elsewhere. You know it's a simple plan and understand each part of it, but may not be able to picture it in action through the chaos of the market.

To get around this, we'll watch how an investor uses the plan over a time period fraught with real news, and how the plan compares with more typical long-term investment approaches. We'll do so by following the lives of three fictional investors at the same company, on the same earnings path, using the same 401(k), and dealing with the same maelstrom of events ripped from the headlines. The only difference among the three is what they do with their same level of savings within the same set of investment options—with wildly different results. Two of the characters are archetypes of the most common investment personalities I've encountered: the part-time trader plagued by z-vals and the diligent saver unnerved by volatility. The third runs 3Sig.

I want you to feel clearly the power of 3Sig, to see how it makes investment life easier and more profitable, so we're going to go into some depth. Sit back with me as we navigate actual news stories and

z-val forecasts to understand the impact they have on people trying to plan for the future while living life. Notice how forecasters
have always seemed believable, and how they've always said many of
the same things you hear them saying today. Notice, too, that they've
been wrong about half the time. File this away in your wisdom vault.
Investing wouldn't be a challenge if the experts looked like buffoons.
It's a challenge because they look like experts and we want to trust
them, but they're wrong as often as amateurs.

　　This chapter will give you more than a textbook view of 3Sig. It
will take you into the real-life experience of running the plan so you
know what to expect when implementing it in your own life.

The Setup

Our three investors begin at age thirty as new employees at Snap-
Sheet, an information analytics company based in Denver, Colorado. Each is a data scientist with a different specialty. Their family
situations are different, too. Garrett is married without children,
Selma is a single mother of two, and Mark is married with three
children. Each started his or her career at SnapSheet with an annual
salary of $54,000 at the end of 2000. That was $4,500 per month,
from which each contributed 6 percent, or $270, to SnapSheet's
401(k). The company matched 50 percent of contributions up to
6 percent, which is why all three contributed the minimum amount
to get the maximum company match, pushing their net monthly
contribution up to $405, or $1,215 per quarter. From their retirement accounts at previous employers, each transferred $10,000 into
SnapSheet's 401(k). So their initial investment balances were
$10,000, and their starting quarterly contributions were $1,215.

　　Garrett had always been interested in the stock market. In his
twenties, he read trading books, attended a technical analysis semi-
nar, and opened an individual brokerage account where he'd tried
his hand at picking a few winners. His results were mixed, but he felt

he'd been improving at the time he hired on with SnapSheet and took a look at its 401(k). He was happy to find that it offered a long list of mutual funds and also included a brokerage option where he could buy and sell anything he wanted. He was eager to do so, especially since he believed cheaper prices after the dot-com crash provided potential to get ahead in a recovery.

Selma's main concern was taking care of her two children on a single salary. The last thing she wanted to worry about was the whim of Wall Street, so she'd read financial planning books and taken a community college class on asset allocation for the long haul. She was happy to find a suitable collection of mainstream mutual funds in the SnapSheet 401(k). With them, she would create a retirement mix that benefited from the long-term growth of the stock market with some safety added by putting some of her account in steadier funds. She got to work choosing the right mix.

Mark was a dedicated family man, leaving work at work and spending as much time as possible with his wife and three kids. He shared Selma's desire to keep the whim of Wall Street out of his life, but he knew he needed the growth potential of stocks in his retirement account. He researched asset allocation as a way to balance growth with safety. The problem he noticed was that doing so didn't produce as much profit as he was hoping to amass. He studied stock index funds as a low-cost way to get more performance with more risk that paid off in eventual recoveries from setbacks, and then stumbled onto 3Sig. He liked it best of all because it would focus his capital not just on stocks, but on the highest potential small-cap segment of stocks, supported by the bond account for stability and quarterly trades based on the signal. It would also provide him with buying power in a downturn, something his past experience with dollar-cost averaging never had. The 3Sig technique seemed like the best way to get high profits with little stress out of low-cost index funds, so Mark decided to adopt the plan.

When these three began work at SnapSheet in early December 2000, the Nasdaq had fallen 45 percent since peaking on March 10.

The presidential election had been a fiasco, and when the three arrived at SnapSheet, the country still didn't know whether George W. Bush or Al Gore had won. On December 12, the Supreme Court would decide that Bush was president, but after that it would be discovered that Gore had actually won the popular vote. The crashing Nasdaq and contentious election made it a tough time to decide where to invest a 401(k).

Garrett thought the deflated Internet stock universe, which was taking a pounding almost daily in the media, offered a lot of latent value. He looked back at the darlings of the bubble—JDS Uniphase, Nortel, Sycamore, and others—and thought he finally had a chance to buy on the cheap all the stocks those bragging blowhards at his former company had teased him about for not owning in the final three years of the 1990s. What he called bragging blowhards you and I know as Peter Perfect. Garrett was vulnerable to their taunting.

He figured it would be hard to pick through the rubble of the Internet wasteland, but worth it, and he knew just the man for the job: Ryan Jacob, of Jacob Internet Fund fame. Sure, Jacob was being keelhauled by every reporter as the best fish-in-a-barrel proxy for what went wrong with net stocks, but Garrett had a feeling Jacob would be the star of "Comeback Kid" cover stories within a few years. About the time the latecomers piled in for the next phase of online stock growth after such stories, Garrett figured he'd be up 100, maybe 300 percent. That's what happened in the good old days of just a year or two earlier, and so he thought it would happen again, and with a vengeance now that Jacob's Internet Fund was beaten flat on its back.

Landon Thomas Jr. wrote in the *New York Observer* in October that Ryan Jacob used to be famous as an Internet investing rock star after turning $200,000 into $25 million in 1998, taking the top performance spot among mutual funds that year. Currently, however, his fund ranked dead last after losing 54.1 percent year-to-date. "Yet Mr. Jacob remains nothing if not steadfast," Thomas wrote, citing Jacob's praise of his third-largest holding, a company called iVillage, which topped out at $100 per share in April 1999 but was now $3. Jacob told Thomas, "The stock has underperformed, not the company."

Garrett decided it was time to really go for it, and so he put half his $10,000 into Jacob Internet Fund for the recovery. The other half he decided to put into more traditional stock funds, just in case the Internet didn't have as much recovery potential as he suspected.

He chose Wasatch Small-Cap Growth after it topped a list of "Small-Cap Growth Funds with Long-Tenured Managers" at TheStreet.com, which said the fund "has a record that's tough to ignore. Jeff Cardon has held the reins since the fund's 1986 inception and his track record is solid. Thanks to his measured approach, the fund beats 75 percent of its peers over the last one-, three-, five- and 10-year periods, according to Morningstar."

Garrett selected Janus Global Technology for a wider perspective on tech potential than Ryan Jacob specialized in. He read the following in "Mike Molinski's FundWatch" at MarketWatch in October:

> A recent study by fund-tracking firm Wiesenberger found that global technology funds actually have a lower standard deviation than domestic technology funds, 47.65 versus 61.62, meaning that day-to-day, their closing prices don't stray as much from their average price. . . .
>
> What's more, adding a global technology fund to an all-domestic portfolio can reduce the overall risk level of your investment portfolio because foreign stocks don't move in tandem with U.S. stocks, thus reducing your exposure to a big drop in the U.S. market. . . .
>
> The largest global sector fund is Janus Global Technology, which raised a staggering $10 billion in its first year in 1999 and returned 211.55 percent. This year, the fund isn't doing so hot, down 0.68 percent as of Sept. 30.

Right, Garrett thought, but it's exactly the "isn't doing so hot" part that leaves tech funds at amazing bargain prices for the few people smart enough to understand what the word *recovery* means. Since the Nasdaq peak on March 10 through the end of November, Jacob Internet was down 81 percent, Wasatch Small-Cap Growth was down 4 percent, and Janus Global Tech was down 51 percent.

Garrett would begin 2001 with his $10,000 allocated thusly: $5,000 in Jacob Internet, $2,500 in Wasatch Small-Cap, and $2,500 in Janus Global Tech. He also specified that each of his $405 monthly contributions be divided by the same percentages. He'd keep the plan going this way for the time being, while he got his bearings at SnapSheet. Once he was comfortable on the job and had more time for stock research, he'd add some of his own picks to the mix for even better performance.

While Garrett was understandably bewitched by the compressed-spring appearance of these three funds, their veneer of potential performance was less impressive when peeled away from the guaranteed cost of their underlying expenses. Garrett would certainly pay up for potential performance:

TABLE 45. Garrett's Initial Expense Ratios

Fund	Expense Ratio (%)
Jacob Internet (JAMFX)	2.87
Wasatch Small-Cap Growth (WAAEX)	1.26
Janus Global Tech (JAGTX)	1.00

Well, who knows, maybe he'd get performance so huge it would swamp expense concerns entirely. That's what the z-vals selling expensive funds always promise. Garrett went into 2001 betting they'd be proven right by the recovery dead ahead, and he'd be made richer.

Selma took a different approach. She'd become very cautious with her meager savings after the dot-com meltdown cost her her job and a big piece of her retirement account. In a fresh start, she wanted to minimize danger to her savings. After she landed the new job at SnapSheet, she met with a financial planner at her church and told her she wasn't sure she wanted to own any stock funds in her retirement account. Not one. "Not owning stocks in your retirement account is like not planting flowers in your flower bed," the planner told Selma. "Flower beds are for flowers, not just ground cover. Retirement accounts are for stocks, not just bonds. If you put nothing but bonds in your retirement account, it'll be as dull as a flower bed without flowers." Selma thought dull sounded pretty good compared with the fireworks since March, but she got the planner's point.

The planner took Selma through a series of questions to determine her risk tolerance, even though Selma quipped, "Let me save you some time: low." After the questions confirmed Selma's prediction, the planner overruled the result and suggested that Selma put 80 percent of her retirement capital in stocks. Selma felt queasy about this. She had a lot of working years in front of her, though, and the planner said that, in the long run, stocks always recover, so Selma took a deep breath and grudgingly agreed to put 80 percent of her retirement in stocks.

As was her way, she carefully researched at the library over several weekends. She printed out fund ratings from Morningstar for each of SnapSheet's 401(k) offerings that appealed to her. She read articles and a seemingly endless collection of fund rankings. "Funds That Go up When the Market Goes Down," "Three Top-Rated Growth Funds for the Long Haul," "The Best Low-Volatility Funds for Gun-Shy Investors," and similar fare usually featured a few comments by the managers of the winning survey, photos of them in the office, and then a wrap-up along the lines of the manager having "stood the test of time" or being a "veteran of the markets" or "battle-hardened," unless the manager was new, in which case he or she "showed promise" and would probably "breathe new life into performance." It was overwhelming at first, but Selma was no dummy and quickly detected repeating patterns and began grouping her options in a way that made them easier to rank and assemble.

She wanted to put the bulk of her capital in large-cap U.S. stocks, which she came to see as the most basic way to gain exposure to the stock market. She wasn't interested in specializations or any type of focus, just the reliable blue chips that comprise the backbone of the market. Among such funds in the SnapSheet plan, she settled on Fidelity Growth & Income and Longleaf Partners as the best choices.

Fidelity Growth & Income garnered rave reviews at the end of 2000 for having wisely limited its exposure to overvalued tech stocks. Manager Steve Kaye positioned the portfolio defensively going into the tech wreck, owning bargain-priced health care companies and steadily growing financial stocks instead. Morningstar analyst Scott Cooley concluded in November 2000 that Kaye's "low-turnover, cautious approach has served shareholders well for the long haul. During his nearly eight-year tenure, the fund has roughly matched the S&P 500's return while exhibiting less risk than the index. In short, this still looks like a solid core holding for conservative investors." That sounded perfect to Selma, who was certainly conservative. She would put a quarter of her retirement in Fidelity Growth & Income.

Similarly conservative, the manager of Longleaf Partners, Mason Hawkins, came off as a wise grandfather figure who would steer Selma's account higher through whatever happened next. He had incentive to do so because he and others on the team were required to keep all their invested assets in the firm's funds. Selma liked this. Longleaf Partners actually gained money in the second quarter of the year, when almost everything else had been crashing from the Nasdaq peak in March, and Hawkins told *The New York Times* in July, "We have not changed the way we do things for the 26 years that we've operated." His fund was highly rated, and he was highly respected, and seemed about as far away from the flash-in-the-pan Internet madness as one could hope to get. Morningstar analyst

Christopher Traulsen wrote in August that what the fund did best was "scour the market's unloved for diamonds in the rough, buy them cheap, then hold tight until everybody else catches on." From the Nasdaq peak to the end of November, Longleaf Partners rose 34 percent. No doubt about it, Hawkins was her man. Selma would put a quarter of her retirement in Longleaf Partners.

As for the other 30 percent of Selma's allocation to stocks, the planner recommended international funds. "They can zig when the U.S. zags," she explained. Among international stock funds in Snap-Sheet's 401(k), two caught Selma's attention: Artisan International and T. Rowe Price International Stock Fund.

Mark Yockey had been in charge of Artisan International since 1995. Media offered nothing but praise for his stewardship. He told interviewers about his belief in fundamental value and how his team looked for companies that could grow for decades. They hunted long-term trends and then found companies sporting the best business models to benefit from them. The cheapest among those comprised the sweet spot of the global market, the stocks Artisan wanted to own.

Morningstar analyst Hap Bryant wrote at the end of March that the fund "finished 1999 in the foreign-stock category's top quintile, thanks to big stakes in technology and telecommunications stocks," and he credited Yockey's growth strategy for this. In October, analyst William Samuel Rocco added, "This fund continues to handle whatever the world's markets throw its way." He noted that it "encountered anything but favorable conditions in 2000" and that "Yockey slashed the fund's telecom exposure in March" and "found opportunities in the media and financial sectors." Rocco continued:

> Thanks to these moves, the fund, unlike many of its growth-oriented peers, hasn't relinquished the big lead it established early in the year (when telecom and tech stocks flourished). Despite posting a loss, it's ahead of 75 percent of its rivals for the year to date through October 23, 2000. The fund has out-

paced even more of its rivals over the long term by placing in its group's top decile three times in the past four calendar years.

This was all very encouraging, but the part that really cemented Artisan International into Selma's portfolio was an aside near the end of Rocco's report, that "the fund has suffered only average volatility along the way" and that its expense ratio was declining. She'd put 15 percent into it.

The other 15 percent of her foreign stock allocation would go into T. Rowe Price International Stock Fund. Rocco wrote in November that it had "been an incredibly steady performer in the past," faring well in "the sell-offs of 1990 and 1994 as well as the robust rallies of 1998 and 1999" such that it had "outgained its average peer by about one percentage point per year during the past decade." Best of all, as far as Selma was concerned, Rocco considered the fund to be "a solid option for those who are seeking a conservative foreign-stock holding."

Her remaining 20 percent she would put into bonds, half of it in Oppenheimer Global Strategic Income Fund and half in PIMCO Total Return.

Morningstar's William Harding reported in October that the Oppenheimer fund's "eclectic mix of bonds has produced good results so far in 2000." It was the fund's safety that appealed to Selma, with its eight hundred issues "limiting the impact of individual disasters." Harding wrote that its five-year returns landed it in the top third, "while its volatility has been below the group's norm. Seasoned management and a hefty yield are two more reasons to consider this offering." Selma would more than consider it; she would put 10 percent of her account into it.

Like Hawkins at Longleaf, Bill Gross at PIMCO Total Return was a legend in the business. Sarah Bush at Morningstar wrote in March, "When manager Bill Gross acts, the investment community tends to take notice." He'd loaded up on long-term Treasuries ahead of a buyback, which he said would shrink supply and drive up the prices of the bonds he bought, and that's exactly what happened. His success over the years had been driven by identifying and exploiting such anomalies. Bush wrote that "despite the occasional misstep, this fund has consistently outperformed both its index, the Lehman Brothers Aggregate and its intermediate-term bond peers. With a 10-year return that ranks among its group's best, it's no surprise that when Gross talks, the bond market listens." From the Nasdaq peak to the end of November, PIMCO Total Return rose 9 percent while paying a dividend of about a nickel per share every month, for a total of $0.48 paid over nine months. Selma would put 10 percent of her retirement under the guidance of Bill Gross.

Selma liked the bond market's steadying influence on a portfolio, especially in conjunction with her fairly safe stock fund choices. Surely, she thought, with a quarter of her money run by the legendary Mason Hawkins and 10 percent of it run by the legendary Bill Gross, she'd be fine. That was more than a third of her retirement allocated to legends in the business, and two-thirds allocated to other well-respected managers known for above-average returns from only average or below-average volatility.

Selma did a good job. Her portfolio was sensible. Her $405 per month would be divided among the six funds in the same allocation as her initial mixture, for steady, reliable growth. She knew the dollar-cost averaging would help her take advantage of price swings without needing to worry about eventual recovery. Her top-notch managers would see to that. One thing she didn't pay close attention to was the cost of her portfolio, which is easy to overlook among glowing reports on legendary and well-respected managers. Here's what she paid:

TABLE 46. Selma's Initial Expense Ratios

Fund	Expense Ratio (%)
Fidelity Growth & Income (FGRIX)	0.71
Longleaf Partners (LLPFX)	0.91
Artisan International (ARTIX)	1.19
T. Rowe Price International Stock (PRITX)	0.49
Oppenheimer Global Strategic Income (OPSGX)	1.85
PIMCO Total Return (PTTDX)	0.75

This is better than what Garrett faced in the expense department, but still far above the tiny fees associated with index funds. Also, the Oppenheimer fund included a deferred sales load that Selma would have to pay if she sold shares within six years, but she ignored it because she knew the account was for the long haul and because the financial adviser had said Oppenheimer was well known in the business and quite popular. Selma figured that if anybody could earn the higher charges, it was the six first-rate management teams she'd selected. The final solidifying input from the financial planner was that Selma's allocations to domestic stocks, international stocks, and bonds was correct for her age, and the diversification into two funds for each asset class provided further safety. "There's no optimum number of funds," the planner said, "but your six look very good for your temperament and time horizon." Great! Selma was set.

Mark's plan was the easiest to start. He'd concluded in the years before joining SnapSheet that active management wasn't for him, regardless of rave reviews and glowing reputations. After he discovered the low-cost advantage of index investing and the fact that it beats almost all active managers, he set about finding the best way to grow an index fund portfolio. The only two approaches that appealed to him were dollar-cost averaging and 3Sig. He'd gone with dollar-cost averaging in a diverse mix of stock index funds at his former employer. The portfolio grew like clockwork in the late 1990s, but then he entered the dot-com crash fully invested and unable to do anything but watch his portfolio melt away. Had he sold at the peak a year earlier, the end of 1999 or even sometime in early 2000, he'd have been fine. When prices began retreating, though, he knew it was the time to keep going with his monthly purchases, so he did. The problem was, they were so small in comparison to the thousands disappearing monthly from his account. He found himself wishing he'd had some real buying power into the depths of the crash, and that's when he remembered 3Sig.

He'd sold all his stock funds and hid out in cash during his unemployed months before SnapSheet, worried for his wife and three children the same way Selma worried about her two children. While job-hunting, he consolidated everything he had in the safest place possible. Once he was hired at SnapSheet, he turned his attention to the new 401(k) at his disposal and again faced the trade-offs between dollar-cost averaging and 3Sig. "What really went wrong?" he asked his wife at the dinner table one night in their new home, after the kids had been excused.

"The market crashed," she replied.

"I know, but if that's what markets do now and then, and if it craters my retirement account every time, then I'm doing something wrong." She offered that maybe they should own safer investments. "That could work," he agreed, "but then we end up underperforming most of the time, when the market rises." He reminded her of 3Sig, how it would keep them mostly invested in high-performing small caps, but with a 20 percent bond buffer to be able to "really wade in when the market collapses, like this year," he said. He thought that was about the best balance they'd be able to strike—plus, it was easy to do.

With that, he set up 3Sig in his SnapSheet 401(k). He divided his initial $10,000 along the 80/20 stock/bond allocation you now know well. Since SnapSheet's plan included iShares Core S&P Small-Cap (IJR) among its choices, and it was the cheapest small-cap index vehicle in the plan, it's what Mark would use for the stock side. For the bond side, SnapSheet's plan included Vanguard GNMA (VFIIX), so he'd use that for the 20 percent safe portion of the plan. He'd begin 2001 with $8,000 in IJR and $2,000 in VFIIX. He would build half his $1,215 quarterly contribution into the 3 percent quarterly signal target, leaving the other half in bonds for buying power. If his bond allocation ever reached 30 percent of his account, he would move the extra into IJR on the next buy signal. If the market ever dropped 30 percent on a quarterly closing basis, he would enter the "30 down, stick around" mode and ignore the next four sell signals. That was it. Here's what he'd pay in expenses:

TABLE 47. Mark's Initial Expense Ratios

Fund	Expense Ratio (%)
iShares Core S&P Small-Cap (IJR)	0.16
Vanguard GNMA (VFIIX)	0.21

Mark's allocation-adjusted expense ratio came to 0.17, some 92 percent less than Garrett's 2.00 and 82 percent less than Selma's 0.92. Already his portfolio enjoyed a distinct advantage. Garrett and Selma didn't know this, however. Z-val commentators, Peter Perfect, and active managers promise investors that higher fees are more than overcome by better performance, an opinion straight from the old "you get what you pay for" philosophy. Time would tell.

With these preparations, our three investors were off and running at their new jobs with their new 401(k) plans.

Year 1

Everybody's salary and retirement contributions stayed constant in their first year on the job. The dot-com crash wasn't quite over yet, it turned out, and the year would introduce a major disruption in September: the 9/11 terrorist attacks.

April 2001

Trouble began early for Garrett. At the end of March, his initial $10,000 plus his three $405 monthly contributions had fallen to an account value of $7,629. At lunch with Selma and Mark, he vented. "I'm down almost twenty-four percent, and that *includes* the twelve hundred fifteen dollars in new money. I thought Jacob Internet was going to scream higher, and it did in January, with an eighteen-percent gain, but now it's down forty-six percent since the end of last year when I bought it. I thought the dot-bomb crash was over!"

"You should switch to something safer," Selma said. "I got burned by Internet junk a year ago, too, so I put together a steadier fund mix this time."

"I don't want steady," Garrett said. "I want excitement." He chuckled. "Anyway, I'm not doing much better in my other funds. In the first quarter, Wasatch Small-Cap is down eleven percent, and Janus Global Tech is down thirty percent."

"I don't know how you stand it," Mark said. "What are you going to do?"

"Not sure yet. Analysts say tech profits are still bad, and a lot of them think the economy and all corporate profits, not just tech, are going to stay bad all year. I'm thinking I should get to the sidelines and buy back in later, when prices are lower. What about you guys?"

"I'm not doing anything," Selma said. "My planner and I put together a good portfolio of six funds. My Oppenheimer and PIMCO bond funds paid dividends, and so did Fidelity Growth & Income. I automatically reinvest dividends into the fund that paid them. My funds are safer than yours, so rough quarters like this one don't do much to them. The dividends and my cash contributions build on top of steady gains. I finished the quarter up five percent overall, so I'm pretty happy."

Garrett didn't look happy to hear this, and reiterated his belief that he could catch up later in the year if he got to the sidelines and reentered at lower prices.

"But isn't that what you tried in December?" Mark asked. "I remember your saying the dot-com crash had made tech stocks so cheap that you wanted to focus on them. Now they're cheaper. If your goal was to invest in cheap tech stocks, wouldn't it be better to keep buying the funds you own at these lower prices?"

"Sure, if they're going to go up soon, but not if they're going to keep going down. I guess I could play that game forever, couldn't I? I'll stay put for a while, keep my contributions steady. What about you, Mark?"

"I just did the only thing I'll ever do," Mark replied. Garrett and Selma looked over at him. "No, really. I follow the same procedure at the end of every quarter. I see if my stock fund achieved its three-percent growth goal plus half the cash I contributed to my bond fund for the quarter. If so, I do nothing. If not, I use money from the bond fund to buy the stock fund up to the target balance. If the stock fund is over the target, I sell it down to the target and put the proceeds into my bond fund. That's all."

"What did you do this time?" Garrett asked.

"Bought more of my stock fund. It fell six percent, so it missed the target balance for the quarter. The bond fund did fine, though, up almost three percent for the quarter and paying dividends, so I had plenty of cash to catch the stock fund up to its target. My account finished the quarter about eight percent higher."

"Those are good funds," Garrett said.

"They're just indexes. My stock fund tracks the S&P Small-Cap Six Hundred Index and my bond fund owns government GNMAs. Nothing special, and no human judgment involved. I like that. People have terrible long-term track records against indexes; plus they charge more."

"My fund managers are some of the best in the business," Selma said. "They beat the indexes. Managers are ranked, you know, so it's easy to choose good ones. Mine are highly rated."

"Yeah, Mark, not all people have terrible long-term track records against indexes," Garrett added.

"Maybe not all, but how's yours shaping up?"

September 2001

The September 11, 2001, terrorist attacks shut down the stock market for a week. When it reopened, prices fell sharply, sending poor Garrett's portfolio to the mat yet again. On the first day of trading after the attacks, Monday, September 17, the Dow fell 7.1 percent and posted its largest single-day point drop in history to that time, and the Nasdaq fell 6.8 percent. Jacob Internet lost 27 percent in September alone, and was off 71 percent for the year. Wasatch Small-Cap Growth was down 6 percent for the year, Janus Global Tech 54 percent. Even though Garrett kept buying the cheaper prices with his monthly contributions, his account value had slipped 26 percent since the beginning of the year.

During a lunchtime walk in a park near the offices, he told Selma and Mark that the amount of money he'd lost in the first nine months of the year wasn't just the $2,629 difference between his initial $10,000 and his current $7,371 balance. "No, I have to include all my monthly contributions, too." Run $405 per month for nine months and you get $3,645. He pulled a slip of paper from his pocket. "Total lost, then: six thousand two hundred seventy-four dollars. I'm starting to really hate stocks. First the never-ending dot-bomb bust, now the attacks. Oh, and by the way, Mark, thanks for your swell advice to keep buying cheaper prices back in April."

"Hey, now," Mark said. "That's not my fault. I was just telling you what my signal said, which was to buy more. I bought then, too, you know."

"Didn't you sell over the summer, though?" Selma asked.

Mark nodded. "The signal said to sell a bit of my stock fund at the end of the second quarter, yes."

"How about now?" Garrett asked.

"A big buy signal, what else? You're not the only person whose stocks are falling. My stock fund dropped sixteen percent last quarter."

"After you sold the previous quarter?"

"Right."

"Now you're going to buy more?"

"Yeah, almost twenty-five hundred dollars more. It's a big buy signal, at least for me."

"So, let me guess: you think I should buy more, too."

"I don't think anything, Garrett. I just follow the signal. It's telling me to buy a lot more, so I will. Besides, even if you wanted to buy more, you don't have the cash, right?"

"Thanks a lot."

"No, I'm just asking. Is it even an option to buy more?"

"I could at least keep my monthly contributions buying more, but I might not," Garrett said. "I'm getting fed up with this. The chief economist at Wells Fargo said the attacks have hurt consumer confidence, and it's costing billions in business activity. I tell you what, my confidence sure is hurting. I've just had it." He walked quietly for a moment. "But your signal says to buy now, right?"

Mark nodded. He didn't want to say much, preferring just to report the signal. Wasn't Garrett hearing enough noise as it was?

"I'm keeping my plan going," Selma said. "I didn't actually lose badly last month. Artisan and Longleaf went down something like twelve and thirteen percent, but PIMCO gained. With my regular contribution and the dividends, my account value dipped only five percent. It's important to keep buying when the market dips, Garrett. You pick up more shares on the cheap."

"I know, I know, but see how you feel when cheap gets cheaper, and cheaper, and cheaper."

Garrett couldn't stop thinking about it. He watched investment reports on TV, read investment websites, and devoured the most recent issues of the newsletters he received. His wife mentioned that they were the same newsletters that thought buying cheap tech a year ago was a good idea, and he admitted as much, but said just as all the bears were eventually proved right at the end of the dot-com bubble, so the bulls would eventually be proven right at the end of the current bear market. He wanted to change something but didn't want to miss out on the big recovery that he just knew lay ahead.

His thinking was confirmed by the media and newsletters. The BBC reported that the "souring U.S. economy further weakened by the recent attacks on the World Trade Center in New York and Washington has erased billions of dollars of wealth among U.S. investors. Many have reacted by pulling what remains of their worth out of stocks and mutual funds, further exacerbating a desperate situation." As much as he hated the sound of that, he was determined not to join them in the exit stampede. Some analysts suggested it was a perfect time to put fresh money to work. Garrett didn't have fresh money, but he could rearrange what was already invested.

He was eager to get out of Jacob Internet, even embarrassed to say he ever owned the thing, now down 71 percent year-to-date. Was there a way to bail out of the Internet's journey to the center of the earth without losing all recovery potential? He thought so when he read that the stock market can do well in a time of war, which the United States entered with a retaliatory strike on Afghanistan and something bigger cooking in Iraq, by all early indications. Apparently, when the United States does well in a war, stocks rise, and nobody expected anything but a positive outcome in whatever Middle East wars resulted from the terrorist attacks. So he should own stocks. Which ones? Airlines.

That's what one of his newsletters suggested as the sector most poised for a rocket off the bottom. Airplanes were used in the attacks, air transportation was locked down in response, big changes in security procedures were on the way, so airline stocks and related stocks crashed. They wouldn't disappear, the newsletter said; they would rebound big time when people started traveling normally again, and airlines might even get a helping hand from government. The letter recommended a list of airline stocks, and also the Fidelity Select Air Transportation Portfolio "for investors who'd rather own a basket of stocks than individual picks." That was it! Garrett would replace Jacob Internet with Fidelity Select Air Transportation Portfolio.

He got on it right away and began Q4 with his new portfolio. On top of what he hoped would be better appreciation potential—how could it be worse?—he would save on expenses. The fee at Jacob Internet had been 2.87 percent. His new Fidelity fund's expense ratio was only 0.94 percent. With half his capital allocated to this part of the portfolio, the discount represented a big savings. This was his new portfolio's expense structure:

TABLE 48. Garrett's Expense Ratios in Q401

Fund	Expense Ratio (%)
Fidelity Select Air Transportation (FSAIX)	0.94
Wasatch Small-Cap Growth (WAAEX)	1.26
Janus Global Tech (JAGTX)	1.00

As Garrett stayed up late researching and weighing his options, discussing the market with his wife, debating whether war was good or bad for stocks, then which stocks in this particular brand of war would do well, his colleagues did almost nothing.

Selma did literally nothing, allowing her dollar-cost averaging plan to work its magic on the six reliable funds. Terrorist attacks or no, her $405 went into her portfolio per the usual allocations, and she didn't give stocks another thought after the lunchtime walk with Mark and Garrett.

Mark already knew his signal line for the quarter, which was always 3 percent higher than the previous quarter's balance in his stock fund, IJR, plus half his quarterly contributions into his bond

fund, VFIIX. That quarter, the signal line was $10,620. At IJR's clos-
ing price of $95.50 (unadjusted), he needed 111 shares of IJR. He
owned only 85, so he would buy another 26 shares, which would
require $2,483. He sold that amount of his bond fund and bought the
26 shares of IJR. He glanced at SPY to see if it had fallen enough to
trigger the "30 down, stick around" rule, and saw that it hadn't.
Then, like Selma, he didn't give the market another thought.

December 2001

At the conclusion of their first calendar year at SnapSheet, these
were the retirement account balances of our three investors:

TABLE 49. December 2001 401(K) Balances of Garrett, Selma, and Mark

Investor	December 31, 2001 401(k) Balance ($)
Garrett	10,748
Selma	14,553
Mark	16,216

The Dow Jones Industrial Average lost 7 percent in 2001. On top
of the terrorist attacks, investment media fretted about the bankruptcy of Enron, with *The Economist* writing at the end of November that the situation had gone from the firm having a stock market
valuation of $60 billion in February to shareholders set for nothing
after its bankruptcy. Barely a year earlier, Enron founder Ken Lay
was "being touted as the next energy secretary," but now "his career
as an innovative entrepreneur has ended in failure."

"That's an interesting sideshow," Garrett thought, but he was
more concerned with his new sector fund, Fidelity Select Air Transportation Portfolio, which gained only 21 percent in the fourth
quarter. Jacob Internet, the fund he'd replaced with Air Transportation, gained 51 percent. Even the other funds he kept did better than

Air Transportation. Wasatch Small-Cap gained 30 percent, and Janus Global Tech gained 31 percent. He still felt good to be finished with the Internet, but wished he'd held on longer before making the switch.

At least advisers suggesting airline stocks were still bullish. The International Air Transport Association said its Corporate Air Travel Survey had discovered an optimistic business community, with 57 percent of respondents expecting normal travel conditions to resume within six months. Garrett thought this had to be good for airline stocks, so he would hold on to his three funds for a payoff someday.

The fourth quarter was pretty good to Selma. Artisan International gained 9 percent and paid $1.06 in dividends, while Longleaf Partners gained 13 percent and paid $0.52 in dividends. She glanced at her account balance before heading off to a New Year's Eve party with her children, thought it looked good, and promptly forgot about it.

Mark ran his usual procedure at quarter's end and was happy to get a decent sell signal, thereby vindicating the previous quarter's big buy signal. IJR gained 20 percent in the fourth quarter, generating a $1,176 sell signal, which he entered. He would later move the proceeds of the sale into his bond fund. After fifteen minutes of easy calculations and a couple of orders, he was done for the quarter.

Year 2

Everybody's salary increased by 5 percent in January 2002, to $56,700 per year, or $4,725 per month, pushing their monthly 401(k) contributions to $425 after the employer match. The year would mark an increasing fever pitch in President George W. Bush's war on terror in Iraq, Iran, and North Korea, which he called collectively "an axis of evil" in his first State of the Union address, and outlined three goals: winning the war, protecting the homeland, and conquering the recession.

March 2002

It was another ho-hum quarter for Garrett, with Air Transportation up 12 percent but Wasatch Small-Cap down 4 percent and Janus Global Tech down 7 percent. His overall balance, including monthly contributions, rose 13 percent for the quarter, to $12,137. He looked at it positively, though, impressed with his own good judgment to have focused on airlines as they accelerated into a strong recovery. "I've figured out a thing or two," he told his wife over dinner. She asked if he was thinking of taking profits from the "airplane fund." He said, "No, not yet. I want to give it room to run." He'd read in *Investor's Business Daily* that it's important to keep winners. Air Transportation was definitely a winner, so he wanted to keep it.

Six months had passed since 9/11. The Associated Press reported, "The Dow has climbed 28.9 percent since its post-attack lows, the Nasdaq is up 35.6 percent and the S&P has advanced nearly 21 percent." It mentioned that "After two years of unsustainable rallies and tumbling stock prices, there are concerns that some issues have become too expensive given the modest projections for the future. [Some investors] want to hear more companies report improving results before committing too much to stocks."

Neither Selma nor Mark cared. They paid little attention to the financial media, focusing instead on their family situations. Selma's account grew 12 percent in the quarter, to $16,243. Mark's grew 13 percent, to $18,359.

September 2002

In a *USA Today* article, "Bear Drags Stocks Deeply into Den," Adam Shell wrote on September 30, 2002, that logic says stocks can't go down forever, but after watching the Dow Jones Industrial Average sink for three years—nearly 18 percent in the previous three months alone—"countless investors are starting to wonder if stocks will ever go up again." The Dow and S&P 500 delivered their worst quarterly performances since the fourth quarter of 1987, and the Nasdaq lan-guished at a six-year low.

The z-vals duked it out in the article. The market is "at least in the very late stages of the decline," said Woody Dorsey, president of Market Semiotics, which specializes in behavioral finance. "We are in a very difficult period, where all of the negative headlines are self-reinforcing." Bears countered with worries about war in Iraq and "a potentially debilitating bout of deflation" in addition to terrorism, weak corporate profits, and a possible double-dip recession. Until the economy perked up, Donald Straszheim of Straszheim Global Advisors said he expected little more than "sporadic, unsustainable rallies." Michael Farr, president of money management firm Farr Miller & Washington, said, "The past few years, investors have been rewarded for selling and punished for buying." Todd Clark, a trader at Wells Fargo Securities, added, "There is an unbelievable amount of pessimism."

Garrett couldn't believe it. He flipped through research reports in his home office, looking back at the quarter. Would the stock market nightmare ever end?

A market strategist at Ryan Beck & Co. quipped to the Associ-ated Press, "I think what we're seeing is a tug of war between one camp looking for the economy and corporate earnings to fall sig-nificantly further from where we are, and the other camp looking for the economy to expand . . ." Garrett sighed and pushed back from his computer. "Duh, ya think?" he mocked. "What other choices are there? Here's an idea: If you don't know anything, don't say anything."

His focused bet on Air Transportation had fizzled, with the fund down 30 percent year-to-date. It had even fallen below what he'd paid for it after the 9/11 attacks, but analysts were still bullish on airlines. "Their day will come," wrote the newsletter editor who first gave Garrett the idea a year earlier. "We were early, but not wrong."

"Early but not wrong?" Garrett asked out loud. "Tell that to the guy who walked onto the train tracks after you gave the all-clear. 'It wasn't safe then, but it will be later. Sorry.' Thanks a lot! I'm squashed flat! Sometimes, early *is* wrong."

Of course some analysts still said to hold on tight. The recovery that had been "just around the corner" for the past two years was still around the corner. Garrett realized that he was plain sick of it. The same comments from the same people in the same media about the same things hadn't helped him one bit. He was down and still falling. He knew the best way to guarantee a miraculous market recovery was to sell everything, so he wouldn't do that. What he would do, though, was stop investing more every month. At least that way, his monthly contributions would build up a buying buffer so he could take advantage of a potentially lower low in the future. If the market didn't keep falling, he would feel good to have held on to what he already owned. It seemed like a good compromise.

Selma followed her usual action plan, which was to do nothing. Her $425 monthly contribution continued to be divided among her six funds as initially allocated. Even after all the market fuss, her overall account balance including contributions had slipped less than 3 percent since the end of March. No biggie.

Mark followed the signal, as always, but was getting concerned that he might run out of cash. At the end of the first quarter, his bond allocation had hit 32 percent of his account, over the 30 percent threshold, triggering the need to rebalance for the first time. The chance to do so happened the very next quarter, when 3Sig issued the buy signal that gave him the all-clear to rebalance bonds back down to 20 percent.

The market had been bad in that second quarter, pulling IJR down 7 percent. The 3Sig plan issued a signal to buy 16 more shares, or $1,832 worth. Before the order, Mark's IJR stock balance was $11,712 and his VFIIX bond balance was $7,264. Dividing his bond balance by his account balance of $18,976 showed that he had 38 percent in bonds. He wanted only 20 percent. Multiplying $18,976 by 0.2 showed he should have just $3,795 in bonds. Subtracting this from the bond balance of $7,264 revealed that he should buy $3,469 of IJR instead of the $1,832 indicated by the signal. He sold $3,469 worth of the bond fund, bought the same amount of the stock fund, and began the second quarter with $15,181 in stocks and $3,795 in bonds, perfectly back at the 80/20 ratio that was his target. He then resumed the standard plan, and would stick with it until bonds reached a 30 percent allocation again, triggering another rebalance.

Unfortunately, the market kept falling. Right after the big buy in the second quarter, 3Sig issued another big buy signal, for $3,925 worth of IJR at the end of the third quarter. His contributions to the bond fund had pushed its balance up to $5,204 so he could fund the buy signal, but doing so brought his bond allocation down to only 7 percent. A big enough buy signal in upcoming quarters with no sell signals to help could leave him unable to buy into further price weakness. There was nothing he could do about it, but it reminded him of the idea to keep a bottom-buying account alongside the plan, some extra cash just in case he ever used up his bond fund. He hadn't set up a bottom-buying account yet. Maybe if he got another raise in the New Year, he would.

December 2002

At the conclusion of their second calendar year at SnapSheet, these were the retirement account balances of our three investors:

TABLE 50. December 2002 401(K) Balances of Garrett, Selma, and Mark

Investor	December 31, 2002 401(k) Balance ($)
Garrett	12,085
Selma	17,931
Mark	19,604

After falling 6 percent in 2000 and 7 percent in 2001, the Dow Jones Industrial Average lost 17 percent in 2002. On the Nasdaq, things were much worse: –39 percent in 2000, –21 percent in 2001, and –32 percent in 2002. A *Businessweek* special report, "Where to Invest in 2003," began:

> Some say Wall Street is a crooked thoroughfare that begins at a churning river and ends in an old graveyard. It's a fitting metaphor for 2002—the third year of a grisly bear market. There hasn't been a time in recent memory when the stock market has been so violently roiled, destroying the fortunes of so many. Nor has Corporate America ever been shaken by such an array of scandals. Words like Enron, WorldCom, Adelphia, ImClone, Grubman, Kozlowski, and Fastow have entered the vocabulary as shorthand for corruption and greed. Even Martha Stewart— the Queen of Clean—got her hands dirty in an insider-trading scandal. Things got so bad that Wall Street became a running joke on late-night talk shows. As Jay Leno said: "Do you know the difference between Las Vegas and Wall Street? In Vegas, after you lose your money, you still get free drinks."

Garrett's plan to stop investing his monthly contributions felt right. Fidelity Select Air spiked a tad after his decision, but then began falling again in December, down 2 percent. The same happened with his other funds. He liked watching his cash fund build up for the right time to buy later, if there'd ever be a right time. He and his wife set a rule for that year's Christmas celebrations with family: no stock talk. She was tired of his bad mood that always accompanied such discussions, so asked that they be avoided altogether. He eagerly agreed.

Selma, on the other hand, couldn't have been happier with her six funds. They kept cooking along, and she continued plowing more money into them every month. All her research two years prior was paying off—the highly rated funds were doing what she'd wanted them to do. If the bear market ever ended, she expected to really see some gains.

Mark was also happy, but a tad nervous about his low bond fund

balance as he kept using it to satisfy 3Sig's buy signals in the bear
market. From 7 percent at the end of the third quarter, it rose to 11
percent at the end of the fourth. At least it was rising, but seeing it
fall below 10 percent bothered him. He decided he would definitely
open a bottom-buying account in the New Year, just to be safe.

Years 3-7

In each of the years 2003 to 2007, everybody's salary increased by
5 percent. All three of our investors were good at managing their
personal finances, and decided to set aside 4 percent of their gross
salary in a savings account at SnapSheet's credit union. They took
the modest dividends from these savings accounts out as bonus
spending money for a little fun, leaving the balance in the accounts
growing at just the pace of their contributions. Here's how these factors looked over the five years:

TABLE 51. Salary and Contributions from 2003 to 2007

Year	Annual Salary ($)	Monthly Salary ($)	Monthly 401(k) Contribution (6% + 50% Match) ($)	Monthly Savings Contribution (4%) ($)
2003	59,535	4,961	447	198
2004	62,512	5,209	469	208
2005	65,637	5,470	492	219
2006	68,919	5,743	517	230
2007	72,365	6,030	543	241

All three considered their savings to be rainy-day funds, but
Mark assigned his the extra role of bottom-buying account for his
3 percent signal plan. He soon forgot all about this, however, because after the second quarter of 2003, his bond balance stayed in a
comfortably high range, growing from his contributions and the

plan's signals. He kept setting aside 4 percent of his salary as savings, but stopped regarding it as a bottom-buying account to be used if he exhausted his bond fund balance. In the bull market finally under way, there looked to be little risk of a steep crash.

The period didn't begin as a bull market under way, though. It began with all kinds of uncertainty.

March 2003

The first quarter of 2003 was dominated by the lead-up to war with Iraq. President Bush declared March 17 to be the "moment of truth" for the U.N. Security Council to tell Iraq to disarm immediately or face invasion. Nothing happened at the United Nations, and Iraqi president Saddam Hussein refused to step down, so the United States bombed Baghdad on March 19. The next day, ground troops invaded Iraq. On March 22, the well-announced "shock and awe" air strikes commenced. Finally, the war was under way. During the uncertainty ahead of it, the Dow fell 14 percent from mid-January to March 12. As soon as the start of the war looked imminent, the market turned up.

Garrett, for one, felt like a genius. With nothing but talk of war everywhere the previous Christmas, he'd followed the advice of a cyclical-timing newsletter and switched his Fidelity Select Air Transportation money to the Fidelity Select Defense & Aerospace Portfolio. The fund's focus on the defense industry not only stood a good chance of thriving in what looked to be a protracted war ahead, given the lack of objectives, but it also charged an expense ratio of just 0.84 percent, compared with 0.94 percent at Select Air.

In the prewar drumbeat, Select Defense fell only 8 percent in the first quarter, compared with Select Air's 9 percent drop. The slip back was a welcome development for Garrett, who still hadn't resumed investing the monthly contributions he'd been keeping in cash since the previous October. At the end of a six-month hiatus

that saw his cash balance grow to $2,616, he was pleased as punch
that he hadn't lost as much as he would have if he'd kept investing
every month. His timing was vindicated, and his confidence increased. To make the move perfect, he just had to deploy his cash at
the right moment—and he had a feeling that right moment was
upon him. Most of his newsletters said the start of the war would be
the start of a bull market. The war had started, and he already owned
the only defense industry fund on the market. Bulking up his position in the fund at a low price point in the cycle would make it even
better, so he decided to put all $2,616 of his cash into Select Defense
at the end of the first quarter of 2003 and resume his regular monthly
purchases, too. He'd called the winds of war correctly, and it was
finally time to catch up.

Morningstar analyst Kerry O'Boyle confirmed Garrett's bull-
ishness on Select Defense in a March 18, 2003, review titled, "This
Unique Offering Continues to Shine in the Shadow of War," which
began:

> Fidelity Select Defense & Aerospace has been drawing quite a
> bit of attention lately. As the only sector fund devoted exclu-
> sively to the defense industry, it can be viewed as a leading
> candidate to benefit from a war with Iraq. But that would ig-
> nore the fund's long-term outlook, especially with regard to
> defense-spending trends. Manager Matthew Fruhan thinks
> that the military is only midway through a building boom re-
> quired to replace aging equipment, a buying spree that has
> only accelerated since the Bush administration took office.
> Whereas a war may provide a short-term boost to defense
> stocks, it's this spending cycle that drives defense-company
> profits.

As Garrett maneuvered his money to benefit from news trends,
Selma's all-star portfolio kept doing everything right, so she continued her tradition of merely glancing at its improving balance and

doing nothing. Despite market gyrations in what O'Boyle called the "shadow of war," Selma's portfolio with contributions grew 4 percent in the first quarter. She happily noted that, at the current pace, it would soon exceed $20,000 for the first time.

Mark had been watching for SPY to activate the "30 down, stick around" rule in the bear market, and it did so in the third quarter of 2002, by finally slipping under the price that was 30 percent below its quarterly closing high of the previous two years. SPY closed 2000 at $131.19 (unadjusted), putting the rule's 30 percent level at $91.83. When it closed in September 2002 at $81.79, the level was convincingly breached, instructing Mark to stick around in IJR by ignoring 3Sig's next four sell signals. The market did badly for two more quarters, causing 3Sig to issue buy signals. The current one forced Mark's bond balance back down to 7 percent.

That was the last quarter for a long time that a low bond balance would worry him, though. From the $91.48 he paid for IJR at the end of March 2003, its price would rise 74 percent, to $158.85, in the following two years, starting the period with four sell signals in a row that he would ignore per the "30 down, stick around" rule, as his stock and bond balances both rose. IJR would then split three-for-one and go on to rise another 29 percent in the next two years. He had no way of knowing this in advance, of course, and the news continued launching noisemakers every step of the way higher. He didn't care about that, though. The beauty of 3Sig was that it wasn't waylaid by worrywarts.

December 2004

At the conclusion of their fourth calendar year at SnapSheet, these were the retirement account balances of our three investors:

TABLE 52. December 2004 401(K) Balances of Garrett, Selma, and Mark

Investor	December 31, 2004 401(k) Balance ($)
Garrett	33,285
Selma	37,416
Mark	44,809

Until he compared balances with his colleagues at a holiday party, Garrett had been confident in his portfolio. Select Defense went gangbusters as the Iraq War dragged out. After President Bush changed the war's objective from finding nonexistent weapons of mass destruction to building democracy in a country that didn't want it, defense analysts became giddy with glee because such a mission would never be accomplished. What could be better for defense profits than a war without end? Garrett's extra investment in Select Defense back in March 2003 paid off as the fund rose 78 percent by the end of 2004. His other funds did well, too. In the same time period, Wasatch Small-Cap grew 61 percent and Janus Global Tech grew 52 percent. Yet here he was way behind Selma and Mark, who never did anything interesting in their accounts.

He dove back into his market research and discovered an energy newsletter pushing oil refiners and drillers because their shares had done well recently. Then he found Richard Bernstein, the chief U.S. strategist at Merrill Lynch, telling *Businessweek* that stocks would go up only a little in 2005, about 1 percent plus a couple of percent from dividends. "It could be a rough ride even for that," Bernstein warned. "The Federal Reserve is going to be tightening short-term interest rates at the same time profit growth is slowing down to about half the 18 percent we've been getting in 2004. That's a coincidence that never ended well under [Fed chairman Alan] Greenspan. It contributed to the early-1990s recession, the 1998 financial crises, the deflation of the tech bubble, and the last recession." He liked the energy industry because "prices will cycle up and down, but the secular trend is higher." He suggested avoiding refiners and drillers. "It is better to hide out with big, reliable guys like ExxonMobil."

After serious thought and dinner conversations with his wife, Garrett decided he would sell his position in Janus Global Tech, his overall laggard, and put the proceeds into ExxonMobil stock. He'd keep his monthly contributions divided up the same way, with half going into Select Defense and a quarter into each of Wasatch Small-Cap and his new ExxonMobil holding. Maybe his problem had been too much diversification, he thought, and by concentrating a portion of his account on a single stock, he would do better. After all, Bernstein called energy "the No. 1 story for the decade" and seemed to think ExxonMobil would lead it. The stock had nearly kept up with Janus Global Tech since March 2003, and paid a steady quarterly dividend, so Garrett thought its outlook was decent. At the end of December 2004, then, his portfolio became this:

TABLE 53. Garrett's Portfolio at the End of December 2004

Investment	Allocation (%)
Fidelity Select Defense (FSDAX)	53
Wasatch Small-Cap (WAAEX)	29
ExxonMobil (XOM)	18

Selma was surprised to find herself wondering if her all-star portfolio wasn't as great as she'd thought. Mark didn't do much more than she did, and used only two dirt-cheap index funds in the signal system he was always citing as an excuse to avoid stock talk. Whenever Garrett or another colleague started repeating forecasts they'd heard on TV or read somewhere, Mark would hold up a hand and say, "I have no opinion and couldn't care less. I just follow the signal." For a while it had been impressive enough that his signal stayed slightly ahead of her all-star portfolio. Now it was no longer just slightly ahead; it was 20 percent ahead. She read more about her

funds in the investment media to see if she'd gone wrong somewhere. It didn't look like it. Consensus expected ever better results
from the likes of Mason Hawkins and Bill Gross, so she decided
that, for the time being, she'd keep on keeping on. For the first time,
however, she did so with a twinge of doubt.

As for Mark, he couldn't have been happier. His bond balance
hit 25 percent that quarter, and he wondered if he'd soon need to
move extra bond money into stocks again. When the only challenge
he had to contend with was shifting an abundance of bond balance
into a surging stock balance, life was good. How much time did he
spend listening to z-vals and others paid to make noise for a living?
Zero—and he was beating them all.

September 2005

On August 29, 2005, Hurricane Katrina struck Louisiana, causing
severe damage to that state and the Gulf Coast from Florida to
Texas. The levee system in New Orleans failed, allowing the flooding
of 80 percent of the city and prompting a lawsuit against the U.S.
Army Corps of Engineers for its role in one of America's worst civil
engineering disasters. The storm killed more than 1,800 people and
caused more than $100 billion in damage, making it the costliest
hurricane in U.S. history.

Chris Isidore at CNNMoney warned on September 6 that
"higher gasoline prices aren't the only economic fallout from the
devastating storm. Real estate and home construction, trade, agri-
culture and livestock—even the purchasing power of the dollar—are
all likely to be impacted by the storm in the coming months." Worse,
it seemed a recession was in the cards:

> The prospect that the U.S. economy will significantly slow is
> one reason many investors and analysts now believe the Fed-
> eral Reserve may not raise rates at its Sept. 20 meeting, which
> would be the first time since May 2004 it left rates unchanged.

But there are growing concerns that the combination of higher energy prices and some transportation disruptions, coupled with lower economic activity in the Gulf region itself, could be enough to plunge the economy into an actual recession. . . .

"I don't think it's too soon to talk about a recession, even if I still think there's less than a 50-50 chance," said Doug Porter, deputy chief economist of BMO Nesbitt Burns. "Every other recent recession has been preceded by an energy shock. Certainly at the least there is a risk that growth will be curtailed."

Garrett smiled. Energy shock? No problem. He owned Exxon-Mobil, which had risen smartly along with oil prices. Since he bought it at the end of December, the stock had gained 24 percent and paid $0.85 in dividends per share. It now comprised 21 percent of his portfolio, even though his other two holdings were up a lot, too.

Selma and Mark were also doing well. None of the three investors saw any cause for concern in his or her 401(k), but just to be sure, both Garrett and Selma asked Mark about the current signal. "A very tiny sell," he reported; "less than ten dollars. It's saying to stay put." That's what they all did.

December 2006

At the end of their sixth calendar year at SnapSheet, these were the retirement account balances of our three investors:

TABLE 54. December 2006 401(K) Balances of Garrett, Selma, and Mark

Investor	December 29, 2006 401(k) Balance ($)
Garrett	59,769
Selma	60,458
Mark	66,957

This came as a shock to Garrett, still in last place even after watching his account balance grow 36 percent that year, from $43,805 to $59,769. Select Defense rose 11 percent and paid a whopping $6.61 in dividends for an 8 percent yield. Wasatch Small-Cap was up only slightly but paid $2.92 in dividends. ExxonMobil rose 36 percent and paid a $0.32 dividend every quarter. It was nothing but up, up, and up, yet he hadn't kept pace with his do-nothing colleagues. How well had their positions done?

Selma's Longleaf Partners fund rose 13 percent and paid dividends, her Artisan International fund rose 15 percent, and her other funds did well and paid dividends, too. Mark's IJR small-cap index rose 14 percent and paid a dividend, while his bond fund was flat but sported a 5 percent dividend yield. These weren't amazing performances, but somehow Selma had outpaced Garrett, while Mark's quarterly signals extracted enough extra profit from the performance of his funds to put him even farther ahead.

Just about the time Garrett plotted what he could do to sprint ahead of Selma and possibly overtake Mark, another colleague of theirs, whom we'll call Peter Perfect, began bragging about his investments. Peter told Garrett, "I'm killing it with First Marblehead. The thing occupies a sweet spot inside a sweet spot, taking advantage of loan securitization but with student loans, not subprime. This credit boom has most people eyeing mortgages, but the really smart money is in student lending. These guys take a basket of student loans, turn it into a tradable security for a huge fee, then sell it off. Almost no risk. It's brilliant."

"Has the stock done well?" Garrett asked.

"Well?" Peter said, laughing. "You could say so. I paid thirty-five dollars for it a year ago. It was seventy-five earlier this month, and just split three for two." He let that sink in, then elbowed Garrett and added in a lower voice, "It even pays a dividend every quarter."

"All the profit's probably gone," Garrett said.

"I doubt it. Fundamentals are rock solid. P/E is only thirteen, profit margin is a fat forty-six percent, revenue growth is seven hundred sixty percent, it has two hundred sixty-five million in the bank and almost no debt, and insiders own a third of the company. At least you know if it goes down, the people running the place are going to go down with it, right?"

"Right. Are you buying more?"

"A lot more."

Garrett confirmed that Peter got First Marblehead's fundamentals right. All the research he could find on the stock was positive, except for a few analysts worried about overvaluation after the stock's recent rise. Business had never been better for the company. It just closed a $1 billion securitization of private student loans originated by several banks under different loan programs structured with the help of First Marblehead. He read in the most recent 10-Q (a quarterly report that the U.S. Securities and Exchange Commission requires public companies to file) that Marblehead was shielded from lending risk because it did "not take a direct ownership interest in the loans our clients generate, nor do we serve as a lender or guarantor with respect to any loan programs that we facilitate." It made money only from "the volume of loans for which we provide outsourcing services from loan origination through securitization." This seemed promising, what with the cost of college rising exorbitantly, all but guaranteeing demand. Marblehead looked like the ultimate middleman between borrower and lender, making mega profits with minimal risk.

At the end of December 2006, Garrett moved half his Wasatch Small-Cap allocation into First Marblehead stock. Wasatch was his laggard; ExxonMobil, his leader. Maybe another smart stock pick could become a leader, too. Prospects for Marblehead looked even better than those for ExxonMobil, and Garrett thought he might just lead the 401(k) pack with this addition. His new portfolio became:

TABLE 55. Garrett's Portfolio at the End of December 2006

Investment	Allocation (%)
Fidelity Select Defense (FSDAX)	54
ExxonMobil (XOM)	22
First Marblehead (FMD)	12
Wasatch Small-Cap (WAAEX)	12

As for Selma and Mark, they were both pleased with the progress of their portfolios in the bull market, and Mark was surprised to find himself cruising comfortably ahead of Selma. He knew that in a long enough bull market he could fall behind an unwavering, fully invested portfolio, but was reminded by Selma's position in second place that the full investment needed to focus on high-performing stocks, such as his small caps in IJR. Selma was proving to be nothing if not steadfast, and she had certainly done her homework in selecting the best of the best funds, but she had diversified beyond high-performing categories. Would her team of pros prove their worth in the quarters ahead?

September 2007

News about the troubled housing market was everywhere. A *Barron's* article titled "Getting Ready for the Roof to Fall" looked at the strategy of bond fund manager Jeffrey Gundlach, the chief investment officer of TCW Group: "He sees U.S. home prices dropping an average of 12 percent to 15 percent annually from the highs achieved last year and not reaching their eventual trough until late 2008, at the earliest. And they may not start recovering until 2010 or 2011, inflicting, in the meantime, real damage on the economy."

Gundlach thought the downward trend in mortgage delinquencies and foreclosures would accelerate. "That's because next year and early 2009 will see a crescendo in the troubled 2006 and early-2007 subprime mortgage vintages reaching their two-year rate reset points, when the low teaser rates expire. Facing jumps in monthly payments of 30 percent or more, many homeowners are likely to just throw in the towel and default on their mortgages."

Maybe, Garrett thought, but it sure looked like the Federal Reserve was ahead of the curve in supporting the economy. It cut the federal funds rate by 0.5 percent, to 4.75 percent, on September 18, which sent stocks up sharply. He'd read an article in *Barron's* a month earlier titled "A Contrarian Should Be Bullish on Stocks," in which investment newsletter watchdog Mark Hulbert wrote that the stock market's 7 percent drop from early July to early August, "painful as it undeniably has been, is not likely to be the beginning of a major bear market." Hulbert reasoned that since the average investment newsletter had turned bearish, it was time to do the opposite, because "a contrarian would conclude that the current sentiment picture does not conform to the typical psychological profile of a major market top." He suggested that investors think of it this way: "The editor of the average market-timing newsletter is more often wrong than right at market turning points. To be bearish right now requires you to bet that this time he will uncharacteristically get it right. Is that really how you want to bet?"

It wasn't how Garrett wanted to bet, so he stayed put. From the end of July to the end of September, his account grew 11 percent, to $74,092 from $66,756. That was with a little help from the Fed, true, but wasn't that legitimate? The Fed always has the market's back. It's one of the long-term reasons to stay bullish, he figured. Following the half-point rate cut, *USA Today* reported, "The Dow soared 335.97, or 2.51 percent, to 13,739.39. The last time it rose more than 300 points in one session was Oct. 15, 2002, when it gained 378 points, and Tuesday's percent increase was the biggest since April 2, 2003. The blue-chip index is now only about 1.9 percent below its record close of 14,000.41, reached in mid-July."

Garrett's First Marblehead bet had gone south, down 31 percent since he bought it the previous December, but it had shot 15 percent higher since July and had grown its dividend from 15 cents in March to 27.5 cents in September. It was still recommended by the *Motley Fool Hidden Gems* newsletter, and nineteen hundred out of two thousand investors in the Motley Fool CAPS research community thought First Marblehead would beat the market. The company announced earlier that month that its most recent sale of asset-backed securities would raise almost $3 billion. Everything was on track for a good recovery, and Garrett felt fine putting more money into the stock at lower prices. He allocated 12.5 percent of every monthly contribution to it, and would continue doing so.

Besides, his other picks were more than making up for Marblehead's struggles. Year-to-date, Select Defense gained 18 percent; ExxonMobil, 21 percent; and Wasatch Small-Cap, 9 percent. Once the market caught on to Marblehead's outstanding business results and reinvigorated the stock, his portfolio would fire on all cylinders and he'd mount some serious profits.

December 2007

At the end of their seventh calendar year at SnapSheet, the 401(k) balances of our three investors stood as follows:

TABLE 56. December 2007 401(K) Balances of Garrett, Selma, and Mark

Investor	December 31, 2007 401(k) Balance ($)
Garrett	70,740
Selma	71,208
Mark	74,092

Both Garrett and Selma had narrowed the gap between their balances and Mark's. Selma's all-star portfolio seemed to be proving that high expense ratios were worth it, and that careful research of active management track records and sticking with a plan were the keys to profiting over the long term. She was still ahead of Garrett and looked destined to surpass Mark, with no effort.

Garrett wasn't as upset as he had been at the ends of other years, now that all his hard work had finally paid off. He'd basically kept pace with Selma's famous fund managers and was closing in on Mark's smug signal, and that was after First Marblehead nearly gave up the ghost in the fourth quarter, crashing 60 percent. He wasn't sure what was going on there, given that the company had nothing to do with poisonous subprime lending. All the Marblehead bulls kept insisting that the market was throwing out the baby with the bathwater and suggested averaging into lower prices for an eventual recovery, so Garrett kept his plan going. There wasn't much risk left anyway, because Marblehead had dwindled to just 3 percent of his portfolio. Even if it blinked out entirely, it wouldn't matter a whole lot.

Everybody felt fantastic that holiday season, as most investors do at the tail end of bull markets. Mark rarely thought about stocks, but with everybody around him bragging about their bang-up performances, it was hard to ignore them. Garrett had become especially noisy, chiding Mark for ending the quarter with a fifth of his capital in bonds. "I'm still ahead of you," Mark said, to which Garrett replied, "Not by much anymore." He never missed a chance to remind Mark that stocks mostly go up. If anybody ever mentioned the dot-com collapse, Garrett retorted, "And what came after it? A raging bull. Money needs to be put to work."

The signal had been telling Mark to buy most of the year, including that quarter. The only sale was in the second quarter, and it was a modest one. He noticed that IJR had been steadily moving lower since then, to the tune of –9 percent since the end of the second quarter. The next two quarters of buying lowered his bond balance from 27 percent of the portfolio to 20 percent, where it stood after the fourth-quarter buy. At least the signal was moving more of his bond allocation into stocks, the asset class everybody loved talking about. Something was odd, though. If stocks were so great, why had IJR been falling for six months?

He mentioned his thinking about the signal to his wife, one of the rare times he let stock talk invade their home. They agreed that growing the account to $74,000 in seven years without paying any attention to all the fuss on Wall Street was pretty darned good, and better than most. They decided to leave 3Sig to its own devices.

Garrett asked Mark what the signal was saying at the end of December 2007. "To buy," Mark answered. "A fair amount, too: sixty-four hundred dollars."

Garrett clapped him on the shoulder. "It's good to see that signal trying to stay ahead. Most of my newsletters are bullish, too, so your signal is probably right."

"It's been mostly right so far. What are your newsletters saying?"

"That we're going to make more money. I'll e-mail you some highlights later." Garrett's note arrived full of bullish commentary from pundits, interspersed with his own analysis emphasizing quotes and tossing in phrases showing he'd been onto the bull market from the start: "as I expected" and "which was obvious" and "as anybody paying attention could see" peppered the connecting material.

Bob Brinker wrote in the early December issue of his *Marketimer* newsletter that the stock market's recent sell-off was good news. "The short-term correction that began in October and continued into November has served as a health-restoring pullback, and has paved the way for new record highs in the S&P 500 index in our view." Garrett agreed because anybody paying attention to history could see that the market never rose in a straight line. It needed to take a break from rising to avoid getting overbought, he explained.

In the December 6 issue of *The Chartist Mutual Fund Letter*, editor Dan Sullivan wrote, "What we find remarkable and most encouraging is the fact that the market has been able to make upside progress in the face of extremely adverse news. If history is any guide, this bull market has further to run. We say this because at bull market peaks, the news is highly favorable and the public is jumping in with both feet. Currently, the public is apprehensive with the financial press painting a very bleak picture. This is more indicative of a market bottom than a top." He kept the letter's portfolio fully invested.

Garrett added his two cents: "Sullivan is right. Retail investors are too negative here. The time to get out will be when they're all bullish. There's more upside ahead in 2008." He liked what an investor friend of his observed on this score: "We may be at the beginning of the end of this bull run, but not the end of the end."

Stephen Savage at the *No-Load Fund Analyst* stayed fully invested, too, because "our valuation work continues to suggest that large-cap U.S. stocks are at least reasonably valued under a broad range of likely growth scenarios. We continue to expect stocks to outperform bonds over our five-year tactical time horizon." Garrett said his analysis also indicated that stocks were not yet overvalued. "Besides," he added, "valuation almost never causes a crash."

Even the Value Line Investment Survey thought stocks could rally in 2008 if "the economy steadies itself and corporate earnings press forward even modestly." It kept its recommended stock allocation at 75 percent, where it had been since June. Garrett said the odds of profits being "considerably better than modest" were very good. "Don't fight the Fed," he advised, "especially when it's working overtime to keep stocks rising."

Then came 2008.

Years 8–9

In 2008 and 2009, SnapSheet froze salary increases to shore up its finances in the credit crunch. All three of our investors kept their $72,365 annual salaries of 2007, with monthly contributions of $543 into their 401(k) accounts and $241 into their savings accounts.

December 2008

The year saw Bear Stearns go bankrupt in March. On Friday, March 14, 2008, its stock fell 47 percent in the first half hour of trading, in a furious exchange of more than a million shares per minute. In *New York* magazine, Jim Cramer wrote an article after the crash titled, "The Bear Stearns Bull," and subtitled, "With the collapse of the country's fifth-largest bank, the market hit bottom." He didn't just mean Bear stock itself, either, but "the whole stock market" and "the long-suffering housing market, too." People like Garrett who followed such advice by either buying into stocks or staying put that March, suffered for the rest of the year. Select Defense, for instance, slipped another 36 percent from the end of March to the end of December.

More than bearish calls ignored, it was the amassing of such bullish calls gone wrong that wore down the resilience of steadfast investors. The feeling of "I should never have listened" destroys more confidence than "I wish I had listened." For so long, every new dollar invested had withered away, and the bear market wasn't just dragging out; it was accelerating.

That autumn, Lehman Brothers disintegrated into the wreckage of subprime mortgage–backed securities. Its stock dropped in sickening cascades that would have been newsworthy as one-off events, but they came in series, dragging the market down as the world questioned how large a shock modern finance could withstand. Shares of Lehman dropped 45 percent on Tuesday, September 9, and another 40 percent two days later before the company tried finagling a government bailout over the weekend. When that looked impossible, it desperately sought a suitor. It failed on both fronts, and declared bankruptcy in the early hours of Monday, September 15, in New York.

That day, the Dow Jones Industrial Average shed 504 points in a phalanx of face-whitening financial news. Beside the Lehman saga, Bank of America was forced to buy Merrill Lynch for $50 billion to prevent further unraveling of the financial system when too many of Merrill's trading partners lost confidence in its solvency, and harsh whispers hinted that the insurance giant American International Group was about to collapse. An AIG collapse, the rumors assured everybody, would make Lehman's demise look like a child tripping on a grassy field. The credit market upheaval was so severe that the Federal Reserve needed to inject $50 billion into the banking system just to keep overnight rates close to its 2 percent target. Few moments in financial history have produced as much mayhem as the autumn of 2008.

In the first seven trading days of October, the market fell another 22 percent. It recovered a bit by the end of the month, but in the twelve trading sessions from Election Day on November 4 to November 20, it fell another 25 percent. Every familiar metric used to measure stocks became useless. They traded as a block, without regard for specific company fundamentals, and prices across the board drained away. It became a game of pick-a-price on Wall Street, and many people characterized stock investing as just a glorified form of gambling. Rolling the dice for recreation might be fine, but few people wanted to roll the dice for retirement.

At the end of their eighth calendar year at SnapSheet, the 401(k) balances of our three investors had diminished dramatically from the previous year, as follows:

TABLE 57. December 2008 401(K) Balances of Garrett, Selma, and Mark

Investor	December 31, 2008 401(k) Balance ($)
Garrett	50,926
Selma	46,556
Mark	69,993

The $69,993 was Mark's balance after he responded to the largest buy signal his plan had ever issued, which sparked a soul-searching conference between him and his wife. Their balance before the buy signal was $59,117. The issue they faced before deciding to buy was whether it was worth the risk of tapping their savings account to satisfy the signal's call to throw even more money into the bear market's maw.

The plan issued buy signals in every quarter of 2008 as IJR fell 32 percent, from $65.02 in the fourth quarter of 2007 to $43.97 in the fourth quarter of 2008, as follows:

TABLE 58. Mark's 3Sig Plan in the Crash from Q407 to Q408

Quarter	IJR Price ($)	Signal	Capital Required ($)	Remaining Bond Balance ($)	Remaining Bond Allocation (%)
Q407	65.02	Buy 97.74 shares	6,355	14,932	20
Q108	59.93	Buy 120.48 shares	7,220	9,672	14
Q208	60.17	Buy 40.21 shares	2,419	8,967	12
Q308	59.51	Buy 58.03 shares	3,453	7,293	10
Q408	43.97	Buy 463.22 shares	20,368	−10,876	0

Mark's $7,293 bond balance at the end of Q308 grew to $9,492 at the end of Q408 with the addition of his $1,629 quarterly cash contribution, a 3 percent rise in the price of his Vanguard GNMA fund, and the total of 12.6 cents Vanguard GNMA paid in monthly dividends that quarter. The buy signal at the end of the quarter required $20,368 in capital, however, which was $10,876 more than his $9,492 bond balance. This was the first time he'd faced the decision of whether to use his bottom-buying capital in the savings account he'd started at SnapSheet's credit union back in January 2003 with 4 percent of his gross monthly income. Its balance that December stood at $16,044, enough to cover 3Sig's shortfall, but was doing so a good idea? This is what Mark and his wife discussed in their conference, during which they decided that, yes, it was worth it.

After-Tax 401(k) Contributions

Almost all 401(k) contributions are made pretax, which is to say they're deducted from a worker's salary before income taxes are taken out. There's a limit on how much these pretax contributions can add up to in a year. It was $15,500 for people under age fifty in 2008, the year Mark and his wife discussed whether to use their bottom-buying account in 3Sig.

Their bottom-buying account was not pretax money, however. It was after-tax money, part of Mark's take-home pay that he set aside in a savings account. He'd already paid income taxes on it. The limit on after-tax contributions to a 401(k) is more generous than the limit on pretax contributions. In 2008, the maximum total amount that could be contributed to a 401(k) was the lesser of 100 percent of the employee's pretax income, or $46,000. Even with the addition of his bottom-buying capital, then, Mark did not come close to this limit.

Meanwhile, Garrett's head spun. He wondered how he could have stayed put through the year. He paged back through the bullish commentary saying to buy the cheaper prices, which helped explain some of his persistence. Then there were reactive bounces along the way, such as Select Defense's 8 percent rise over the summer, and ExxonMobile's 8 percent rise in November, and even First Marblehead's 64 percent rise in August—64 percent! Too bad they were all reactive twitches higher in a dominant downtrend. For the year, First Marblehead lost 92 percent; Select Defense, 44 percent; Wasatch Small-Cap, 42 percent; and ExxonMobil, 15 percent. Marblehead didn't pay a single dividend during the year, and only ExxonMobil grew its dividend, to $0.40 per quarter from $0.35. Wasatch's fell to 5.8 cents in December 2008, from $4.59 a year earlier, and Select Defense's fell to $0.40 from $3.35 a year earlier.

Selma was doing even worse. Longleaf Partners lost 53 percent;

Fidelity Growth & Income, 52 percent; Artisan International and T. Rowe Price International, 50 percent; and Oppenheimer Strategic Income, 21 percent. Only PIMCO Total Return avoided trouble, falling just 5 percent.

The final straw for Garrett was something Robert J. Samuelson wrote in *The Washington Post* on December 8: "Despite the Fed's frantic efforts to relax credit, it seems to be tightening in the midst of a harsh recession: the opposite of what's wanted. Private behavior is neutralizing public policy. Lenders are terrified by losses and the fear of what they don't know; the sudden failure of Lehman Brothers in September compounded their anxieties. . . . The danger is that tight credit and consumer pessimism combine to lower spending, raise joblessness and cause more defaults." Part of Garrett's reason for staying in stocks had been his belief that the Fed would hold their prices up. With the central bank looking powerless, he could no longer believe this. If boldly slashing the federal funds rate to 1 percent, from 5.25 percent since September 2007, hadn't worked, what would?

Garrett read that it was important to stay nimble for the right buying opportunity. After much agonizing, he sold every position in his 401(k) at the end of December 2008 to await better reentry prices. "We're putting everything in cash and regrouping," he told his wife, who by then was just plain sick of hearing about the stock market. Holding out in cash had worked for him back in autumn 2002. Maybe it would work again.

Selma couldn't stand it any longer, either. The only one of her funds that hadn't let her down was PIMCO Total Return, helmed by the legendary—and now heroic, to her—Bill Gross. As the whole world went to you-know-where in a handbasket, Gross piloted his fund to a mere 5 percent loss for the year and paid twelve monthly dividends for a total of $1 per share in 2008. Even more amazing, the dividend *grew* from 4.1 cents in January to 53.9 cents in December. Selma remembered the harrowing duration of the dot-com bear market. This new one was so much more severe in the first year—

she'd already lost a third of her account—that it would probably wreak havoc even longer. She refused to let another third of her account sink into the subprime sewer. At the end of December 2008, she moved her entire balance into PIMCO Total Return, where she would hide out until the coast was clear. Then, maybe she'd pick through cheap stock funds for another go.

It looked like she'd have plenty of time to go about it. Bill Fleckenstein at MSN Money called the recession one the Fed couldn't easily fix. Paul Krugman at *The New York Times* wrote, "The prosperity of a few years ago, such as it was—profits were terrific, wages not so much—depended on a huge bubble in housing, which replaced an earlier huge bubble in stocks. And since the housing bubble isn't coming back, the spending that sustained the economy in the pre-crisis years isn't coming back either." In *The Wall Street Journal*, Holman Jenkins rued policies getting "twisted and rendered incoherent" in the mounting bank bailouts and auto bailouts, and predicted that "the bad policy vicious circle probably has a long way to run. . . . Bottom line: Politics is in charge—in a way that makes a lost decade of subpar prosperity more likely than not."

It was against this backdrop of capitulation and despair that Mark and his wife discussed whether to heed their 3 percent signal plan's largest buy signal yet. What if the economy kept shrinking and SnapSheet reduced its headcount? If Mark lost his job, the family might need the $16,044 they'd saved at the credit union. "We have some other savings," Mark said. "We own our cars outright. I haven't heard any bad news at work."

"So, you think we should use the savings," his wife said.

"Yes. Moments like this are exactly when the plan works, and they don't happen often. Buying now is scary, but that's why we follow the signal, so we can get our bearings. We're supposed to do what it says. Needing to use our bottom-buying money to do what it says this time means it's probably a very important buy signal. The eleven grand we put into IJR here could become fifteen grand in a couple of years."

"Or six grand, with you out of a job."

"Or six grand," he repeated. "I know. Anything could happen. I just think the signal has steered us basically right so far, and it's backed by market history. It'll probably be right this time, too."

They sat quietly for a few minutes. Then his wife breathed in deeply, squeezed her husband's hand, and said, "Okay, let's buy it." Mark moved the $10,876 into their 401(k) and fully funded the biggest buy signal the plan had ever issued. Then he threw up.

March 2009

The market kept dropping. Mark and his wife's $11,000 became $9,000 as IJR lost another 17 percent. Their account balance fell to $59,753, and the plan issued a second giant buy signal, this one for $13,154 more than the meager $1,826 they had in Vanguard GNMA. They could have used the $5,891 in their savings account to get closer to the full buy signal, but both agreed that enough was enough. Mark used only the $1,826 in Vanguard GNMA, and even buying that much more of the stock market felt foolish.

He was amused to see a note he'd written in December reminding himself to ignore the next four sell signals. On a quarterly closing basis, SPY had peaked in the third quarter of 2007, at $152.58, setting the 30 percent threshold for the plan's "30 down, stick around" rule at $106.81. When SPY closed the fourth quarter of 2008 below it, at $90.24, it triggered the stick-around mode of skipping the next four sell signals. How quaint this looked to Mark now. A sell signal would require a rising stock market. When was the last time he'd seen one of those? In his present situation, without buying capital, he would have to ignore every signal, not just sell signals.

Garrett's all-cash account grew to $52,555 from $50,926 at the end of December, due to his monthly contributions alone. Just seeing something positive while stocks crashed filled him with relief. Guess who had *not* lost 17 percent that quarter in Select Defense?

Garrett, that's who. A painless three months! He assumed his plan was working. He'd be able to buy at cheaper prices later.

Selma felt even better. That Bill Gross at PIMCO was some kind of genius, all right. Since she put her entire $46,556 account balance in PIMCO Total Return at the end of December, it had grown to $48,861 thanks to her monthly contributions, a stable price, and a total of 15.3 cents per share paid in three monthly dividends. Everything she'd sold, by contrast, kept falling apart in the first quarter: Fidelity Growth & Income was –12 percent; Artisan International, –10 percent; T. Rowe Price International, –9 percent; Oppenheimer Strategic Income, –6 percent; and Longleaf Partners, –2 percent. "Good riddance to them," she thought. She had a good thing going at PIMCO, higher returns without the worry. She was even starting to wonder about ever buying back into stock funds. The very thought of it made her queasy.

John Plender captured the reasons in his March 2, 2009, article in the *Financial Times*, which began, "As stock markets everywhere continue their slide, global equities have in effect now shed all of the gains they had notched up between the Asian economic crisis of 1997–98 and the onset of the credit crisis in 2007." He continued:

> The message of all this misery is summed up by Michael Lewitt of Harch Capital Management, a fund manager who was quick to identify the risks in the credit bubble. "Virtually every strategy institutional investors followed, or were advised to follow by their consultants or funds of funds," he says, "turned out to be a complete disaster." . . .
>
> [D]iversification cannot work well in a credit bubble because virtually all asset categories are driven up by leverage. Then when the bubble bursts, deleveraging affects asset categories indiscriminately. Equally fundamental is that fund managers tend to move in herds because that reduces the risk of their losing client mandates. Minimizing business risk takes priority over the interests of beneficiaries.

In a March 5 article in *Forbes*, "The U.S. Financial System Is Effectively Insolvent," Nouriel Roubini wrote about the "rising risk of a global L-shaped depression that would be even worse than the current, painful U-shaped global recession." The reasons were obvious:

> The scale and speed of synchronized global economic contraction is really unprecedented (at least since the Great Depression), with a free fall of GDP, income, consumption, industrial production, employment, exports, imports, residential investment and, more ominously, capital expenditures around the world. . . . With stock prices down over 50 percent from peak and home prices down 25 percent from peak (and still to fall another 20 percent), the destruction of household net worth has become dramatic.

He preempted any improvement in stock prices by labeling it a head fake: "Of course, you cannot rule out another bear market suckers' rally in 2009, most likely in the second or third quarters. The drivers of this rally will be the improvement in second derivatives of economic growth and activity in the U.S. and China that the policy stimulus will provide on a temporary basis. But after the effects of a tax cut fizzle out in late summer, and after the shovel-ready infrastructure projects are done, the policy stimulus will slacken by the fourth quarter. . . ."

Thus was the mood in March 2009. Not only were markets down, but they were going to stay down for a long time. Even if they perked up, it would only be temporary, before they moved lower again. Whatever you do, went conventional wisdom, don't bet on stocks. Garrett certainly wouldn't; nor would Selma. Mark wished he hadn't, but he did his best to tune out until the next quarter. If there was indeed a suckers' rally, he'd just have to be one of the suckers.

December 2009

A funny thing happened on the way to oblivion. Stock prices rose—a lot. It was a suckers' rally, no doubt, as Garrett and z-vals and incarnations of Peter Perfect were quick to point out. Anybody buying it or owning it had only happened upon profits by blind luck—everybody could see that—and they were just playing with fire ahead of the next waterfall plunge. Hadn't Roubini and others foreseen this very knee-jerk move higher and pre-labeled it for the benefit of the smart money?

You bet they had, which was why Mark had a hard time following 3Sig's "30 down, stick around" rule. The plan followed the two largest buy signals it had issued since Mark began it, the ones of Q408 and Q109, with the two largest sell signals it had issued, in Q209 and Q309. They told him to sell $10,595 of IJR at the end of June 2009 after the fund had gained 22 percent in the second quarter, then to sell $9,985 of it at the end of September 2009, after the fund had gained 18 percent in the third quarter. He joked with his wife, "Suckers' rallies are fun!" They contemplated whether to just follow the signal and take some profits in case the market did head south again, as the z-vals were warning would happen, but they decided it was too late to start second-guessing 3Sig now.

Garrett said Mark was an idiot to keep everything in stocks. "And small caps, no less," he added.

In June, he told Mark that famous short-seller Doug Kass, who almost perfectly timed the 40 percent rise from March by switching from a bearish view to a bullish one that month, suddenly saw potholes ahead. Kass thought investors were too optimistic. "The same talking heads who were scared witless in March have turned back into perma-bulls," Kass said in a *Barron's* article that month, in which he also suggested it was going to become a "square-root sign shaped rally," a plunge followed by a spike followed by a long, flat, go-nowhere market. The article ended on the idea that Kass "says most people like to rationalize reasons to buy stocks when prices are going up. Now Kass is looking toward doing the opposite of the crowd—just as when he was buying ahead of the March lows."

"Fine," Mark shot back at Garrett in a rare display of emotion regarding stocks. "Guess who else said to buy stocks in March? I did, after looking at 3Sig. I just didn't have enough money to follow it all the way. I bought in December, though, and as much as my account could afford in March, and I'm glad I did. The plan says to stay put, so that's what I'm going to do."

In September, with Garrett still in cash and Selma still entirely in PIMCO Total Return, Mark dutifully ignored the second-biggest sell signal his plan had ever issued, thereby wrapping up four straight quarters of the biggest moves he'd witnessed to date, two drops and two rises.

"Are you really staying in small caps?" Garrett asked. "Really?" He e-mailed a link to a September 17, 2009, MarketWatch story by David Callaway, "As Dow 10,000 Looms, a Time to Worry," which intoned, "In March, it was just a relief that stocks rose after six months straight down. In April and May, it was perplexing. In June, July and August, it was invigorating as the market recouped 50 percent of its losses. Now, in September, supposedly a bad month for stocks, it's getting scary." He believed "a correction is inevitable" and worried about bad earnings, Washington gridlock on health care and financial regulation, bank failures, and unemployment approaching 10 percent. When the correction finally arrived, he predicted it would "come with a loud crack in equities, as all the positive momentum behind the market right now suddenly shifts to an embarrassing, emperor-without-clothes type of feeling, which will precede a rush to sell."

Mark wrote back to Garrett: "If the correction does come, my signal will say to buy it . . . and I will." It didn't happen, in the fourth quarter, when IJR gained another 5 percent and the plan issued its third sell signal in a row. It was a small one, just $515, but it was a sell signal nonetheless, and Mark ignored it as he was supposed to do during the stick-around phase. There was just one more to go.

With Garrett in cash, Selma in PIMCO Total Return, and Mark sitting on a 94 percent allocation to IJR with only 6 percent in bonds, here's how the 401(k) balances of our three investors finished their ninth calendar year at SnapSheet:

TABLE 59. December 2009 401(K) Balances of Garrett, Selma, and Mark

Investor	December 31, 2009 401(k) Balance ($)
Garrett	57,442
Selma	59,755
Mark	95,470

Bloomberg news columnist Caroline Baum selected *new normal* as the most overused term of 2009. It reentered the lexicon in May, when PIMCO, home of Selma's favorite investor, Bill Gross, forecasted a new normal of slower growth, higher regulation, and a diminished role for the United States in the global economy. Soon thereafter, everybody began calling everything the new normal, and Baum thought "overuse has rendered new normal meaningless."

Maybe, but the idea that something had permanently changed for the worse pervaded people's thinking. Richard Rahn, chairman of the Institute for Global Economic Growth, wrote in *The Washington Times* at year-end: "The long-term outlook for the stock market is not good, and here is why. For the past 100 years, there has been an inverse relationship between changes in the size of government and the growth or decline in the stock market." Because the U.S. government's share of GDP had gone from 21 percent to 28 percent in eighteen months, Rahn was pessimistic.

Years 10–13

In 2010, SnapSheet resumed salary increases after freezing them in 2008 and 2009, but did so gradually with only a 2 percent raise that year. In the three years following, it provided 3 percent annual increases, which was typical across the nation back then. Here's how these modest advancements trickled through the income and savings picture of our three investors:

	TABLE 60. Salary and Contributions from 2010 to 2013			
Year	Annual Salary ($)	Monthly Salary ($)	Monthly 401(k) Contribution (6% + 50% Match) ($)	Monthly Savings Contribution (4%) ($)
2010	73,812	6,151	554	246
2011	76,027	6,336	570	253
2012	78,307	6,526	587	261
2013	80,657	6,721	605	269

June 2010

After ignoring the fourth and final sell signal in the stick-around phase of his plan, which happened in the first quarter, Mark found himself in June 2010 face-to-face with another buy signal demanding more than his bond balance could handle. The 3Sig plan said to buy $12,479 worth of IJR, but he had only $9,495 in Vanguard GNMA. Should he make up the $2,984 shortfall with his bottom-buying account?

The decision was a lot easier this time than last time, for a couple of reasons. First, it was obvious that the only reason he didn't have enough in bonds was that he'd ignored four sell signals in a row. Three of the four had been good calls, as the stock market kept rising and had pushed the value of the money he kept invested in it even higher. He'd have had more than enough in his bond fund to cover the new buy signal if he'd been selling IJR on the way up, but his overall balance would have been much lower. Second, by June 2010 he'd already replenished his savings account up to a balance of $9,536. Seeing his savings balance rise along with his retirement balance created boldness from the wealth effect. He was more willing to throw extra money at stocks in a bad quarter after several good quarters than he had been at the bottom of several bad quarters that made everybody poorer. Besides, he figured this would probably be the last time he'd have to use the bottom-buying account for a while because the stick-around phase was over, so later sales of stock strength would bulk up his bond balance again. His wife agreed, and he used $2,984 from their savings account to fund the buy signal.

Garrett stayed in cash and Selma in PIMCO Total Return, and both were happy, given the prevalent belief that stocks were still trapped in a long-term bear market with occasional bounces along the way. That quarter's 12 percent drop in the S&P 500 emboldened bears to say, "See? Told you so."

In a June 11, 2010, article titled, "Why the Worst Isn't over Yet," David Rosenberg, chief economist at Gluskin Sheff, told *Fortune* that stocks were only 60 percent of the way through a secular bear market and that "rallies are to be rented and not owned." His overall advice? "Be very defensive. I would be 30 percent equities, 50 percent bonds, and 20 percent cash." On the other hand, he thought gold was "in a secular bull market" and predicted it would reach $3,000 per ounce in the inflationary environment sure to come from the Federal Reserve's balance sheet expansion from $850 billion in mid-2007 to $2.3 trillion that summer, when gold bounced around $1,200 per ounce. Garrett made note of this idea.

December 2010

At the end of their tenth calendar year at SnapSheet, the 401(k) balances of our three investors had diverged noticeably:

TABLE 61. December 2010 401(K) Balances of Garrett, Selma, and Mark

Investor	December 31, 2010 401(k) Balance ($)
Garrett	64,090
Selma	71,622
Mark	131,574

This disparity was not lost on Garrett, despite his seeing bearish commentary in every direction: the z-vals were warning of inflation from the Fed's "dollar-killing policies"; collapse in the euro zone; crushing debt in Japan; the anemic recovery in America, which saw an alarmingly low labor force participation rate; and most of all, the fact that stocks weren't higher due to fundamental improvement but only because their prices were being propped up by Federal Reserve chairman Ben Bernanke's easy-money fixation. Couldn't people see this? It was a false rally. The Fed pumped cash with abandon, creating another bubble that would end badly. Garrett had learned the hard way that what goes up can come down, and things had gone up just a little too quickly in the past two years with no demonstrable improvement in the situation.

Doug Kass reappeared on Garrett's screen during a free trial of the $999.95-per-year RealMoneyPro service, warning in a December 15, 2010, article titled, "Kass: Color Me More Bearish," that stocks were "overbought and overloved," and citing "the rapidity of the rise in interest rates" as one of several reasons to be cautious. Kass lamented that the "country's leadership has taken the easy route and has demonstrated still further that there will be no meaningful movement on our burgeoning deficit. The bond vigilantes smell blood, recognize this inertia and are demanding a price to be paid in much higher interest rates." He concluded: "I believe the prudent course shouldn't be the adoption of too much risk at the current time," then reiterated his article's title, "Color me more bearish."

Garrett had to do something, though. He heard how well Selma had performed with her all-bond portfolio and thought about copying her for a while until he figured out an edge. He didn't want to be one of the dumb money retail investors who buy higher stock prices just before another rollover, but he couldn't just stay in zero-interest cash forever.

The problem with bonds, according to his newsletters, was that their best days were probably over. They'd had a great run as investors sought safety, and inexplicably, they had not seen lower interest rates that autumn as the crisis in Europe accelerated and the Fed kicked off another quantitative easing program, dubbed QE2, for $600 billion worth of long-term Treasuries. Bond watchers called the failure of rates to fall in the face of such buying a sea change in the market, one suggesting a bond price top. This had Garrett thinking an all-bond stance wasn't a prudent choice. He decided he'd put only half his capital into a bond fund.

He settled on DoubleLine Total Return, under lead manager Jeffrey Gundlach and comanager Philip Barach, two of just a handful of bond jockeys who could hold a candle to Bill Gross at PIMCO. Gundlach and Barach did well investing in mortgage-backed securities while running a fund at TCW from 1993 to 2009, and that took skill given the subprime smash-up. Garrett remembered Gundlach predicting in September 2007 that mortgage delinquencies and foreclosures would accelerate, and boy had he been right. After departing TCW in 2009, Gundlach started DoubleLine Total Return in April 2010, and it was already up 16 percent in eight months. The comanagers put half the fund in long-term, government-backed mortgages and the other half in nongovernment-backed, including subprime and Alt-A mortgages, at deep discounts to their original prices. The fund was supposedly well shielded from rising interest rates, with analysts estimating that a 1 percent uptick in rates would push the fund down a mere 3 percent or so. Putting half his capital with Gundlach and Barach, two proven bond market operators, looked smart to Garrett. It would get him back in the market without exposing him too much to the dangers that Kass and others saw in stocks at high prices.

With a quarter of his account, he would finally buy gold. Since summer, he'd begun looking at the best inflation protection known to man, what the great economist John Maynard Keynes called the "barbarous relic." Garrett read articles online about gold and silver and bought a new book called *Hard Money: Taking Gold to a Higher Investment Level,* by Shayne McGuire, head of global research at the Teacher Retirement System of Texas and manager of its $500 million GBI Gold Fund, one of the world's largest pension funds.

McGuire called gold "the best method for shorting the government," and argued, "Betting against government—that is, on a sudden, sharp rise in inflation—has strong odds in the midst of surging government deficits." Inflation, even hyperinflation, "can erupt when the public grows wary of the money being printed in growing quantities by monetary authorities, which are forced to buy—to 'monetize,' in the financial vernacular—a surging supply of government bonds that the markets no longer all want to buy." He pointed out that "Gold is the only credible currency whose quantity cannot be expanded at will to meet the spending needs of governments in distress. By its very nature it remains scarce and rises in value as the supply of paper money grows." Garrett thought gold could provide just the adrenaline shot his account needed. According to McGuire, "Over the past decade, stocks were down 24 percent while gold rose 280 percent, a fact that would have benefited any fund with a significant gold investment. Gold was beating stocks even during the 2002–07 stock-market rally." This was very convincing, as was the metal's continued rise after the bear market bottom in March 2009. McGuire wrote, "I strongly believe that present financial conditions are about to transform the investment strategies of the world's largest investment funds in a way that will cause gold to surge substantially higher."

After long deliberation, Garrett concluded that he needed to be bold if he was ever going to make up for lost time. His bond allocation was safe enough, so he'd go for it with a quarter of his remaining capital by putting it in gold via SPDR Gold Shares, the most liquid gold ETF. At the end of December 2010, then, his portfolio moved from all cash to this:

TABLE 62. Garrett's Portfolio at the End of December 2010

Investment	Allocation (%)
Cash	25
DoubleLine Total Return (DLTNX)	50
SPDR Gold Shares (GLD)	25

Selma was also ready for a change. The financial planner at her church finally convinced her to move some of her account out of PIMCO Total Return and into stocks. "At your age, you just can't keep everything in bonds," the planner said. Selma replied that bonds had been good to her, far better than stocks had been, and that the last thing she wanted to do was go through another crash like the last two. The planner said such crashes were rare, to which Selma replied, "Not in the past decade, they haven't been." Nonetheless, she reluctantly agreed to move half her account back into stocks, this time dividing the stock portion evenly between just Artisan International and Longleaf Partners. Artisan had had a rough 2010, but analysts chalked this up to the fund's deployment of capital in undervalued European stocks, and most thought the short-term underperformance would be rewarded later. Longleaf had regained its stride, beating 90 percent of mutual funds in its large-blend category in 2010, and Morningstar noted "an absence of steep losses among the fund's larger holdings," which reassured Selma. At the end of December 2010, her portfolio became:

TABLE 63. Selma's Portfolio at the End of December 2010

Investment	Allocation (%)
Artisan International (ARTIX)	25
Longleaf Partners (LLPFX)	25
PIMCO Total Return (PTTDX)	50

Both Garrett and Selma specified for their automatic monthly contributions to be divided along the same allocations they'd set up at the end of December.

As for Mark, he was happily back to his default mode of ignoring markets. He'd exited the stick-around phase of his plan and resumed following the signal as usual after the first quarter. It looked like the hard times he'd experienced when deciding whether to use his bottom-buying account were over. After two big IJR sales in the third and fourth quarters of 2010, for respective amounts of $5,397 and $12,719, his bond allocation returned to a comfortable 17 percent of his account, and he returned to cheerfully disregarding all stock market information beyond quarterly closing prices. Whenever Garrett offered forecasts or warnings from whichever z-val currently topped his research pile, Mark just held up three fingers for 3Sig and said, "Good luck."

December 2011

At the end of their eleventh calendar year at SnapSheet, the 401(k) balances of our three investors showed Mark to be doing nearly twice as well as his colleagues:

TABLE 64. December 2011 401(K) Balances of Garrett, Selma, and Mark

Investor	December 30, 2011 401(k) Balance ($)
Garrett	75,512
Selma	77,863
Mark	145,738

Garrett felt much better, nonetheless. Including his contributions, his double-barreled bond/gold portfolio had grown his balance 18 percent for the year, from $64,090 to $75,512. What's more, he was pleased to note that his DoubleLine Total Return bond fund had outperformed Selma's PIMCO Total Return. DoubleLine gained 1 percent in price while paying 88.2 cents per share in monthly dividends for the year. By contrast, PIMCO was flat in price while paying 39.5 cents in dividends. At the end of December 2011, DoubleLine's yield was 8.0 percent compared with 3.6 percent at PIMCO. Take that, Selma!

More important, Garrett had discovered the joy of bonds. DoubleLine's price moved little throughout the year as it paid about a 7-cent dividend per share every month no matter what happened in the news. He could see why Selma had moved her whole account to PIMCO in the subprime crisis, and also why her account had kept growing impressively in the quarters that followed. Bonds weren't bad, not bad at all. That's not what his newsletters had led him to believe.

Even better, his gold bet had gone swimmingly, up almost 10 percent for the year after an initial drop in January of 6.4 percent that nearly sent him for the exits. He held on to the shares he'd bought the month before, however, and continued buying more shares every month with a quarter of his monthly contribution, and GLD recovered smartly over the course of the year.

There was something gratifying about achieving such big gains without owning a single stock or stock fund. The nonmainstream feel of bonds and gold, and the rare combination of the two that he'd achieved by paying attention to information that most investors ignored, put him in rarefied air, at least in his own mind. "Let the hoi polloi buy stocks," he told his wife that month after reporting the substantial appreciation in their retirement account. "We'll stick with bonds and gold."

Meanwhile, Selma was disheartened by her account faring worse after the reintroduction of stocks than it would have done had she left it entirely in PIMCO Total Return. Artisan International slipped 9 percent in 2011; Longleaf Partners, 6 percent. She calculated what her balance would have been had she not deviated from the 100 percent allocation to PIMCO, and came up with $81,329. After diluting PIMCO down to half her account and dividing the other half between Artisan and Longleaf, she'd ended 2011 at a balance of only $77,863. It wasn't a big difference, but it did underscore the appeal of handing money over to Bill Gross and the PIMCO posse, who seemed never to slip up.

She mentioned this offhandedly to the financial planner at her church one Sunday that December, and the planner said, "Give it time. Market history proves that diversifying into stocks pays off in the end." Selma wondered what end, but let it go. She'd stay the course to eventually benefit when Artisan and Longleaf recovered. *Recovered.* Now there was a word she'd never had to use with PIMCO Total Return. The fund just moved higher, come what may. No wonder Gross was a billionaire, and that people called him the Bond King.

Mark did nothing but follow 3Sig at the end of each quarter. The plan had called for a big buy in the third quarter of the year— $28,095 worth of IJR—but his bond balance of $29,249 had been enough to cover it, so he hadn't even paused before placing the order. In this current fourth quarter, the very next one following the big buy, his plan signaled a time to take profits. He followed it, selling $15,826 worth of IJR, which put his bond balance at a comfortable 13 percent of his account.

Unbeknownst to Mark, the z-vals had been fretting up a storm in the third quarter of his big buy. They certainly hadn't recommended buying. The most prevalent worry was that the "failed policies" of President Barack Obama would smother America in national debt, which already tallied $14 trillion while the economy still struggled. In fact, it was worsening again. In a September 15, 2011, article in *The Fiscal Times* titled, "Economists Double Down on a Double Dip Recession," Michelle Hirsch reported:

> A new series of economic reports out today confirm U.S. economists' fear that the early signs of a second recession are taking hold. Weekly jobless claims hit a 2-month high indicating employers are pulling back in an already weak labor market. Labor Department figures show jobless benefits applications rose 11,000 to 428,000 last week, pushing the average up for the fourth straight week to 419,500. Economists agree that applications need to dip below 375,000 to signal hiring is picking up enough to cut the nation's 9.1 percent unemployment rate. "The trend in jobless claims is an important input into our recession probability model, and if this trend were to continue for a number of weeks it would raise a warning flag on the state of the economy," said John Ryding, chief economist at RDQ Economics.

John B. Judis warned in a September 14, 2011, article in *The New Republic* titled simply, "Doom!" that the current prolonged recession:

> does not merely resemble the Great Depression; it is, to a real extent, a recurrence of it. It has the same unique causes and the same initial trajectory. Both downturns were triggered by a financial crisis coming on top of, and then deepening, a slowdown in industrial production and employment that had begun earlier and that was caused in part by rapid technological innovation. . . . The recessions in 1926 and 2001 were both followed by "jobless recoveries." . . .

In each case, the financial crisis generated an overhang of consumer and business debt that—along with growing unemployment and underemployment, and the failure of real wages to rise—reduced effective demand to the point where the economy, without extensive government intervention, spun into a downward spiral of joblessness. The accumulation of debt also undermined the use of monetary policy to revive the economy. Even zero-percent interest rates could not induce private investment.

At year's end, commentators still worried about the weak economic recovery. Gene Epstein mentioned in the December 17, 2011, *Barron's* that "The recovery from the 2008–09 recession has been the slowest since any recession in the post–World War II era. It has taken nine calendar quarters since the recession ended in the second quarter of 2009 for real gross domestic product to climb back to its fourth-quarter '07 peak."

Neil Irwin recapped the year in a December 31, 2011, article in *The Washington Post* titled, "After Wild Ride in 2011, Stocks Back Where They Started," which began, "After all the turbulence of the past year, the solid rallies and breathtaking drops, the U.S. stock market, like any roller coaster, ended back almost precisely where it started."

Various forecasts piled up as the year wound down. Reasons to freeze in place included a Greek default widely characterized as "inevitable," the potential global cash crunch that crashing European banks would unleash, a renewed collapse in the U.S. employment market, the falling U.S. savings rate, a dysfunctional government in Washington that would drive America to bankruptcy, and a U.S. debt downgrade that would wreak havoc on financial markets.

Even Garrett wasn't tuning in as much as he used to. Sometimes the experts were right, sometimes wrong. What was the point in paying attention?

December 2012

At the end of their twelfth calendar year at SnapSheet, the 401(k) balances of our three investors still differed greatly:

TABLE 65. December 2012 401(K) Balances of Garrett, Selma, and Mark

Investor	December 31, 2012 401(k) Balance ($)
Garrett	87,400
Selma	97,101
Mark	174,282

Garrett was beside himself. He'd begun tuning in to the z-vals again, who argued endlessly about the prospects for gold going forward. No other asset engendered views as far apart as the ones on gold. Half the commentators thought it was worth nothing in the long run because it's a nonproductive asset valued only because of its scarcity. The other half thought it was worth an infinitely high number because its scarcity made it the only monetary medium that would hold value in a world of endless money printing.

As this debate raged in 2012, Garrett's GLD position flatlined for the year. The metal had been declining steadily in the fourth quarter, from $1,800 an ounce at the beginning of October 2012 to less than $1,700 at the end of December. Mainstream financial media z-vals couldn't resist calling it "tarnished," but two of Garrett's newsletters remained steadfastly bullish on it, both agreeing with Tocqueville Gold Fund comanager Doug Groh, who told MarketWatch in December, "Monetary policy around the world is prompting investors to seek alternatives to whatever currency they're in." Groh said that developed countries were debasing their currencies as emerging markets bought gold, and predicted that "in the next year we'll see the $2,000 mark and the gold cycle [won't be] over until we see the $2,400 mark."

Somehow, Garrett didn't buy this. "Call it instinct," he told his wife. "I just think gold has done about all it's going to do in response to runaway money printing. It's not like they started pumping money just last week. They've been doing it for four years, but there's no inflation yet. I think that's why gold is falling and I think it'll keep falling."

Beyond that, he decided that all the bears were wrong. They'd been wrong all along. What he should have done was buy leveraged stock funds back in March 2009, when all the idiots said the world was ending. He knew it wasn't ending. He'd always known. Obviously the news couldn't have gotten any worse back then after all they'd been through. Why had he waited for cheaper prices? He promised himself he would pay more attention to the bulls from then on, starting by ignoring the bearish concerns about the fiscal cliff Washington was about to tumble over. Everybody was gloomy about Democrats and Republicans being unable to cut a budget deal, which would trigger automatic across-the-board spending cuts and tax increases, which would send the economy into a recession and push unemployment higher.

Here's what the bulls saw: private-sector growth of 3 percent, improving home prices, a rising stock market, and so much money parked in bonds that any adjustment back into stocks would send the market even higher. Edward Yardeni wrote in the *Financial Times* on December 10, 2012, "There should be enough growth to boost revenues and earnings for the S&P 500 companies by 5–7 percent. Valuation multiples should rise next year. If so, then the bull market should continue—sooner rather than later if there is a deal to avoid the fiscal cliff. If not, there is likely to be a correction that should provide lots of good buying opportunities."

A week later, in the *Barron's* cover story "Outlook 2013," Vito J. Racanelli reported, "The 10 strategists recently surveyed by *Barron's* see more gains ahead next year. Their mean S&P prediction for 2013—1562—implies a 10 percent price gain from current levels." The experts, from the likes of Barclays Capital, BlackRock, Goldman

Sachs, and Morgan Stanley, agreed that some kind of political deal would mitigate damage from the fiscal cliff.

So, back into stocks, Garrett concluded. He was tired of spinning his wheels and wanted to ratchet up the aggression. One of his newsletters thought the Fidelity Advisor Small Cap fund was set for a bang-up year ahead, and it appealed to Garrett for its potential to beat the small-cap index that had kept Mark dumbly happy for so long. The fund had trailed its category in 2012, but manager Jamie Harmon's focus on high-quality stocks and broader diversification was expected to reinvigorate performance in 2013. Over his seven years at the fund, Harmon was ahead of most of his peers, and the short-term setback looked like a chance to get future strong performance on sale. With DoubleLine beating Selma's PIMCO in the bond department, and Fidelity possibly beating Mark's index in the small-cap stock department, Garrett might finally gain traction in his account. He thought of tapping a third fund, just in case, but changed his mind after reading another glowing review of Small Cap's potential. He decided to focus on it with half his account while leaving the other half in DoubleLine. Here's how he went into 2013:

TABLE 66. Garrett's Portfolio at the End of December 2012

Investment	Allocation (%)
DoubleLine Total Return (DLTNX)	50
Fidelity Advisor Small Cap (FSCIX)	50

He was pretty sure this would get him back on track, with a smartly timed exit from gold into an undervalued small-cap fund that was ready to rock, and the best bond fund available.

Selma, on the other hand, was content to stick with her three-fund portfolio. It had gained 25 percent that year, after all, including her contributions. Her two stock funds had finally kicked into gear, with Artisan International gaining 24 percent and Longleaf Partners paying $4.52 in dividends. Her financial planner kept asking her, "Aren't you glad you went back to stocks?" Selma had been hesitant to say yes, but she was beginning to feel that she was glad. When she'd reallocated her portfolio two years prior, she'd put a quarter into each of Artisan and Longleaf while leaving half in PIMCO Total Return. She'd contributed those same allocations to each fund every month. In the two years that followed, their allocations ended up at exactly the same place they'd started:

TABLE 67. Selma's Portfolio at the End of December 2012

Investment	Allocation (%)
Artisan International (ARTIX)	25
Longleaf Partners (LLPFX)	25
PIMCO Total Return (PTTDX)	50

It was hard for Selma to miss that bonds had held their allocation in the supposed bull market under way in stocks. This, more than anything else, is why she continued resisting her financial planner's advice to move more of her bond allocation into stocks. Why? For excitement? "No thanks," Selma thought, and kept half her account in the only fund that had never let her down.

As for Mark, he just followed 3Sig with nary a thought about allocations or prognostications. It had issued two quarterly buy signals and two quarterly sell signals in 2012, and he followed each as always. In the current fourth quarter, it signaled a minor buy of $3,226 worth of IJR, fiscal cliff fracas notwithstanding. Even after the buy, his bond allocation was 16 percent of his account, well within the comfort zone. After the usual quarterly fifteen minutes of easy calculating and order placement, he rejoined his family for holiday activities.

June 2013

Halfway through their thirteenth calendar year at SnapSheet, the 401(k) balances of our three investors showed Mark miles ahead:

TABLE 68. June 2013 401(K) Balances of Garrett, Selma, and Mark

Investor	June 28, 2013 401(k) Balance ($)
Garrett	97,971
Selma	102,929
Mark	200,031

Garrett was pleased to see his gut instinct about the price of gold pay off in spades. It slipped under $1,600 an ounce in February and kept falling to less than $1,250 that June. The shares of GLD he sold for $162 at the end of December fell to $119 six months later, a 27 percent drop that he avoided by paying closer attention to the market than did most investors—at least that was his explanation. His replacement for GLD, Fidelity Advisor Small Cap, was up 16 percent in the same six months, making him feel doubly clever to have made the switch.

His DoubleLine Total Return ran circles around Selma's PIMCO Total Return, too. DoubleLine slipped 2.7 percent in price while paying a total of 25.2 cents in monthly dividends. PIMCO slipped 4.3 percent in price while paying 13.0 cents in dividends. Garrett still had the better bond fund! Too bad his small-cap stock fund wasn't doing any better than Mark's plain old IJR index. Fidelity had gained 16 percent in the first half of the year, but so had IJR. Worse, Fidelity paid nothing in dividends, while IJR paid out 49.6 cents per share. He decided to stick with Fidelity anyway. Maybe Small Cap's carefully chosen stocks that analysts marveled about the previous December would start to pull ahead of the index.

In any event, Garrett felt good to have gained 12 percent overall in the first half, including his contributions. That blew away Selma's 6 percent and wasn't too far behind Mark's 15 percent.

Selma had established deep enough trust in PIMCO Total Return to overlook its recent rough months, partly because it was easy to see the thorny patch it faced in the bond landscape. *The New York*

Times DealBook reported on June 24, 2013, that retail investors had sold "a record $48 billion worth of bond mutual funds so far in June" and that hedge funds and other big institutional investors had also been "closing out positions or stepping back from the bond market." Hans Humes, chief executive of the hedge fund Greylock Capital, told the paper, "The feeling you are getting out there is that people are selling first and asking questions later."

From the end of April to the end of June, Bill Gross's fund lost 5.1 percent, plus it paid dividends of only 2.2 cents and 1.7 cents, respectively, in May and June. The media pounced on Gross, saying he'd left his fund overexposed to rising yields when Federal Reserve chairman Ben Bernanke told Congress on May 22 that the central bank might begin tapering its stimulative bond-buying later in the year.

Gross defended himself in the June 25, 2013, online edition of *Barron's*: "High levels of leverage, both here and abroad, have made the global economy far more sensitive to interest rates. Whereas a decade or two ago the Fed could raise the fed funds rate by 500 basis points and expect the economy to slow, today if the Fed were to hike rates or taper suddenly, the economy couldn't handle it. All this suggests that investors who are selling Treasuries in anticipation that the Fed will ease out of the market might be disappointed."

Bloomberg reported two days later that bond funds had experienced record monthly redemptions through June 24 "amid signs the country's central bank may scale back its unprecedented stimulus." It warned that rising rates could "trigger hundreds of billions of dollars in redemptions" from bond holdings. Investors had already plucked $1.3 billion from Gross's fund in May, which was down 4 percent for the year, "trailing 93 percent of rivals."

"Let them go," Selma thought. Anybody viewing these modest setbacks as cause for concern obviously hadn't lived through the kinds of stock crashes she'd seen over the years. She would keep her capital in PIMCO, because if there was anybody who would find the way forward, it was Bill Gross. She left her account exactly as it had been, confident that the almost imperceptibly listing ship of bonds would right itself.

Meanwhile, unaware of all market drama, Mark ran his quarterly calculation at home. The plan signaled its second sale in a row for the year, but a small one, at just $202. The first-quarter sale had been $11,470. That pushed his bond allocation up to 24 percent, where it remained after the second-quarter sale. It looked like another bull market was under way in his IJR ledger, and he would probably have to rebalance his bond allocation back to 20 percent after it reached 30 percent again, just as he'd done in the dot-com crash recovery eleven years earlier. "The more things change, the more they stay the same," he thought. He closed his notebook for the quarter and went for a walk.

Analysis

Which of these three investment paths would you like to follow? More people than you think choose Garrett's path, flitting from one investment idea to another based on the news of the moment or the expert du jour, most of which fade out with time. If anything, this history was too kind to Garrett, limiting him to a focused portfolio of mostly reasonable ideas. In the real world, investors such as Garrett end up with dozens of positions in their portfolios, some that are downright loony, and their performance suffers accordingly.

All things considered, Garrett didn't do too badly. His Air Transportation fund performed well in the first quarter of 2002. Keeping his monthly contributions in safe cash for six months from that year's difficult autumn worked out as he'd hoped, and he was able to buy cheaper prices later. His Fidelity Select Defense & Aerospace Portfolio fund was a winner during the early years of the Iraq War. His ExxonMobil position held up in the volatility of the subprime mortgage crash of 2008 and paid a reassuring dividend that even grew through the mess. He made an excellent choice in buying

DoubleLine Total Return. He bailed out of gold before its 2013 swan dive.

Getting some moves right is trickier than getting none right, because it feeds false hope. Among Garrett's mistakes were just enough good calls to keep the illusion of market-beating skill alive in him. This is often the case, and it's bolstered when the market hits a bull stride. Garrett became extra confident in his skills, mistaking his growing account balance at the peak of the bull for talent rather than luck, and dispensing officious analytical advice with all the authority of a real z-val. I'm not ridiculing Garrett here, because he's not unique. He's an archetype, cloned countless times and set loose with real money in the market's house of mirrors. While he serves as a cautionary tale, let's at least give him credit for getting several things right in his journey through the zero-validity environment.

He fared worse than Selma, however, even though she expended much less energy in the management of her account. Her well-researched portfolio of superb funds combined with relentless dollar-cost averaging into them powered her higher through good times and bad. Well, not all the bad times. Her decision to retreat to PIMCO Total Return in the depths of the autumn 2008 credit crisis was the exception, but a better call than hiding in cash, as Garrett and millions of other investors did at that time.

Of course, the best performance by far was Mark's, and he achieved it with little stress and low expenses. He followed 3Sig to remain mostly calm through this tumultuous time in financial history. We have to say "mostly calm," because even the stoniest investors were unable to ignore the calamity of the credit crunch. People following the signal plan should do so in full awareness that it's possible for a buy signal to demand more capital than is available in an investor's bond balance, and it's unnerving to put bottom-buying capital to work. It happens only in the worst of circumstances, when the news is at its most dire, the z-vals at their loudest, the throngs of Peter Perfects at their preachiest . . . and prices at their lowest. That's why it's called a bottom-buying account, after all.

This is hard to get through our heads. It's the worst news that produces the best buying prices. Because we're easily gripped by fear, which can prevent us from taking advantage of splendid buying opportunities, we need the signal to overcome our inclinations. It tells us what to do. Even when you can't do exactly what it tells you, as happened to Mark in March 2009 at the very bottom of the bear, you can follow it in spirit to much better results than if you try interpreting the cacophony of information from supposed experts.

The coin tossing commentators bellow their most confusing harangues precisely when it's important to do the right thing by either buying low or selling high. When prices are low, we're fearful and more likely to tune into the doomsayers urging caution. When prices are high, we're greedy and more likely to tune into the cheerleaders urging aggression. Even if only half the voices urge selling at the bottom and buying at the top, our tendencies put the odds on following the wrong ones. Because key moments to buy and sell with significant impact are rare, it doesn't take many missed moves to impair performance permanently by either buying a major top or selling a major bottom. Just ask Garrett and Selma. Their missing most of the rally off the March 2009 low probably destroyed their chances of ever retiring with as much money as Mark will amass.

Stick with the dispassionate signal. It's smarter than the z-vals and even smarter than a collection of top-ranked managers of the type Selma assembled. She did extremely well, considerably better than almost any average 401(k) account in this same time frame, because most portfolios end up in mediocre funds that overcharge and underdeliver. Whereas Selma sat atop a collection of blue-ribbon funds, most investors are lucky to average honorable-mention funds in their lousy lineup of choices. You can be sure that if plain old indexes in the signal plan beat a portfolio containing all-stars like Artisan International, Longleaf Partners, and PIMCO Total Return, they'll stomp ordinary funds to bits.

The fact is stocks trade as a block in extreme times, which are the very best times to be buying low or selling high. Even highly rated funds just mimic indexes in such times, making it hard to understand why anybody pays their expensive fees. In the fourth quarter of 2008, the heart of the credit crunch, almost all stock funds delivered wretched returns, even the ones leading the ranking systems at Morningstar and Value Line. Selma discovered this firsthand.

You may wonder if there's an unfair comparison taking place. You might consider it convenient in this history that both Garrett and Selma lost their nerve at the bottom of the bear market while Mark stuck it out. This isn't unfair, though, because their choice to sell was common at the time, as you'll read in a moment. Providing investors with clear signals to do the right thing, such as buying into bear markets and staying put through bottoms, is the very point of 3Sig and is necessary for the very reason that investors so often do exactly the wrong thing. Garrett bailed out because he listened to z-vals, and an enormous percentage of investors did as he did in the credit crunch.

In a December 22, 2008, story titled, "Stock Investors Lose Faith, Pull Out Record Amounts," *The Wall Street Journal* reported that "a record $72 billion" fled stock funds in the previous October alone, according to the Investment Company Institute (ICI). Later, ICI would report that by the end of the year, stock funds had lost $234 billion. Nearly 42 percent of equity capital cashed out of cascading prices from May to December 2008, and investors panicked out of every fund category tracked by ICI: domestic equity, world equity, hybrid, total bond, taxable bond, and municipal bond in September, October, November, and December of that year.

The supposed smart money didn't behave any more intelligently. In a December 14, 2008, story titled, "Fleeing Investors Put a Strain on Funds," *The New York Times* reported that "a growing number of hedge funds are trying to slow the exodus" of investors racing for the exits. A representative of an investment advisory firm managing about $20 billion in assets said that withdrawals had been gathering steam for months as the markets collapsed. In January 2009, Hedge Fund Research confirmed this trend in reporting that $152 billion had fled hedge funds in the fourth quarter. The president of the research firm said in the statement, "Investor risk aversion remained at historically extreme levels through year end. Investor redemptions were widespread and indiscriminate across fund strategies, regions, asset sizes and performance."

Garrett and Selma weren't alone in bailing out of the market. It's easy to see the pressure they faced to do so. In that very difficult moment, Mark's 3 percent signal advised getting in with both feet, the very opposite of popular pressure. The signal was right.

A main takeaway from this history is that almost all market information is noise. Notice the recurring news themes in this chapter, some of which are undoubtedly reappearing in the financial media as you read these words. There's always strife somewhere in the world, and somebody always worries that it will pressure stock prices lower. Federal Reserve policies are always offered as evidence that either higher or lower stock prices are on the way. Washington is always dysfunctional, forever pushing the country over some kind of cliff or past a point of no return, and somebody always expects this to either damage stocks immediately or mute their future performance.

Z-vals always keep at hand a list of beaten-down stocks recommended for dramatic recovery, some of which do recover while others don't. They crow about the coin tosses they win and stay quiet about the ones they lose. Investors following such tips will also win some and lose some, then feel emboldened by their random winnings that don't add up to as much as they would have made by just owning a stock index with most of their capital. Analysts never say they were wrong, just early or late. Finally, there's always an obsession with "the current market" or "today's market" or "the market now," implying that there's something unique about the breaking news of the moment that investors must consider.

Over time, almost none of these recurring themes matter, and without the benefit of hindsight, even the ones that do matter are indistinguishable from the ones that don't. The best we can do is react intelligently to what already happened in the past rather than guessing what might happen in the future. The 3Sig plan is designed for this purpose.

Here's a chart of our three investors' 401(k) balances over the time frame in this chapter, December 2000 to June 2013, using the twelve balances shown in the narrative as data points:

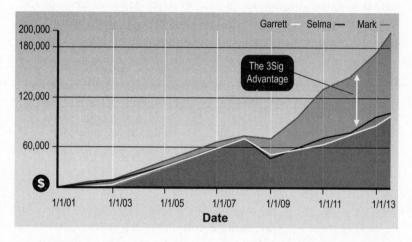

The 401(k) balances of Garrett, Selma, and Mark, December 2000 to June 2013.

Notice that in the 2003–2007 bull market, both Garrett and Selma pulled close behind Mark. This is to be expected when an investor begins 3Sig at or near the beginning of a bull market, because they will not be fully invested in stocks during a phase of strong appreciation. As we saw with our three investors, 3Sig tends to reassert itself for a permanent or at least long-term lead over competing strategies when it signals buying into and holding through bear markets. Almost all other strategies fall apart in extreme bear markets, given their lack of guidance to the contrary of what media and our instincts tell us to do. Locking in bear market losses then missing out on subsequent bull market gains translates into permanently diminished end balances for most investors. Those, such as Mark, who stay with 3Sig will not suffer this fate.

Don't think I forgot about the identical savings account set up by our three investors. Beginning in 2003, each contributed 4 percent of their gross salary. Only Mark used his for anything during the time frame, withdrawing $10,876 in the fourth quarter of 2008 to fund the first of two big buy signals during the bottoming of the credit crisis, and $2,984 in the second quarter of 2010 to fund the first buy signal coming out of his "30 down, stick around" phase. Garrett and Selma never withdrew any of their safe savings. Here's how their savings accounts concluded the period:

TABLE 69. June 2013 Savings Account Balances of Garrett, Selma, and Mark

Investor	June 28, 2013 Savings Account Balance ($)
Garrett	29,670
Selma	29,670
Mark	15,810

Using the savings account for bottom buying proved well worth it for Mark. Even after considering the $13,860 less he had in savings after funding the two buy signals, he still finished far ahead of his peers. This is for obvious reasons. Money invested at key stock market bottoms will always outperform money parked in static cash.

You may wonder how 3Sig stacks up against other variations that, however unlikely in the real world, are intriguing to consider. The next table starts off with the results of our three investors, then shows how ten other plans would have fared with their same monthly contributions:

TABLE 70. 3Sig Beating a Variety of Investing Plans

Plan Number	Plan from December 2000 to June 2013	Initial Balance ($)	Total Monthly Contributions ($)	New Cash Needed ($)	June 28, 2013 401(k) Balance ($)
1	Garrett actual	10,000	76,770	0	97,971
2	Selma actual	10,000	76,770	0	102,929
3	Mark actual	10,000	76,770	13,860	200,031
4	Selma, no bear market selling; initial portfolio throughout	10,000	76,770	0	124,646
5	Mark, no bottom buying, only funding signals with bond balance throughout	10,000	76,770	0	171,253
6	Mark, all bottom buying, fully funding every buy signal	10,000	76,770	29,373	238,492
7	Dollar-cost averaging S&P 500 via SPY; same contributions as other plans	10,000	76,770	0	133,773
8	Dollar-cost averaging S&P Small-Cap 600 via IJR; same contributions as other plans	10,000	76,770	0	166,658
9	Dollar-cost averaging 80/20 allocation to S&P Small-Cap 600 via IJR and Vanguard GNMA; same contributions as other plans	10,000	76,770	0	156,998
10	Dollar-cost averaging S&P 500 via SPY; same contributions as other plans plus Mark's $13,860 new cash evenly distributed across all contributions	10,000	90,630	0	155,487
11	Dollar-cost averaging S&P Small-Cap 600 via IJR; same contributions as other plans plus Mark's $13,860 new cash evenly distributed across all contributions	$10,000	90,630	0	192,613

(continued)

Plan Number	Plan from December 2000 to June 2013	Initial Balance ($)	Total Monthly Contributions ($)	New Cash Needed ($)	June 28, 2013 401(k) Balance ($)
12	Dollar-cost averaging S&P 500 via SPY; same contributions as other plans plus $29,373 new cash for all buy signals evenly distributed across all contributions	10,000	106,143	0	179,793
13	Dollar-cost averaging S&P Small-Cap 600 via IJR; same contributions as other plans plus $29,373 new cash for all buy signals evenly distributed across all contributions	10,000	106,143	0	221,667

This table shows 3Sig outperforming other approaches even when they're perfectly executed. Add in the near certainty that they won't be perfectly executed, and 3Sig's superiority becomes unmistakable.

Look at plans 4 and 5, which show Selma and Mark doing nothing but following their initial plans, no bear market selling for Selma or bottom buying for Mark. They ended up with starkly different balances: $124,646 for Selma and $171,253 for Mark. This is a resounding triumph for 3Sig because it vanquished Selma's portfolio, which included some of the most highly rated actively managed funds in the world, and did so paying 82 percent less than she paid in expense ratios. Remember that it's now possible to run 3Sig at an even cheaper cost than Mark did because new ETFs offer the same index exposure at lower fees than the very low ones he paid, thus the cost advantage is greater these days. Remember, too, that 3Sig achieves a bigger outperformance against more typical portfolios of mediocre funds from the fat part of the bell curve, and better still against laggards at the bad end of the curve. The overwhelming majority of actively managed funds are worse than the champions that powered Selma's portfolio.

Next, turn your attention to Plans 7, 8, and 9, which show

dollar-cost averaging the monthly contributions of our three investors into the S&P 500 via SPY, the S&P Small-Cap 600 via IJR, and an 80/20 allocation to IJR and Vanguard GNMA, respectively. These perfectly executed dollar-cost averaging plans beat Selma's all-star portfolio in Plan 4, but did not beat Mark's 3Sig in Plan 5. This is another impressive feather in 3Sig's cap.

The advantage of Mark's bottom-buying account becomes clear when looking at plans 10 through 13. On top of the same monthly contributions, evenly distributing the $13,860 Mark used from his bottom-buying account across all 150 months of the time frame into SPY and IJR produced lower ending balances of $155,487 in SPY and $192,613 in IJR than Mark's $200,031. If we take it a step further and add to the monthly contributions the $29,373 of bottom-buying capital required to have fully funded all Mark's buy signals, we end up with $179,793 in SPY and $221,667 in IJR, but $238,492 in Mark's 3Sig plan—the all-bottom-buying version shown in Plan 6.

Across several variations, then, 3Sig outperformed dollar-cost averaging: with no bottom buying against top-ranked funds and indexes, with partial bottom buying against indexes, and with complete bottom buying against indexes. If 3Sig beats the very formidable dollar-cost averaging strategy this clearly, it's easy to see why less effective ideas of the day from z-vals and Peter Perfect fall utterly flat against it.

Executive Summary of This Chapter

The 3Sig plan provides a low-stress beacon through the chaos of the stock market. This chapter followed the experiences of Garrett, Selma, and Mark, three investors working at the same company earning the same income. Garrett followed z-val advice in his 401(k). Selma assembled a portfolio of superb mutual funds and dollar-cost averaged into them. Mark ran 3Sig with IJR and Vanguard GNMA. Even though he funded only two bottom-buying opportunities, Mark came out far ahead of Garrett and Selma. This is typical, and why you should run 3Sig in your retirement account. Key takeaways:

✔ Beware high expense ratios. Garrett and Selma paid much more for the funds they chose, but underperformed Mark's cheap index funds.

✔ Frenetic activity is a waste. Garrett's method of trying this and then trying that only frustrated him. His occasional wins provided false confidence that harmed him later.

✔ Severe bear markets can be emotionally hard on 3Sig followers, too. Using a bottom-buying account isn't easy when everybody is swearing off stocks, but it's worth it.

✔ Because key moments to buy and sell with significant impact are rare, it doesn't take many missed moves to permanently impair performance by either buying a major top or selling a major bottom. After panicking out of stocks in the bear market and then missing most of the recovery, Garrett and Selma are unlikely *ever* to catch up with Mark's balance.

✔ There are many recurring themes cited as reason to think stock prices will move up or down, among them: global strife, Federal Reserve policies, and dysfunction in Washington. Over time, almost none of these recurring themes matters, and without the benefit of hindsight, even the ones that do matter are indistinguishable from the ones that don't.

✔ The 3Sig plan is designed to react intelligently to what has already happened. It doesn't consider what might happen, and neither should you.

✔ Because 3Sig even beats formidable dollar-cost averaging plans into all-star funds and indexes, z-vals and Peter Perfect are annihilated by it.

CHAPTER EIGHT
Happy Signaling

A t the end of the introduction, I invited you to come with me on a journey to a better way to invest. We found it. The 3Sig plan will put your account on a powerful growth path that doesn't require much of your energy or cause you undue stress. You'll never again take seriously the squawkers of the financial media. Whenever you encounter them, you'll smile and shake your head, knowing they're just poor z-vals who will be soundly beaten by your program over time.

If you'll permit me a moment of philosophical musing, I'd like to tell you that I've found a deeper wisdom from many years of researching and then implementing 3Sig. Rising above the fray of the stock market, one of humanity's most fervent endeavors into which enormous intellectual capital is poured, and doing better than the breathless commentators by retreating into silence and near inaction, is instructive. People who meditate talk of the need to escape our "monkey mind," that always active thought device between our ears that fires off random notions. If we can acknowledge its existence and tame it, we can achieve greater contentment.

The stock market is humanity's monkey mind writ large. For many, there is no greater cacophony, no greater distraction from life than the news cycle connected to financial markets. The more enlightened way to navigate the complexity is by letting it all go, reducing the disorder to a concise list of prices, visiting that list just four times a year, letting an unemotional formula tell you what the prices mean you should do, and then doing it. This higher state of investing not only performs better; it costs less and uses less of your limited time on earth.

Life is for living, not flailing stressfully in a zero-validity environment. Put your ambition into areas where intuition makes a difference. Don't wear it out on a fruitless quest to divine the future. Put your financial security on autopilot and turn your attention elsewhere. I hope I've helped you do this. You're too important to waste yourself on stocks.

Keep in touch. My address is jason@jasonkelly.com. I provide updates and more information at jasonkelly.com, and my e-mail list is free. Thank you for reading, my friend. I wish you much happiness in the stress-free time created by 3Sig.

APPENDIX 1

Mark's Plan

You read about Mark's 3Sig journey in Chapter 7. His plan's complete worksheet appears over the next four pages in this appendix. It uses unadjusted prices from December 2000 to June 2013. In some places, the plan's balances differ by a dollar from the ones you saw in Chapter 7 due to my rounding them in various examples and then making sure they added up correctly in the narrative.

Areas of particular importance are shaded in the table and summarized in the key at the bottom. Mark's quarterly cash contributions changed over time. Each time they did, the new amount was manually entered the first time it happened and then automatically pulled forward by the spreadsheet. The manual entries are shaded. In the "Order Adjust" column, notice when Mark needed to move his excess VFIIX balance into IJR in Q202, and when he did not fund his entire buy signal in Q109 but instead used only his VFIIX balance.

You can see the price history of SPY in the second column, and the two times it triggered the "30 down, stick around" rule, prompting Mark to skip four sell signals each time: the ones from Q203 to Q104, and the ones from Q209 to Q110. Finally, IJR split 3-for-1 in Q205, which is indicated in that row with an underline.

To get a single-page printable version of the table for reference as you reread Chapter 7, and a working copy of a similar spreadsheet, please visit jasonkelly.com/3sig.

Quarter	SPY Price	UR Price	UR Div	VFIIX Price	VFIIX Div	UR Shares Before Action	Quarter Cash Contrib	UR Balance Before Action	3% Growth + 50% Cash Contrib (Signal Line)	Shares Needed to Reach Signal Line	Order Adjust
Q400	$131.19	$108.09		$10.24	0.171	74.01		$8,000			
Q101	$116.69	$101.50	0.040	$10.35	0.170	74.01	$1,215	$7,512	$8,848	87.17	
Q201	$122.60	$114.01	0.036	$10.29	0.167	87.17	$1,215	$9,938	$9,720	85.26	
Q301	$104.44	$95.50		$10.54	0.164	85.26	$1,215	$8,142	$10,620	111.20	
Q401	$114.30	$114.40	0.118	$10.38	0.157	111.20	$1,215	$12,721	$11,546	100.92	
Q102	$114.52	$122.49	0.036	$10.33	0.156	100.92	$1,275	$12,362	$12,529	102.29	
Q202	$98.96	$114.50	0.051	$10.55	0.054	102.29	$1,275	$11,712	$13,543	118.28	Excess VFIIX Bal
Q302	$81.79	$93.14	0.058	$10.76	0.139	132.59	$1,275	$12,349	$16,274	174.73	
Q402	$88.23	$97.45	0.066	$10.75	0.113	174.73	$1,275	$17,027	$17,400	178.55	
Q103	$84.74	$91.48	0.049	$10.72	0.045	178.55	$1,341	$16,334	$18,592	203.24	
Q203	$97.63	$109.65	0.070	$10.70	0.128	203.24	$1,341	$22,285	$19,821	180.76	Sell Sig Ignored
Q303	$99.95	$117.38	0.072	$10.56	0.118	203.24	$1,341	$23,856	$23,624	201.26	Sell Sig Ignored
Q403	$111.28	$134.00	0.082	$10.50	0.125	203.24	$1,341	$27,234	$25,242	188.38	Sell Sig Ignored
Q104	$113.10	$142.40	0.072	$10.54	0.127	203.24	$1,407	$28,941	$28,754	201.93	Sell Sig Ignored
Q204	$114.53	$147.20	0.101	$10.29	0.120	203.24	$1,407	$29,917	$30,513	207.29	
Q304	$111.76	$144.24	0.094	$10.43	0.120	207.29	$1,407	$29,899	$32,132	222.77	
Q404	$120.87	$162.71	0.131	$10.44	0.117	222.77	$1,407	$36,246	$33,799	207.73	
Q105	$117.96	$158.85	0.164	$10.33	0.119	207.73	$1,476	$32,997	$35,551	223.80	
Q205	$119.18	$55.02	0.105	$10.43	0.120	671.41	$1,476	$36,941	$37,356	678.95	
Q305	$123.04	$57.76	0.103	$10.31	0.118	678.95	$1,476	$39,216	$39,214	678.92	
Q405	$124.51	$57.80	0.130	$10.30	0.123	678.92	$1,476	$39,242	$41,129	711.57	
Q106	$129.83	$65.23		$10.16	0.128	711.57	$1,551	$46,416	$43,138	661.32	
Q206	$127.28	$62.10	0.105	$9.96	0.129	661.32	$1,551	$41,068	$45,208	727.98	
Q306	$133.58	$61.29		$10.19	0.131	727.98	$1,551	$44,618	$47,340	772.39	
Q406	$141.62	$65.99		$10.21	0.132	772.39	$1,551	$50,970	$49,535	750.65	

Quarter	UR Shares to Buy or Sell (minus)	UR Shares to Buy or Sell (minus) After Order Adjust	VFIIX Shares + Divs Reinv + Cash Before Action	VFIIX Balance Before Action	VFIIX Shares After Action	VFIIX Balance After Action	New Cash Needed	VFIIX Shares After New Cash	VFIIX Balance After New Cash	VFIIX % of 3% Signal Balance	UR Shares After Action	UR Balance After Action	Total Balance
0400			195.31	$2,000		$2,000							$10,000
0101	13.16		316.20	$3,273	187.19	$1,937	$0	187.19	$1,937	18%	87.17	$8,848	$10,785
0201	-1.91		308.61	$3,176	329.75	$3,393	$0	329.75	$3,393	26%	85.26	$9,720	$13,114
0301	25.94		450.15	$4,745	215.12	$2,267	$0	215.12	$2,267	18%	111.20	$10,620	$12,887
0401	-10.28		336.69	$3,495	449.94	$4,670	$0	449.94	$4,670	29%	100.92	$11,546	$16,216
0102	1.37		580.52	$5,997	564.31	$5,829	$0	564.31	$5,829	32%	102.29	$12,529	$18,359
0202	15.99	30.30	688.55	$7,264	359.74	$3,795	$0	359.75	$3,795	20%	132.59	$15,181	$18,976
0302	42.14		483.60	$5,204	118.82	$1,279	$0	118.82	$1,279	7%	174.73	$16,274	$17,553
0402	3.82		239.75	$2,577	205.09	$2,205	$0	205.09	$2,205	11%	178.55	$17,400	$19,604
0103	24.69		331.86	$3,557	121.18	$1,299	$0	121.18	$1,299	7%	203.24	$18,592	$19,891
0203	-22.48	0.00	249.29	$2,667	249.29	$2,667	$0	249.29	$2,667	11%	203.24	$22,285	$24,952
0303	-1.98	0.00	380.45	$4,018	380.45	$4,018	$0	380.45	$4,018	14%	203.24	$23,856	$27,874
0403	-14.86	0.00	514.28	$5,400	514.28	$5,400	$0	514.28	$5,400	17%	203.24	$27,234	$32,634
0104	-1.31	0.00	655.35	$6,907	655.35	$6,907	$0	655.35	$6,907	19%	203.24	$28,941	$35,849
0204	4.05		801.73	$8,250	743.79	$7,654	$0	743.79	$7,654	20%	207.29	$30,513	$38,166
0304	15.48		889.11	$9,273	675.07	$7,041	$0	675.07	$7,041	18%	222.77	$32,132	$39,173
0404	-15.04		820.20	$8,563	1,054.59	$11,010	$0	1,054.59	$11,010	25%	207.73	$33,799	$44,809
0105	16.08		1,212.92	$12,529	965.70	$9,976	$0	965.70	$9,976	22%	223.80	$35,551	$45,527
0205	7.54		1,125.08	$11,735	1,085.32	$11,320	$0	1,085.32	$11,320	23%	678.95	$37,356	$48,676
0305	-0.03		1,247.69	$12,864	1,247.85	$12,865	$0	1,247.85	$12,865	25%	678.92	$39,214	$52,080
0405	32.65		1,414.62	$14,571	1,231.39	$12,683	$0	1,231.39	$12,683	24%	711.57	$41,129	$53,812
0106	-50.25		1,399.56	$14,220	1,722.16	$17,497	$0	1,722.16	$17,497	29%	661.32	$43,138	$60,635
0206	66.66		1,907.16	$18,995	1,491.54	$14,856	$0	1,491.54	$14,856	25%	727.98	$45,208	$60,064
0306	44.40		1,662.92	$16,945	1,395.86	$14,224	$0	1,395.86	$14,224	23%	772.39	$47,340	$61,563
0406	-21.74		1,565.81	$15,987	1,706.31	$17,421	$0	1,706.31	$17,421	26%	750.65	$49,535	$66,957

— UR 3-for-1 Split

(continued)

Shading Key:
- Manually entered values
- Manually entered use of VFIIX balance
- Manually entered sell signal ignored
- Same-row cells affected by order adjustment

Quarter	SPY Price	IJR Price	IJR Div	VFIIX Price	VFIIX Div	IJR Shares Before Action	Quarter Cash Contrib	IJR Balance Before Action	3% Growth + 50% Cash Contrib (Signal Line)	Shares Needed to Reach Signal Line	Order Adjust
Q107	$142.00	$67.91		$10.21	0.132	750.65	$1,629	$50,977	$51,836	763.30	
Q207	$150.43	$71.10	0.264	$10.01	0.132	763.30	$1,629	$54,271	$54,205	762.38	
Q307	$152.58	$69.75	0.123	$10.17	0.133	762.38	$1,629	$53,176	$56,646	812.13	
Q407	$146.21	$65.02		$10.37	0.134	812.13	$1,629	$52,805	$59,160	909.87	
Q108	$131.97	$59.93		$10.47	0.130	909.87	$1,629	$54,529	$61,749	1,030.36	
Q208	$127.98	$60.17	0.157	$10.26	0.128	1,030.36	$1,629	$61,997	$64,416	1,070.57	
Q308	$115.99	$59.51		$10.30	0.132	1,070.57	$1,629	$63,710	$67,163	1,128.60	
Q408	$90.24	$43.97	0.250	$10.58	0.126	1,128.60	$1,629	$49,625	$69,993	1,591.83	Only VFIIX Bal
Q109	$79.52	$36.39	0.124	$10.67	0.118	1,591.83	$1,629	$57,927	$72,907	2,003.49	Sell Sig Ignored
Q209	$91.95	$44.43	0.114	$10.61	0.114	1,642.02	$1,629	$72,955	$62,360	1,403.56	Sell Sig Ignored
Q309	$105.59	$52.34	0.127	$10.75	0.103	1,642.02	$1,629	$85,943	$75,958	1,451.24	Sell Sig Ignored
Q409	$111.44	$54.72	0.170	$10.64	0.155	1,642.02	$1,629	$89,851	$89,336	1,632.60	Sell Sig Ignored
Q110	$117.00	$59.45	0.126	$10.72	0.125	1,642.02	$1,662	$97,618	$93,378	1,570.69	
Q210	$103.22	$54.14		$11.00	0.055	1,642.02	$1,662	$88,899	$101,377	1,872.50	
Q310	$114.13	$59.09	0.149	$11.02	0.096	1,872.50	$1,662	$110,646	$105,250	1,781.18	
Q410	$125.75	$68.47	0.331	$10.74	0.322	1,781.18	$1,662	$121,957	$109,238	1,595.42	
Q111	$132.59	$73.56	0.130	$10.72	0.085	1,595.42	$1,710	$117,359	$113,370	1,541.20	
Q211	$131.97	$73.32	0.140	$10.92	0.087	1,541.20	$1,710	$113,000	$117,626	1,604.29	
Q311	$113.15	$58.54	0.186	$11.16	0.092	1,604.29	$1,710	$93,915	$122,010	2,084.22	
Q411	$125.50	$68.30	0.244	$11.07	0.218	2,084.22	$1,710	$142,352	$126,526	1,852.50	
Q112	$140.81	$76.31	0.224	$11.01	0.109	1,852.50	$1,761	$141,364	$131,202	1,719.33	
Q212	$136.10	$73.27	0.271	$11.05	0.078	1,719.33	$1,761	$125,975	$136,018	1,856.40	
Q312	$143.97	$77.07	0.203	$11.11	0.073	1,856.40	$1,761	$143,073	$140,979	1,829.24	
Q412	$142.41	$78.10	0.595	$10.91	0.157	1,829.24	$1,761	$142,864	$146,089	1,870.54	
Q113	$156.67	$87.06	0.228	$10.85	0.068	1,870.54	$1,815	$162,849	$151,380	1,738.80	
Q213	$160.42	$90.31	0.268	$10.48	0.058	1,738.80	$1,815	$157,031	$156,828	1,736.56	
			6.107		6.351		$76,770				

Quarter	UR Shares to Buy or Sell (minus)	UR Shares to Buy or Sell (minus) After Order Adjust	VFIIX Shares + Divs Reinv + Cash Before Action	VFIIX Balance Before Action	VFIIX Shares After Action	VFIIX Balance After Action	New Cash Needed	VFIIX Shares After New Cash	VFIIX Balance After New Cash	VFIIX % of 3% Signal Balance	UR Shares After Action	UR Balance After Action	Total Balance
Q107	12.65		1,887.92	$19,276	1,803.76	$18,416	$0	1,803.76	$18,416	26%	763.30	$51,836	$70,252
Q207	-0.92		2,010.41	$20,124	2,016.94	$20,190	$0	2,016.94	$20,190	27%	762.38	$54,205	$74,395
Q307	49.75		2,212.72	$22,503	1,871.53	$19,033	$0	1,871.53	$19,033	25%	812.13	$56,646	$75,680
Q407	97.74		2,052.80	$21,288	1,439.95	$14,932	$0	1,439.95	$14,932	20%	909.87	$59,160	$74,092
Q108	120.48		1,613.42	$16,892	923.78	$9,672	$0	923.78	$9,672	14%	1,030.36	$61,749	$71,421
Q208	40.21		1,109.84	$11,387	874.00	$8,967	$0	874.00	$8,967	12%	1,070.57	$64,416	$73,383
Q308	58.03		1,043.36	$10,747	708.06	$7,293	$0	708.06	$7,293	10%	1,128.60	$67,163	$74,456
Q408	463.22		897.13	$9,492	-1,028.00	-$10,876	$10,876	0.00	$0	0%	1,591.83	$69,993	$69,993
Q109	411.66	50.19	171.17	$1,826	0.00	$0	$0	0.00	$0	0%	1,642.02	$59,753	$59,753
Q209	-238.46	0.00	171.18	$1,816	171.18	$1,816	$0	171.18	$1,816	2%	1,642.02	$72,955	$74,771
Q309	-190.78	0.00	343.75	$3,695	343.75	$3,695	$0	343.75	$3,695	4%	1,642.02	$85,943	$89,638
Q409	-9.42	0.00	528.10	$5,619	528.10	$5,619	$0	528.10	$5,619	6%	1,642.02	$89,851	$95,470
Q110	-71.32	0.00	708.59	$7,596	708.59	$7,596	$0	708.59	$7,596	7%	1,642.02	$97,618	$105,214
Q210	230.49		863.22	$9,495	-271.20	-$2,983	$2,983	0.00	$0	0%	1,872.50	$101,377	$101,377
Q310	-91.33		176.13	$1,941	665.84	$7,338	$0	665.84	$7,338	7%	1,781.18	$105,250	$112,587
Q410	-185.76		895.45	$9,617	2,079.71	$22,336	$0	2,079.71	$22,336	17%	1,595.42	$109,238	$131,574
Q111	-54.22		2,275.06	$24,389	2,647.12	$28,377	$0	2,647.12	$28,377	20%	1,541.20	$113,370	$141,748
Q211	63.09		2,844.57	$31,063	2,420.94	$26,437	$0	2,420.94	$26,437	18%	1,604.29	$117,626	$144,063
Q311	479.93		2,620.86	$29,249	103.37	$1,154	$0	103.37	$1,154	1%	2,084.22	$122,010	$123,164
Q411	-231.72		305.82	$3,385	1,735.51	$19,212	$0	1,735.51	$19,212	13%	1,852.50	$126,526	$145,738
Q112	-133.17		1,950.33	$21,473	2,873.33	$31,635	$0	2,873.33	$31,635	19%	1,719.33	$131,202	$162,837
Q212	137.07		3,095.14	$34,201	2,186.25	$24,158	$0	2,186.25	$24,158	15%	1,856.40	$136,018	$160,176
Q312	-27.16		2,393.04	$26,587	2,581.45	$28,680	$0	2,581.45	$28,680	17%	1,829.24	$140,979	$169,659
Q412	41.30		2,879.77	$31,418	2,584.10	$28,193	$0	2,584.10	$28,193	16%	1,870.54	$146,089	$174,282
Q113	-131.75		2,806.68	$30,455	3,864.01	$41,925	$0	3,864.01	$41,925	22%	1,738.80	$151,380	$193,304
Q213	-2.24		4,103.05	$43,000	4,122.35	$43,202	$0	4,122.35	$43,202	22%	1,736.56	$156,828	$200,031
							$13,859						

— UR 3-for-1 Split

Shading Key:
Manually entered values
Manually entered use of VFIIX balance
Manually entered sell signal ignored
Same-row cells affected by order adjustment

APPENDIX 2

Tools

To help you with your 3Sig plan, I offer tools on my website. A spreadsheet similar to the one detailing Mark's plan in Appendix 1 is my preferred approach because it not only calculates what to do from quarter to quarter, but it also creates a running history. To get your copy and see what else is available, please visit my website at jasonkelly.com/3sig.

APPENDIX 3

Rights and Permissions

If you have questions regarding the use or licensing of intellectual property contained in this book, including the 3 percent signal investing technique and/or its name, for example, in an investment product, software application, or other project, please submit your detailed request to me in writing via the Contact page at jasonkelly.com.

APPENDIX 4

The Kelly Letter

To keep current on all things 3Sig, consider subscribing to my newsletter, *The Kelly Letter*, which is delivered by e-mail every Sunday morning.

While it's not necessary to read anything about the stock market once you put 3Sig to work in your accounts, you might still want to do so. Seeing the z-vals go wrong in real time as 3Sig runs circles around them is illuminating and provides confirmation that you're on the right path. Also, rather than just going it alone, you may find it comforting to watch me make the quarterly calculations, redeploy the bond balance when it gets too big, and keep an eye out for the 30-down rule.

I maintain three tiers in the letter's portfolio: the 3Sig base case in Tier 1, a leveraged version with a higher growth target in Tier 2, and an open-market version in Tier 3 that taps volatile vehicles with rich dividend yields to run head-to-head against the base case. So far nothing has proved as compelling as the base case of the plan, but this could change, and if it does I'll report it in the newsletter.

I hope to see you on the list! To hear from me every Sunday morning, please sign up at jasonkelly.com.

INDEX

Notes: Page numbers in *italics* indicate charts and diagrams. The term "3Sig" is shorthand for "3 percent signal."

AARP, Inc., 189
actively managed funds,
    24–25, 294
Adelphia, 240
aerospace and defense sector, 191–93,
    192, 199
age considerations
    and allocation of capital, 152–55
    target date portfolios, 191, 193, 200, 202,
        206, 208–11, 213
airline stocks, 232–33
allocation of capital
    and bond balance in 3Sig, 136–37
    and bottom-buying account, 147–49
    and growth targets, *140*, 156
    and investment performance goals,
        76–77, 87–94, *89, 90, 92*
    and life cycle considerations, 152–55
    and order-size adjustments, 141–47
    and quarterly procedure of 3Sig, 160–64
    and reactive rebalancing, 47–51, 52, 78
    and safer versions of 3Sig, 129–30
    and strategy of 3Sig, 37, 50–51
Alternative Retirement Plan (ARP), 205–7
American International Group (AIG), 258
Apgar, Virginia, 21
Apgar scores, 21
Apple (AAPL), *123*, 124, *127*, 128–29
Argus Research, 125

Armed Forces, 204–5
Artisan International
    and expense ratios, *225*
    and initiation of investment plan,
        222–23
    and investment plan performance,
        231, 235, 249, 261, 264, 274, 277,
        282–83, 288
    and sample portfolio allocations,
        275, 283
Asian Contagion, 134
Associated Press, 236
automated trading, xvi, 42, 51–52

Bank of America, 257–58
Barach, Philip, 272
Barclays Capital, 281
Barras, Laurent, 24
Barron's, 126, 251–52, 266, 279, 281, 285
base rates, 6–7
Baum, Caroline, 268
BBC News, 66
bear markets
    and implementation of 3Sig, 164
    and investment performance goals, 71
    and relative performance of 3Sig, *293*
    and sample investing scenarios, 232,
        240–41, 244, 252, 257, 259, 261, 265,
        270, 273, 289, 291, 294, 296

bear markets (*cont.*)
  and selection of 3Sig investments,
    114, 116–17
  See also crashes
Bear Stearns, 95, 257
behavioral economics
  and confirmation bias, 12–13
  and hindsight bias, 8–9
  and limited data, 6–8
  and limits of pattern recognition, 12
  mistaking luck for skill, 9–12
  psychology of, 5–6
  and zero-validity environments, 13–14
  See also emotion in investing
The Believing Brain (Shermer), 13
Bernanke, Ben, 271, 285
Bernstein, Richard, 245
Black Monday, 134
BlackRock, 281
Bloomberg, 268, 285
bond funds
  and cash shortages, 74–78
  criteria for 3Sig strategy, 87
  and dollar-cost averaging vs. 3Sig, 104
  and growth targets, 137–41
  and money management in 3Sig,
    135–37, 155–56, 157
  and order-size adjustments, 141–47
  periodic cash contributions, 133
  and private sector retirement plans, 188
  and relative performance of 3Sig,
    293–94
  and safer versions of 3Sig, 129–30
  and sample investing scenarios, 216, 220,
    223–27, 228–29, 233–35, 238–39,
    240–42, 244, 247, 249, 251, 254, 256,
    259, 268, 269–77, 281–87, 289
  and selection of 3Sig investments,
    84–87, *85*
  and strategy of 3Sig, 38, 50, 78–79, *259*
  See also Vanguard GNMA bond fund
    (VFIIX)
Bond Market Index Fund, 192
bottom-buying account
  and money management in 3Sig,
    147–49, 158
  and relative performance of 3Sig,
    293–94
  and sample investing scenarios, 239,
    241–42, 259–60, 262, 269–70, 275,
    287–89, 292, *293*, 294–95, 295–96
  and strategy of 3Sig, 40

Brinker, Bob, 255
brokerage accounts, 172–84
Bryant, Hap, 222
Buffett, Warren, 42–43
bull markets, 242–43, 251, 254–55, 270,
  281, 283, 286, 291
"The Bumpy Road to Outperformance," 25
Bush, George W., 66, 217, 235, 242, 245
Bush, Sarah, 223
Businessweek, 66, 197, 245
buy-and-hold strategy
  contrasted with 3Sig strategy, 79, 126
  danger during crashes, 151–52
  and investment performance goals, *68*,
    69–72, 74, 79
  and money management in 3Sig, 147, 151
  and selection of 3Sig investments, 89, *89*,
    105, 109, 111

Callaway, David, 267
capital preservation investing strategies, 154
Cardon, Jeff, 218
cash shortfalls and infusions
  and bottom-buying account, 147–49
  eliminating, 146–47
  and growth targets, 137–41, *140*
  and investment performance goals, 56,
    57–59, *58*, 67–68, *68*, 73–74, 74–79,
    75, 77
  and money management in 3Sig,
    134–35, 136, 155–56, 157
  and order-size adjustments, 141–47
  and relative performance of 3Sig,
    293–94
  and sample investing scenarios, 259,
    269, 299, *301, 303*
  and selection of 3Sig investments, 84, *89*,
    89–91, *90, 91*, 92, 95, *102*, 107, 110,
    117, *123–24*, 124, 126, *127*, 128
  and strategy of 3Sig, 39, *39*, 52
C Fund, 202, *202*, 203, *203*
The Chartist Mutual Fund Letter, 255
Clark, Todd, 237
CNET News, 128
coin toss investing
  and investing goals, 59–60
  and investment performance goals, 64, 73
  and Peter Perfect, 30–32, 36
  and reactive rebalancing, 47–51, *48, 50*
  and sample investing scenarios, 288, 290
  and selection of 3Sig investments,
    98–100, 98–101, *102*, 110

and stock forecasting, 15–17, *16*, 20
and strategy of 3Sig, *44*, 44–47, *45*, *46*, *50*, 80
See also randomness
company size, 198–201
complexity of the market, 34
compounding, 1, *55*, 55–59, *57*, *58*
confidence, 8
confirmation bias, 12–13, 13–14, 27–30
Cooley, Scott, 221
Corporate Air Travel Survey, 235
Cramer, Jim, 95, 257
crashes
    emotional danger of, 151–52
    and market volatility, 3
    strategy of 3Sig during, *259*
    and zero-validity environments, 5
    See also "30 down, stick around" rule
credit crunch, 256
CRSP U.S. Small-Cap Index, 82–83, 206
CXO Advisory, 15

day orders, 175–76
decision-making process, 5–6
Defense Business Board, 204
defined contribution plans, 185, 202, 204, 205, 207. *See also* employer retirement accounts
Democrats, 281
Demos, 189, 200
Dillard's (DDS), *123*, 124, *127*
distribution of capital, 69
diversification, 109–10, 251, 264
dividends
    and investment performance goals, 65, 67, 70, 74, 77
    and money management in 3Sig, 154
    and sample investing scenarios, 224, 228–29, 231, 235, 241, 245–46, 248–49, 253, 259–61, 264, 276, 282, 284–85, 286
    and selection of 3Sig investments, 84, 87–88, 122, 129
    and stock performance calculations, xiii
dollar-cost averaging
    and cash shortages, *77*
    compared to 3Sig, 103–10, *110–11*
    danger during crashes, 151–52
    and investment performance goals, *68*, 68–69, 76–77, *77*, 79, 103–11
    and money management in 3Sig, 144, 155

and relative performance of 3Sig, *293–94*
and sample investing scenarios, 216, 224, 225–26, 233, 287, 295–96
and selection of 3Sig investments, *80*, *89*, *90*, 90–93, *92*, *104*, *107*, 110–11, 130–31
Dorsey, Woody, 237
dot-com crash
    and money management in 3Sig, 134
    and sample investing scenarios, 216, 219, 226–29, 232, 254, 261–62, 286
DoubleLine Total Return, 272, *274*, 276, 282, *282*, 284, 287
Dow Jones Industrial Average, 43, 66, 234, 236–37, 239, 257
Dow Jones U.S. Completion Total Stock Market Index, 202, *202*
Dow Jones U.S. Small-Cap Total Stock Market Index, 82

The Economist, 234
"Economists Double Down on a Double Dip Recession" (Hirsch), 278
Edelen, Roger, 60
Edleson, Michael, 59, 106
"The Effect of Myopia and Loss Aversion on Risk Taking: An Experimental Test" (Thaler et al.), 60–62
elections, 217
emotion in investing
    and automation of investing, xvi
    and buy-and-hold myth, 69–71, 109
    and the decision-making process, 6
    and dollar-cost averaging, 131
    and investment performance goals, 66
    and market volatility, 3
    and money management in 3Sig, 131, 134–35, 151–52, 158
    and need to take action, xvi
    and trading tactics, 177, 181–82
employer retirement accounts
    in aerospace and defense sector, 191–93
    and company size, 198–201, *199*
    described, 185–87
    and government employees, 201–7
    and implementation of 3Sig, 213
    and money management in 3Sig, 133
    in nutritional supplement sector, 197–98
    in oilfield services sector, 193–95
    privacy regarding, 187–91

employer retirement accounts (*cont.*)
  in sporting goods retail sector, 195–96
  and target date funds, 208–11
Enron, 95, 234, 240
Epstein, Gene, 279
Evans, Richard, 60
exchange-traded funds (ETFs)
  described, 43
  and implementation of 3Sig, 173–74
  and investment performance goals,
    63–64
  performance by market cap, *81–82*
  and sample investing scenarios, 274, 294
  and selection of 3Sig investments,
    81–84, 85, 118, 124, 130
  small caps compared with SPY, *83*
expense ratios
  and advantage of 3Sig, 213
  and aerospace and defense sector,
    191–93, *192*
  and company size, 198–201, *199, 203*
  and employer retirement accounts,
    187–91, 206, *209*, 210–11
  and government employment, 201, 203,
    203, 204, 206
  and implementation of 3Sig, 164–68,
    166, 227
  and nutritional supplement sector, *197*,
    197–98
  and oilfield services sector, 193–95,
    194, 195
  range of, *219, 225, 233*
  and sample investing scenarios, 219,
    223, *225*, 227, 233, 242, 253, 287,
    294, 296
  and sporting goods retail sector, 195–96
  and target date funds, *209*, 210–11
  and Thrift Savings Plans, *203, 203–4*
ExxonMobil (XOM)
  and sample investing scenarios, 246,
    246, 248–51, *251*, 253, 260, 286
  and strategy of 3Sig, *124*, 125, *127*

fair values, 19
false negatives, 22
Farr, Michael, 237
Farr Miller & Washington, 237
Fastow, Andrew, 240
Federal Reserve
  influence on market, 1–2, 7, 49
  and investment performance goals,
    64–66, 71

and sample investing scenarios, 245,
  247, 252, 256, 258, 261–62, 270–72,
  285, 290, 296
and selection of 3Sig investments, 95
fees. *See* expense ratios
F Fund, *202*
Fidelity Advisor Small Cap fund, 282,
  282, 284
Fidelity Growth & Income, 221, *225*, 228,
  261, 264
Fidelity Investments, 176, 206–7
Fidelity Select Air Transportation Portfolio
  and expense ratios, *233*
  and investment plan performance,
    233–34, 236, 240, 242–43, 286
  and sample portfolio allocations,
    246, 251
Fidelity Select Defense & Aerospace
    Portfolio
  and investment plan performance,
    242–43, 245–46, 249, 253, 257, 260,
    263, 286
  and sample portfolio allocations,
    246, 251
filtered funds, 119–21
Financial Analysts Journal, 25, 60
Financial Industry Regulatory Authority
    (FINRA), 185
Financial Times, 264, 281
First Marblehead, 249–51, *251*, 252–53,
  254, 260
The Fiscal Times, 278
Fleckenstein, Bill, 262
fluctuations in the market. *See* volatility
Fooled by Randomness (Taleb), 11
Forbes, 197, 265
formulas for stock valuation, 20
Fortune, 95, 125, 270
401(k) accounts
  and advantage of 3Sig, 213
  allocation of capital in, *248*
  and employer retirement accounts, 185,
    191–93, *192, 194, 195*, 195–96, *197*,
    197–98, *199*, 199–201, 202, 205, 207,
    209, 210, 211
  and flexibility of 3Sig, 211
  and implementation of 3Sig, 165,
    171–72
  private sector expenses, 187–91
  and relative performance of 3Sig, *234,
    239, 245, 248, 253, 258, 268, 271, 276,
    280, 284, 291, 293, 294*

and salary contributions, *241*, *269*
and sample investing scenarios, 214,
   215–17, 220, 222, 226–27, 235, 248,
   250, 253, 256, 258, 260, 261, 263,
   268, 270–71, 275, 280, 283–84, 288,
   291, 295
and selection of 3Sig investments, 82
and strategy of 3Sig, 40
401k Averages Book, 200–201
403(b) accounts, 185
Fraud Discovery Institute (FDI), 97
frequency of trading, 60–62
Fruhan, Matthew, 243
full investment, 251. *See also* buy-and-hold
   strategy; dollar-cost averaging

GBI Gold Fund, 273
gender issues in investing, 30
General Motors (GM), 126
G Fund, *202*
gold, 49, 270, 273–77, *274*, 280–82, 284, 287
Goldman Sachs, 281–82
good-till-cancelled (GTC) orders, 175–76
Gore, Al, 217
government employees, 201–2
Great Depression, 71, 265, 278
Great Recession, 71
Greek government-debt crisis, 279
Greenspan, Alan, 245–46
Greylock Capital, 285
Groh, Doug, 280
Gross, Bill, 223–24, 247, 261, 264, 268, 272,
   277, 285
growth rates and targets
   gauging against fluctuations, 59–60
   growth stocks, 120
   and investment return rates, *55*,
      55–59, *57*
   and life-cycle considerations, 154
   and strategy of 3Sig, 37–38
Grubman, Jack, 240
Gundlach, Jeffrey, 251–52, 272

Harch Capital Management, 264
Harding, William, 223
Hard Money (McGuire), 273
Harmon, Jamie, 282
Hawkins, Mason, 221–22, 247
Hedge Fund Research, 290
heroic holdings, 94–103
Highlights, 203
high-validity environments, 20

Hiltonsmith, Robert, 189
hindsight bias, 8–9, 27–32, 35, 101–3, *102*
Hirsch, Michelle, 278
historical market performance, *54*, 54–55
Hulbert, Mark, 252
Humes, Hans, 285
Hurricane Katrina, 247
Hussein, Saddam, 242

IBM, *124*, 124–25, *127*
I Fund, *202*, *203*
ImClone, 240
implementing 3Sig strategy
   and brokerage accounts, 172–84
   and employer retirement accounts,
      185–211
   and expense ratios, 164–68
   flexibility of, 211–12
   and IRAs, 170–72
   quarterly procedure, 160–64
   and tax considerations, 168–70
income investing strategies, 154
index funds, 17–18, 40, 42–44, 52, 165–68,
   225. *See also specific fund names*
individual retirement accounts (IRAs),
   133, 136–38, 168–72
individual stock strategies, 121–29
inflation, 271. *See also* interest rates
Inflation Sensitive Strategy, 193
insider-trading scandals, 240
Institute for Global Economic Growth, 268
interest rates
   influence on market, 49
   and investment performance goals, 56,
      66, 71
   and money management in 3Sig, 134
   and sample investing scenarios, 245,
      247, 252, 258, 271–72, 279, 285
   and selection of 3Sig investments, 86, 129
International Air Transport Association, 235
international funds, 222
Investment Company Institute (ICI),
   204, 289
Investor's Business Daily, 236
IRA accounts, 40
Iraq War, 235, 242, 245
Irwin, Neil, 279
iShares Core S&P Small-Cap (IJR)
   expense ratios, *227*
   and implementation of 3Sig, 160,
      168–70, 173–74, 175–77, 177–84,
      188, 194, 203, *203*, 209–11

iShares Core S&P Small-Cap (IJR) (*cont.*)
  and investment performance goals, 57
  and money management in 3Sig, 150
  and relative performance of 3Sig,
    293–94
  and sample investing scenarios, 226–27,
    233–35, 238–39, 244, 249, 251, 254,
    259, *259,* 262–63, 266–68, 270, 275,
    277, 283–84, 286, 295, 299, *300–303*
  and selection of 3Sig investments,
    82–84, *83,* 87–93, *88, 89, 90, 95, 102,*
    113, *114, 115, 116,* 119, 121–23,
    126–27
  and strategy of 3Sig, 124, *124, 127*
  target date funds vs., *209*
Isidore, Chris, 247
iVillage, 218

Jacob, Ryan, 217–18
Jacob Internet Fund, 217–19, *219,* 228, 230,
  232–33, 234
Janus Global Technology, 218–19, *219,* 228,
  230, *233,* 235–36, 245–46
JDS Uniphase, 217
Jenkins, Holman, 262
The Journal of Finance, 24
JPMorgan Chase, 95
Judis, John B., 278

Kadlec, Gregory, 60
Kahneman, Daniel, 5, 9–11, 14, 20, 22–23,
  60–62
Kansas City Southern (KSU), *123,* 124, *127*
Kass, Doug, 266–67, 271
Kaye, Steve, 221
Keynes, John Maynard, 273
Kinnel, Russel, 166–67
Kozlowski, Dennis, 240
Krugman, Paul, 262

Large-Cap Equity Income Fund, *197*
Large-Cap Equity Strategy, 193
Large-Cap Growth Equity Fund, *195*
large-cap stocks, 81, 83, 109, 193, 256
Lay, Kenneth, 234
Lehman Brothers, 128, 257
Lehman Brothers Aggregate, 224
Lewitt, Michael, 264
L Fund, 202–3
"Likely Gains from Market Timing"
  (Sharpe), 25
limit orders, 175–77

Longleaf Partners
  and expense ratios, *225*
  and initiation of investment plan,
    221–23
  and investment plan performance,
    231, 235, 249, 260, 264, 274, 277,
    282–83, 288
  and sample portfolio allocations,
    275, 283
A Look at 401(k) Plan Fees, 165
loss aversion, 60–62. *See also* risk aversion
  and tolerance
luck in stock picking, 9–12, 24, 30, 34, 35,
  96, 122, 266, 287–88

Mad Money, 95
Malkiel, Burton G., 17–18
managing money in 3Sig
  and bond balance, 135–37
  and bottom buying, 147–52
  and growth targets, 137–41
  and life-cycle considerations, 152–55
  and order sizes, 141–47
  starting balances, 134–35
  summarized, 155–56
market capitalization, 81–82, *81–82*
market fluctuations. *See* volatility
Marketimer, 255
market orders, 175–77
market sectors, 118–19
Market Semiotics, 237
MarketWatch, 218, 267, 280
matching funds, 137, 171–72, 185, 211,
  215, 235, *241, 269*
McDonald's (MCD), *124,* 124–26, *127*
McGuire, Shayne, 273
medical field, 20–22
Medifast (MED), 94–103, *95, 96, 98–100,*
  102, 123, 124, *127*
memory, 34, 35. *See also* confirmation bias;
  hindsight bias
Merrill Lynch, 245, 257–58
metrics of investment performance, 53–59
Mid-Cap Equity Index Fund, *195*
Mid-Cap Value Fund, *197*
Mike Molinski's FundWatch, 218
military service, 204–5
Minkow, Barry, 97
"Modernizing the Military Retirement
  System" (Defense Business
  Board), 204
MoneyBeat column, 30–31

Morgan Stanley, 282
Morningstar funds, 25, 166–67, 208,
    211–13, 221–24, 243–44, 274, 289
Motley Fool Hidden Gems, 253
MSN Money, 262
mutual funds
    described, 43
    and expense ratios, 167
    and implementation of 3Sig, 166–67,
        171, 173, 185, 189, 200
    and investment performance goals,
        60–61
    and market fluctuations, 37
    and sample investing scenarios, 216–17,
        232, 274, 285, 295
    and selection of 3Sig investments,
        83, 85
    and strategy of 3Sig, 38, 52
    and typical stock market experiences,
        1–2
    underperformance of fund managers,
        24–27, *25, 26*
    See also specific fund names

natural disasters, 247
*The Neatest Little Guide to Stock Market
    Investing* (Kelly), 175, 178
New York magazine, 257
New York Observer, 217–18
The New Republic, 278
New York Stock Exchange, 41
The New York Times, 66, 95, 221, 262,
    284–85, 289
Nobel Prize in Economics, 5
No-Load Fund Analyst, 256
nonprofit groups, 185
Nortel, 217
nutritional supplement sector, 197–98, *199*

Obama, Barack, 278
O'Boyle, Kerry, 243–44
obstetrics, 20–21
Ohio Public Employees Retirement System
    (OPERS), 205
The Ohio State University, 201, 205–7
oilfield services sector, 193–95, *194,
    195, 199*
Oppenheimer Global Strategic Income
    Fund, 223, 225, *225*, 228, 261, 264
opportunity cost, 166
order size, 141–47
outperformance, 54–59

Panera (PNRA), *123*, 124, *127*
passively investing, 60–62
passively managed funds, 24–25
patternicity, 13
pattern recognition, 12–13, 34–35
pension plans, 172, 186, 201, 204–5,
    207, 272
performance goals, 53–59, 87–94
perspective in investing, 6–8
Peter Perfect approach
    described, 4
    and employee retirement accounts, 186
    psychology of, 27–32
    and sample investing scenarios, 217,
        227, 249–50, 266, 287, 295, 296
    and selection of 3Sig investments, 110,
        121, 126
PIMCO Total Return
    and expense ratios, *225*
    and initiation of investment plan,
        223–24
    and investment plan performance, 228,
        231, 261–62, 264, 267–68, 270, 272,
        274, 276–77, 282–85, 287–88
    and sample portfolio allocations,
        275, 283
Plender, John, 264
political environment, 217, 235, 242, 262,
    265, 279, 281–82
Porter, Doug, 248
predictive rebalancing, 47
pregnancy tests, 20–21
private sector retirement plans, 187–201
profit taking, 277

quantitative easing program (QE2), 272
The Quarterly Journal of Economics, 60–62
quarterly prices and adjustments
    and growth targets, *140*
    and implementation of 3Sig, 160–64
    and investment performance goals, 78,
        87–94, *88, 89, 90, 91, 92*
    and money management in 3Sig,
        134–35, 157
    and performance of 3Sig plan,
        160–64, 212
    and the "30 down, stick around" rule, 112
    and strategy of 3Sig, 39, *39, 58*, 59–60,
        60–63, *63–67*

Racanelli, Vito J., 281
Rahn, Richard, 268

rallies, 3, 5. *See also* bull markets
randomness
    and behavioral economics, 23
    coin toss example, 15–17, *16*, 44–47
    mistaking luck for skill, 9–12, 35
    and pattern recognition, 12, 34–35
A Random Walk Down Wall Street
    (Malkiel), 17–18
"range bound" markets, 49
rationalization, 8–9
RDQ Economics, 278
reactive rebalancing
    and investment plan performance, 79,
        238–39, 286
    and money management in 3Sig,
        156, 157
    and strategy of 3Sig, 37–38, 47–51,
        48, 52
RealMoneyPro service, 271
retirement accounts
    and life-cycle considerations, 154–55
    and matching funds, 137, 171–72, 185,
        211, 215, 235, *241*, 269
    and performance of 3Sig plan, 40, 159
    and tax considerations, 168–70
    See also employer retirement accounts;
        401(k) accounts; individual
        retirement accounts (IRAs)
The Retirement Savings Drain
    (Demos), 189
return rates, *55*, 55–59, *57*
Reuters, 97
risk aversion and tolerance
    and behavioral economics, 5
    buy-and-hold strategy as benchmark,
        73–74
    and return rates, 56
    risk-adjusted investment performance,
        24–25, 74, 91, 110
    and safer versions of 3Sig, 129–30
    and sample investing scenarios, 216,
        218, 220–21, 249–50, 259, 264–65,
        271, 290
Rocco, William Samuel, 222–23
rollover of IRAs, 173, 174, 272
Rosenberg, David, 270
Roth IRAs, 169, 172, 202
Roubini, Nouriel, 265, 266
rounding market orders, 162
Russell 2000 Small-Cap Index Fund,
    43, 82, *82*, 191–92, *192*, *194*, *197*,
    198, 206

Ryan Beck & Co., 237
Ryding, John, 278

safe fund, 50, 59
sample sizes, 6–7
Samuelson, Robert J., 261
S&P 400 Mid-Cap Index Fund, *197*
S&P 500, 43–44, 80, *81*, 144, *145*
S&P 500, Large-Cap Index Fund, *195*, *197*
S&P Mid-Cap 400, *81*
S&P Small-Cap 600 Index, *81*, 82, *83*, *124*,
    127, 229, *293–94*, 295
Savage, Stephen, 256
savings incentive match plan, 172
Scaillet, Olivier, 24
scandals, 186, 240
Schwab U.S. Aggregate Bond (SCHZ), 86
Schwab U.S. Small-Cap Core (SCHA),
    82–84, *83*, 173, *173*
Schwartz, Alan, 60–62
Scientific American, 12
Select Defense. *See* Fidelity Select Defense
    & Aerospace Portfolio
September 11 terrorist attacks, 228, 230,
    232–34, 235, 237
S Fund, 202, *202*, *203*
Sharpe, William, 24–25
Sharpe ratio, 24–25
"Shedding Light on 'Invisible' Costs"
    (Edelen, Evans, and Kadlec), 60
Sheff, Gluskin, 270
Shell, Adam, 236
Shermer, Michael, 12–13
short-term capital gain tax, 168–70, 213
signal line, calculating, 160–61
SIMPLE IRA, 172
simplified employee pension
    (SEP-IRA), 172
Small-Cap Blend Fund, *197*
Small-Cap Equity Fund, *194*, *195*
small-cap indexes, 82, 85, 90, 198–199,
    201–202, 210–213
small-cap stocks, 90, 117–18, 130
small company mutual funds, 38, 40,
    79–84
"Smart 401(k) Investing" (FINRA), 185
Social Security, 208–9
Society for Human Resource Management
    (SHRM), 200
Spartan Short-Term Treasury Bond
    Index Fund–Fidelity Advantage
    Class, 206

Spartan Small-Cap Index Fund–Fidelity Advantage Class, 206–7
SPDR Gold Shares, 274, *274*
SPDR S&P 500 ETF (SPY)
  and implementation of 3Sig, 161, 163–64
  investing plan comparisons, *68*
  and investment performance goals, 63–66, *64*, 67–68, 70, 73–74, *75*, 75–77, *77*, 79
  and relative performance of 3Sig, *293–94*
  and sample investing scenarios, 234, 244, 263, 295, 299, *300*
  and selection of 3Sig investments, 81, *81*, 83, *83*, 87–93, *90*, *92*, *95*, *102*, 112–17, *114*, *115*, *116*, 118, 123–24, 126, *127*, 131
  and strategy of 3Sig, *124*, *127*
speculation, 10, 35
sporting goods retail sector, 195–96, *196*, *199*
Stable Value Strategy, 193
Standard & Poor's Depositary Receipts (SPDR), 63. *See also specific SPDR funds*
Starbucks (SBUX), *123*, 124, *127*
State Street Global Advisors, 63
Stewart, Martha, 240
stick-around rule. *See* "30 down, stick around" rule
stimulus spending, 64
stock funds, xvii, 52, 59, 78–79, *79*–84, 137–41
stock splits, xiii, 244
stock valuations, 19–20
stop-loss orders, 181
storytelling bias, 7–8, 30
Straszheim, Donald, 237
Straszheim Global Advisors, 237
subprime mortgage crisis
  and implementation of 3Sig, 165, 179–80, 186, 204
  and investment performance goals, 64, 71, 75–76
  and money management in 3Sig, 134, 147, 150
  and sample investing scenarios, 249, 251–52, 254, 257, 262, 272, 276, 286
  and selection of 3Sig investments, 115
Sullivan, Dan, 255
survival skills, 12–13

survivorship bias, 11
Sycamore, 217

Take Shape for Life, 97
Taleb, Nassim Nicholas, 10–11
target date plans, 191, 193, 200, 202, 206, 208–11, 213
tax issues, 168–70, 260
TD Ameritrade, 176
Teacher Retirement System of Texas, 273
Teachers Insurance and Annuity Association–College Retirement Equities Fund (TIAA-CREF), 206–7
10-Q forms, 250
Thaler, Richard, 5, 23, 60–62
Thinking, Fast and Slow (Kahneman), 5, 22
"30 down, stick around" rule
  and implementation of 3Sig, 161, 163–64
  and investment performance goals, 75
  and sample investing scenarios, 227, 234, 244, 263, 266–67, 269–70, 275, 292, 299, *300–303*
  and selection of 3Sig investments, 111–17, 131
  and strategy of 3Sig, 40
Thomas, Landon, Jr., 217–18
Thrift Savings Plan (TSP), 185, 194, 201, 202–5, *203*, 208, 211
timing the market
  and confirmation bias, 27–32
  failures of, 34
  and market volatility, 3
  myth of, 3–4
  and the Peter Perfect scenario, 27–30, *28*
  and sample investing scenarios, 229
  and strategy of 3Sig, 37–38
Tocqueville Gold Fund, 280
Total New Cash, 57–58, *58*
trading costs, 83, 173–74. *See also* expense ratios
trading history samples, *28*, *169–70*
trailing stops, 177–84, *179*
Traulsen, Christopher, 222
treasury bonds, 272
Treasury Inflation-Protected Securities (TIPS), 153
T. Rowe Price International Stock Fund, 222, 223, 225, 261, 264
Tversky, Amos, 5, 60–62

uncertainty, 23–24. *See also* volatility; zero-validity environments (z-vals)

U.N. Security Council, 242
U.S. Army Corps of Engineers, 247
USA Today, 236, 252
U.S. Congress, 49, 203, 285
U.S. Department of Labor, 165
U.S. Securities and Exchange
    Commission, 250

value averaging, 59, 106–7, *106–7. See also*
    dollar-cost averaging
Value Averaging (Edleson), 59, 106–7
Value Line Investment Survey, 256, 289
value stocks, 120
Vanguard 500 Index Fund, 144
Vanguard GNMA bond fund (VFIIX)
    expense ratios, *227*
    and investment performance goals,
        64–65, 67, *68*, 73–74, *77*
    and relative performance of 3Sig, *293*
    and sample investing scenarios, 227,
        229, 234, 238, 259, 263, 269, 295, 299,
        300–303
    and selection of 3Sig investments, 85, *86*,
        87, *89*, 90, *92*, 95, 102
Vanguard Group, Inc., xi–xii, *25*, 25–26,
    26, 55
Vanguard Intermediate-Term Bond
    (BIV), *86*
Vanguard Long-Term Bond (BLV), *86*
Vanguard Mortgage-Backed Securities
    (VMBS), *86*
Vanguard Short-Term Bond (BSV), *86*
Vanguard Small-Cap (NAESX), 83
Vanguard Small-Cap (VB), 82, 83, *83*, 174,
    195–96, *196*
Vanguard Total Bond Market (BND), *86*,
    130
Vanguard Total Stock Market (VTI), 130
variations on 3Sig strategy, 117–30
volatility
    and advantage of 3Sig, 209–10
    and cash shortages, 77
    and growth targets, 59–60, 137–38, 141
    and heroic holdings, 96–103, *98–100*
    historical market performance, *54*,
        54–55

and investment performance goals, 67,
    72, 72–73, 79
and money management in 3Sig, 158
as opportunity, 36, 40–42
and order-size adjustments, 144
and sample investing scenarios, 214,
    223–24, 286, 306
and small-cap index funds, 82
and strategy of 3Sig, 40–42, *50*, 52, 84
and trading tactics, 177–84

The Wall Street Journal, 30–31, 262, 289
Walmart (WMT), 121, *124*, 124–25, *127*
war, 235, 243
Wasatch Small-Cap Growth
    and expense ratios, *219*, *233*
    and initiation of investment plan,
        218–19
    and investment plan performance,
        228, 230, 235–36, 245–46, 249–50,
        253, 260
    and sample portfolio allocations,
        246, *251*
The Washington Post, 261, 279
The Washington Times, 268
Wells Fargo, 195–96, 209–11, 231
Wells Fargo Advantage Dow Jones Target
    Funds, *209*, 209–10
Wermers, Russell, 24
What You See Is All There Is (WYSIATI), 6
windfall cash, 143, 156
WorldCom, 240

Yardeni, Edward, 281
Yockey, Mark, 222

zero-validity environments (z-vals)
    described, 4–5, 13–14
    and heroic holdings, 95–97
    and investment performance goals,
        66–67
    and pattern recognition, 34
    and selection of 3Sig investments,
        125–26
    and selective reporting, 103
    and strategy of 3Sig, 47